MW00427260

Emily Dickinson's Vision

University Press of Florida

Gainesville

Tallahassee

Tampa

Boca Raton

Pensacola

Orlando

Miami

Jacksonville

JAMES R. GUTHRIE

MILY DICKINSON'S VISION

Illness and Identity in Her Poetry

03 02 01 00 99 98   6   5   4   3   2   1

Library of Congress Cataloging-in-Publication Data

Guthrie, James R. (James Robert)
Emily Dickinson's vision: illness and identity in her poetry /
James R. Guthrie.
p. cm.
Includes bibliographical references (p.) and index.
ISBN 0-8130-1549-9 (cloth: alk. paper)
  1. Dickinson, Emily, 1830–1886—Criticism and interpretation.
2. Women and literature—Massachusetts—History—19th
century. 3. Identity (Psychology in literature). 4. Vision
disorders—Patients. 5. Heaven in literature. 6. Summer in
literature. 7. Health in literature. 8. Sun—In literature. I. Title.
PS1541.Z5G88   1998
811'.4—dc21   97-44483

The University Press of Florida is the scholarly publishing
agency for the State University System of Florida, comprised
of Florida A & M University, Florida Atlantic University,
Florida International University, Florida State University,
University of Central Florida, University of Florida, University
of North Florida, University of South Florida, and University
of West Florida.

University Press of Florida
15 Northwest 15th Street
Gainesville, FL 32611
http://nersp.nerdc.ufl.edu/~upf

CONTENTS

ACKNOWLEDGMENTS

I AM INDEBTED to several readers whose suggestions and contributions have helped shape this book: Jim Hughes, Jane Donahue Eberwein, Barton Levi St. Armand, and Richard Brantley. Thanks also to Martha Ackmann for her generosity in making available to me information gleaned from interviews with Dickinson descendants.

For their advice and support I am also grateful to my colleagues Henry Limouze and Barry Milligan. For a faculty development grant that paid many of my research and administrative costs, I thank Wright State University's Office of Research and Sponsored Programs.

Deidre Bryan, Alexandra Leader, and Walda Metcalf at the University Press of Florida also deserve credit for seeing this project through to fruition. Finally, I am grateful to my wife, Rebecca Cochran, and to all the rest of my family for their patience and understanding.

Portions of this book have appeared elsewhere in slightly different form. Material from chapter 1 appeared earlier in "Measuring the Sun: Emily Dickinson's Interpretation of Her Optical Illness," *ESQ: A Journal of the American Renaissance* 41, no. 3 (1995), copyright 1995 by the Board of Regents of Washington State University.

Material from chapter 2 appeared originally in "'A Revolution in Locality': Astronomical Tropes in Emily Dickinson's Poetry," *Midwest Quarterly* 37, no. 4 (1996).

Material from chapter 7 appeared originally in "Law, Property, and Provincialism in Dickinson's Poems and Letters to Judge Otis Phillips Lord," *The Emily Dickinson Journal* 5, no. 1 (1996), reprinted by permission of *The Emily Dickinson Journal*.

Texts of Dickinson's poems are reprinted by permission of the publishers and the trustees of Amherst College from *The Poems of Emily Dickinson,* ed. Thomas H. Johnson (Cambridge: The Belknap Press of Harvard University Press), copyright 1951, 1955, 1979, 1983 by the President and Fellows of Harvard College. Poems are also drawn from *The Complete Poems of Emily Dickinson* by T. H. Johnson, copyright 1929, 1935, by Martha Dickinson Bianchi, copyright renewed 1929, 1935, by Mary L. Hampson, and are reprinted by permission of Little, Brown and Company. Quotations from Dickinson's letters are reprinted by permission of the publisher from *The Letters of Emily Dickinson,* ed. Thomas H. Johnson (Cambridge: The Belknap Press of Harvard University Press), copyright 1958, 1986, by the President and Fellows of Harvard College.

I reckon—when I count at all—
First—Poets—Then the Sun—
Then Summer—Then the Heaven of God—
And then—the List is done—

But, looking back—the First so seems
To Comprehend the Whole—
The Others look a needless Show—
So I write—Poets—All—

Their Summer—lasts a Solid Year—
They can afford a Sun
The East—would deem extravagant—
And if the Further Heaven—

Be Beautiful as they prepare
For Those who worship Them—
It is too difficult a Grace—
To justify the Dream—

INTRODUCTION

DICKINSON BEGINS HER list of favorite things in "I reckon—when I count at all—" with poets and the sun. Next comes summer, when the sun shone at its longest and brightest, and then, somewhat pointedly in last place, the "Heaven of God." Yet in the second stanza Dickinson purports to change her mind, striking out the final three items because they are all subsumed within the first. Poets do not need the sun because they can conceive of one more "extravagant" than any the "East" could offer. Neither do they need the summer, for the fertility of their imaginations never wanes. For readers who "worship" poets and poetry, the act of reading itself creates a momentary paradise that renders the orthodox, "Further" heaven superfluous. And even if heaven did prove to be as beautiful as the paradise of literature, says Dickinson, the conceptual effort required to make the comparison still could not be justified. It would be simply "too difficult a Grace" to figure out why God should consent to have his heaven resemble that of the poets. Having poets and poetry, one already possessed heaven.

Even though Dickinson is speaking in this poem about poets she admires, the terms she employs apply most readily to herself. Sun, summer, and heaven were her particular desiderata, ranked in that order because an optical illness made exposure to the sun painful or even hazardous for her, compelling her to retreat indoors especially during the beautiful, brief New England summer, when a heaven was created temporarily upon earth. Within Dickinson's poems, a corresponding tension is set up in which sun and summer entice the poet while threatening her simultaneously with physical or imaginative collapse, generating a dialectic of desire and deferred gratification that precisely parallels her thinking about the "Further Heaven." Although deliberately unfulfilled desire, or what Richard Wilbur perceptively labeled "sumptuous Destitution,"[1] has long been recognized by many critics as the dominant topos of Dickinson's poetry, most have assumed she adopted it by choice, having come to regard a state of expectancy as being inherently more satisfying than fulfillment—or as she wrote, "The Banquet of Abstemiousness / Defaces that of Wine—" (no. 1430).[2] Yet I propose that Dickinson lived in a state of desire as a matter of necessity, schooled by the realities of being ill. Because her ailment probably lingered on for several years, she had to rally her spirits so often that she became one of poetry's keener students of the psychological effects fostered by hope, or rather, by the frustration of hopes.

Dickinson's interactive quartet of poets, sun, summer, and heaven also constitutes a narrative of sorts, or rather a species of personal myth dramatizing the conflict she waged with God over possession of the sun, which became emblematic both of her health and of her existence as a poet. In this struggle, poetry functioned as an extension of her self, an alternative mode of perception that took the place of her injured eyes and which was equally as capable of revealing the truth to her. So complete was Dickinson's identification with her poems that she usually refused to submit them for publication, protesting that to do so would be tantamount to a kind of prostitution. Only after the poems had ceased functioning as buffers or as bulkheads between her and the dangerous, allied energies of divinity and the sun did Dickinson begin to consider them as truly literary artifacts having a public, as well as a private, presence.[3]

My approach in this study will be essentially biographical, although no new biographical materials will be adduced. Instead, I intend to synthesize some of what is already known about the poet and apply that knowledge to close readings of the poems. I do so in full knowledge of the warning issued by Maryanne Garbowsky that "The overemphasis on the life of Dickinson and its secrets has led critics to distrust biographical studies" (20). Garbowsky almost certainly alludes here primarily to a succession of biographical studies that began appearing during the 1930s, many of them containing somewhat prurient speculations concerning who the designated recipient of Dickinson's famous "Master" letters might have been.[4] I can only hope, in suggesting that a close relationship exists between Dickinson's life and her work, that I have taken to heart Austin Warren's admonition, repeated by Barton Levi St. Armand on page 1 of his own book *Emily Dickinson and Her Culture*, that "biographical studies and culture-histories—for those who practice them, ends in themselves—are to be used by a critic with caution and delicacy."

Dickinson's life continues to capture the interest of biographical and nonbiographical scholars alike, for three reasons that strike me as being wholly valid: (1) the paucity of hard information we do possess about her, compared to what is known, for example, about Hawthorne, Emerson, Melville, or Whitman, all of whom achieved some measure of renown during their lifetimes; (2) the unusual character of much of what we *do* know about Dickinson's life, particularly those elements over which she could exercise some control, such as visitors' access to her; (3) the fact that full-blown biographies of Dickinson have been available to scholars only relatively recently, beginning with the publication of Sewall's *The Life of Emily Dickinson* in 1974, complemented in 1986 by Cynthia Griffin Wolff's *Emily Dickinson*. In the absence of a suitably large body of documentary evidence that could paint for us a portrait of the artist all could agree was perfectly accurate and realistic, several critics have tried their hands at "reconstructing" Dickinson's personality, as in, for example, psychobiographical studies such as John Cody's groundbreaking book *After Great Pain: The Inner Life of Emily Dickinson* (1971) and Maryanne Garbowsky's exploration of the issue of agoraphobia in Dickinson's poetry, *The House without the Door* (1989); in cultural studies such as St. Armand's book, which examines the Victorian milieu out of which Dickinson's literary style and subject matter arose; and in textual-biographical studies such as Martha Nell Smith's *Rowing in Eden* (1992), which reevaluates the poet's relationship with her sister-in-law, Susan Dickinson. Notably, all of these studies look for evidence concerning Dickinson's life among the poems, which have been treated, for good or ill, as textual facsimiles of the poet herself.

Indeed, much of the current critical "war" being fought over Dickinson involves different "versions" of the poet, as much as it involves the poems themselves. The effort to see the woman Harold Nicolson described (admiringly!) to Vita Sackville-West as "this frail ugly little trout" (264) clearly as she is, as she was, remains one of the primary goals of contemporary Dickinson scholarship. The "version" of Dickinson I hope to promote is one of a poet who was sick, yet not neurotic; withdrawn, yet not introverted. "My" Emily Dickinson also demonstrates herself to be highly attuned, within her poems, to ontological and epistemological quandaries that vexed some of the best minds of her day, including Emerson's. Thus, while this study does participate to some degree in the current (although sometimes unstated) critical project among Dickinson scholars to "normalize" or "mainstream" the poet within late-Romantic or mid-Victorian American culture, it also seeks to reaffirm the wisdom of locating Dickinson's poetics within the larger continuum of what Jerome McGann has called the "aesthetics of deliberate engagement"—that is, "an activist and contestatory poetics" developed in reaction to "various, often radical, dislocations within the social and cultural orders."[5]

Relatively little attention will be devoted in this study to some cultural issues that have already received well-deserved attention from feminist critics, such as the nineteenth-century American medical establishment's often reprehensible and dismissive treatment of women in poor health. This topic has been admirably and illuminatingly discussed in such books as Diane Price Herndl's *Invalid Women: Figuring Feminine Illness in American Fiction and Culture* (Chapel Hill: University of North Carolina Press, 1993) and Sandra M. Gilbert and Susan Gubar's *The Madwoman in the Attic: The Woman Writer and the Nineteenth-Century Imagination*. Rather than considering illness's effects upon women in the aggregate, I propose to concentrate on the fact of illness itself as a governing factor in Dickinson's development as a poet. We are already accustomed to thinking about ways in which illness or deformity modulate the registers of expression we hear while reading Milton, Keats,

Emily Brontë, Lord Byron. For Dickinson, illness was a formative experience as well, one which shaped her entire poetic methodology from perception to inscription and which very likely shook the foundations of her faith. Reading Dickinson's poems in the full knowledge and belief that, while writing them, she was suffering acutely from a seemingly irremediable illness renders many of them recuperable as almost diaristic records of a rather ordinary person's courageous struggle against profound adversity.

Finally, I would add that I am only too well aware that readings based upon biographical evidence are apt to become excessively reductive and simplistic. Nevertheless, in the prevailing postmodernist critical climate, I think we actually stand at greater risk of underestimating the degree of intimacy existing between an author's literary productions and the network of experiences, great and small, that shapes an individual life. And of all the crises that can beset Everyman and Everywoman on their journeys through life, few resonate so powerfully as illness. For the severely, chronically ill, the reality of illness is omnipresent, constantly compelling them to modify their lives to the demands of their diseases, to deviate ever further from futures they had mapped out for themselves. Patients' lives may be marked by periods of introspection while they gradually learn to cope with diminished expectations and thwarted hopes, neither permitting themselves to become prematurely euphoric if their illnesses go into remission, nor too discouraged should their symptoms return unabated. A convalescent who seems to us to be withdrawing from the world may actually be intensively engaged in conserving her resources, paring away whatever has been found unnecessary in order to sustain those things that have proven to be indispensable.

The organizational scheme of this book is roughly chronological. The first three chapters are dedicated to looking at the poet's initial reactions to illness during her young adulthood, dwelling chiefly upon her religious construction of the reasons why she had fallen ill, her explorations of alternative modes of perception, and her redefinition of her own poetic project in terms borrowed from the natural sciences. Chapter 4 concentrates upon Dickinson's spatial tropes, which internalize the physical spaces from which she had been disenfranchised by illness, and predicates that she attempted to establish a new sort of locus within her poetry. Chapter 5 takes up the issue of Dickinson's theories about symbolism and language, which draw upon Emerson's models before establishing a new paradigm for meaning based upon the rite of the sacrament. Chapter 6 discusses Dickinson's attitude toward publication, particularly in light of her initially intense identification with the substance of poetry itself. Finally, chapter 7 reexamines Dickinson's autumnal love affair with Judge Otis Phillips Lord to determine whether she may finally have adopted a more secular approach to writing, abandoning her sacramental paradigm while simultaneously continuing to employ her poems as proxies of the self.

You persuade me to speak of my eyes, which I shunned doing, because I wanted you to rest. I could not bear a single sigh should tarnish your vacation, but, lest through me one bird delay a change of latitude, I will tell you, dear.

The eyes are as with you, sometimes easy, sometimes sad. I think they are not worse, nor do I think them better than when I came home.

Dickinson, in a letter written in early 1865 to her cousin Louise Norcross

There are some intervals which border the strain of the wood thrush, to which I would migrate — wild lands where no settler has squatted; to which, methinks, I am already acclimated.

Thoreau, "Walking"

"MEASURING THE SUN"

Perception, Punishment, and the Rivalrous Imagination

WHILE EMILY DICKINSON wrote the great majority of her poems during the early 1860s she was also suffering from a chronic optical illness. The coincidence of intensified creativity with a descent into illness may have persuaded her that the two were somehow connected—or such, at least, is the impression she seems to be trying to convey to Thomas W. Higginson, her literary "preceptor," in her earliest letters to him. Interspersed among them are tropes touching upon illness in general and impaired vision in particular. Dickinson commenced in April, 1862, by asking Higginson whether he, like a physician called to her literary sickbed, would be willing to tell her whether her verse was "alive," complaining that she had become so close to her own work that she could no longer view it objectively: "The Mind is so near itself—it cannot see, distinctly" (*Letters*, 403). Her succeeding letter informed him that she was "ill" and writing "from [her] pillow" that day, before thanking him for his "surgery" upon the poems she had sent him (L404). Her next letter characterizes her entire poetic method as a sort of illness, or rather as a cure for illness, her verses "just reliev[ing]" a "palsy" (408). At the same time, Dickinson continued to address Higginson as if he were a doctor, thanking him for the "Balm" of his praise after he had "bled" her with his criticism. She wittily responded to his suggestion that her style had a good deal in common with the "spasmodic" school of poets by saying that she was indeed "in danger" of falling. Unwilling or unable to evaluate her own work, she told him that she trusted his judgment: "The Sailor cannot see the North—but knows the Needle can—." Then she metaphorically put her hand in his, which she quoted him as saying he had stretched out to her "in the Dark," and closed with a poem describing the morning sun's power to "shatter" her with dawn.

To some extent, Dickinson must have been deliberately modeling her portrayal of herself to Higginson upon the stereotype of the female literary convalescent popularized in the Victorian imagination by her idol, Mrs. Browning.[1] Yet the sheer number of tropes Dickinson fashioned out of references to blindness and to physical disability suggests that these letters are more than just initial attempts to exact sympathy from Higginson. Dickinson began writing to him at a crucial moment in her development as a poet, that is, when she had first become confident enough about her work to have it evaluated by a respected critic, and she tries to get off on the right foot by explaining to him not only how she wrote, but why she had become a writer in the first place. What comes across most clearly after a thorough rereading of them is that Dickinson regarded writing as a form of therapy, yet not because it granted her a means of escaping, imaginatively, from the tedium of her sickroom. On the contrary, her poems provided Dickinson with the intellectual tools she needed to come to grips with her situation. In them she could dramatize how her sphere of physical activity had been diminished by illness, analyze the psychological effects of both hope and hopelessness, and mourn the visible world she had been forced to renounce. Even more importantly, she could use her poems to speculate about the religious ramifications of what had happened to her. Correspondingly, some poems would appear to suggest that Dickinson interpreted the onset, recurrences, and ultimate remission of her illness as a series of direct encounters with divinity in which she had achieved a premature revelation of heaven, either accidentally or by design. These meetings left Dickinson with a legacy of resentment, resignation, and, eventually, gratitude—not just for her recovery but also for a heightened awareness of her own creative strength.

A Possible Diagnosis

Any attempt to assess how deeply Dickinson's illness perturbed either her life or her art is made problematic, however, not only by a scarcity of documentary materials but also by her own mysterious reticence on the topic. We cannot say with any real degree of confidence, for example, when Dickinson first fell ill. It is a matter of record that Dickinson journeyed to Boston on at least two occasions, in 1864 and 1865, to be treated by Dr. Henry Williams, an eminent ophthalmologist.[2] These treatments required Dickinson to live among strangers in a boarding house for months at a time: in the case of her first treatment in Boston, from late April 1864 until late November. Dickinson had to remain in her rented room most of the time, out of the light. Yet even indoors her eyes were evidently still vulnerable to being overexposed, for Dr. Williams required her to cover them with bandages she could remove only at sunrise and sunset. In a letter written in November 1864 just before returning home, Dickinson complained to her sister Lavinia, "I have been sick so long I do not know the sun" (L435). Difficult as it may be to determine the date of onset and the duration of Dickinson's illness, discerning her primary clinical symptoms is a comparatively easy matter. In an 1865 letter sent from Amherst to her cousin Louise Norcross, who had nursed her in Boston during the previous year's treatment, Dickinson says that "snow-light" and even house light hurt her eyes, despite a summer spent convalescing (L439). Her eyes may also have been susceptible to tearing, for Dickinson characterizes herself more than once as living underwater, in or at the center of the sea (L434, 441). Further-more, because her eyes pained her unpredictably from one day to the next, she often could not tell whether she was actually getting any better (L439).

Yet Dickinson may have found most daunting of all a realization that illness was becoming a way of life for her. She may have had to begin curtailing her visual activities much earlier than her treatments in Boston during the summers of 1864 and 1865. In a letter written to Joseph Lyman in about 1865, she refers to a period already "Some years ago" when her doctor had forbidden her to read:

> A Calamity. Some years ago I had a woe, the only one that ever made me tremble. It was a shutting out of all the dearest ones of time, the strongest friends of the soul—BOOKS[.] The medical man said avaunt ye ~~books~~ tormentors, he also said "down, thoughts, & plunge into her soul." He might as well have said, "Eyes be blind," "heart be still." So I had eight ~~weary~~ months of Siberia. (Sewall, *Lyman Letters,* 76)

Richard B. Sewall notes the similarity between this passage's first sentence and her statement to Higginson in April 1862 that she had had a "terror since September" (*Lyman Letters,* 74). If the previous year's "terror" to which Dickinson referred was a fear of being confined to her room, and if, by "Some years ago" in her mid-1860s letter to Joseph Lyman she meant the year 1861, being shut up indoors for months at a time could have begun to seem almost routine to Dickinson by the time she sought treatment in Boston in 1864. Thus she may have been seriously ill, on and off, for at least five years, and perhaps for as many as fifteen.[3]

The possibility that Dickinson's illness may have been all in her head has been mentioned more than once. Some critics have proposed that the poet's symptoms, particularly her wariness of sunlight, stemmed from supposedly troubled relationships either with her immediate family or with society at large. Most prominent of the various psychosomatic investigations of Dickinson's illness has been Dr. John Cody's *After Great Pain: The Inner Life of Emily Dickinson* (1971). Dr. Cody, a psychiatrist, theorized that Dickinson's eyes pained her because she unconsciously feared the sun, which represented an unacknowledged, symbolically castrated male principle in herself that was the result of an incomplete, unrequited relationship with her mother (433–34). During the 1980s, however, feminist critics began to challenge this explanation, some of them resituating the basis for Dickinson's optical complaint in the poet's resistance to patriarchal authority. In *Lunacy of Light: Emily Dickinson and the Experience of Metaphor* (1987), for example, Wendy Barker contends that Dickinson's symptoms arose at least in part because the poet resented and resisted being dominated by males, the sun becoming an image in her poems of an oppressive male energy capable of inflicting violence and destruction (66). Yet attributions of Dickinson's shunning of the sun to her attitudes toward men have not been restricted solely to feminist critics. Barton St. Armand, in *Emily Dickinson and Her Culture* (1984), suggests that Dickinson was traumatized by the loss of a male companion whom she came to symbolize, both in her poems and in the Master letters, with the image of the sun.[4]

These psychosociologic explanations for Dickinson's symptoms began to be contradicted, however, by biographers offering more specific organic causes. In his 1974 life of the poet, Richard B. Sewall discussed Dickinson's eye problems at some length and proposed that she suffered from exotropia, or a deviation of the cornea that prevents the sufferer from achieving perfectly binocular vision (606–7n.9).[5] In 1979 Sewall followed up on this idea by collaborating with ophthalmologist Martin Wand to write "'Eyes Be Blind, Heart Be Still': A New Perspective on Emily Dickinson's Eye Problem," in which they used the famous daguerreotype of Dickinson taken at Mount Holyoke Female Seminary to show that the poet's right cornea deviated as much as fifteen degrees from true (403). Cynthia Wolff agreed with Sewall and Dr. Wand in her own 1986 biography that the poet probably suffered from exotropia, yet she integrated their theory with a Freudian profile of the poet which hypothesizes that Dickinson became so alienated from her mother, Emily Norcross Dickinson, that she experienced difficulty in making eye contact with her (581n.2).

Dickinson's mother may indeed have been key to the poet's having fallen ill, yet for reasons that had nothing to do with their emotional relationship. Because exotropia is, as Wand and Sewall point out, a hereditary disease carried matrilineally, women are more likely to manifest symptoms than are men. Wand and Sewall claim that photographs and paintings of the poet's mother and sister reveal that they also suffered from the disease to some degree (403). Moreover, during an international meeting of Dickinson scholars at Innsbruck in 1995, Martha Ackmann of Mount Holyoke College revealed[6] that the (then) oldest living descendant of the poet on her mother's side, Sylvia Swett Viano of Lexington, Massachusetts, reported that her own granddaughter had

had exotropia and that she believed photographs of Loring and Louisa Norcross, the poet's maternal uncle and cousin, showed they had had it, too.[7] If Louisa did, in fact, also suffer from exotropia, Dickinson's statement in her letter to "Cousin Loo" that "The eyes are *as with you*, sometimes easy, sometimes sad" may allude to a shared affliction with which they had both grown so familiar that not much needed to be said on the matter.

A dearth of references to optical problems in the Dickinson family correspondence during the poet's childhood may also have been due to the disease's having remained latent or virtually undetectable until Emily Dickinson became a young woman. According to Wand and Sewall, even though early symptoms of exotropia ordinarily appear soon after birth, the disease may not become readily apparent until a patient reaches the age of thirty, at which time a deviation of the cornea that had been intermittent may become constant (403). Citing Burian and von Noorden's *Binocular Vision and Ocular Motility* (1974), Wand and Sewall summarize exotropes' most common complaints: "eye strain, blurring of vision, difficulties with prolonged periods of reading, headaches, and diplopia [that is, double vision]." Moreover, exotropes may exhibit an acute sensitivity to "bright light in general and sunlight in particular" (404). One irony of the disease is that "when . . . deviation is intermittent, a person may have the most pronounced symptoms, because when this deviation becomes constant, some suppression of vision usually develops in the deviating eye to prevent double vision" (403). In other words, vision within the injured eye will spontaneously diminish to conserve vision in the sound eye.[8]

A similar sort of compensation is discernible within Dickinson's poetics, except that it is her imagination that she substitutes for her injured eyes. Reading some of Dickinson's poems specifically in the context of her optical illness generates a subtext in which God punishes the poet for looking too intensely upon the world, so that she must resort to finding other "ways" of seeing.[9] Although Dickinson tries to placate God by using "faith" as an organ of perception, she discovers that she is tempted repeatedly to "consume" the world all over again, imperilling not only her weakened eyes, but potentially even her ability to write. After coming to terms, finally, both with her illness and with God, Dickinson does achieve a new vantage point from which she can safely function as a poet by paying strict attention to the sun's position in the sky, an indicator of God's "nearness" to her.

NOON AND "COVERED VISION"

Dickinson's absences from home during Dr. Williams's treatments were the longest the poet would ever know, and they forced her to summon up extraordinary reserves of patience, optimism, and, above all, imaginative resilience. Her confinement at least gave Dickinson leisure to consider what the imagination was, how it worked, and how its creative power might rival even God's. She toys with such a notion in a letter written to her sister-in-law in about June 1864, during her first extended treatment:

> I knew it was "November" [*sic*], but then there is a June when Corn is cut, whose option is within. That is why I prefer the Power, for Power is Glory, when it likes, and Dominion, too—(L432)

Here, because Dickinson's bandaged eyes register her sickroom's dimness as dark "November," when farmers cut down dried cornstalks, she simply transposes November for June in her imagination.[10] The exchange yields a twofold benefit: first, it provides a "logical" explanation for the evidence supplied by her senses; second, she can tell herself she really isn't missing sunny, colorful June after all, because June "looks like" November. Her imagination's ability to substitute for her suppressed senses therefore constitutes an "option" still available to Dickinson in the midst of illness, and she even goes so far as to claim, in a playful blasphemy of the Lord's Prayer, that she prefers the "Power" (that is, the power to imagine) over empirical experience.[11]

Although we should read a certain amount of self-deprecating irony into this passage, a residue of seriousness is discernible in the very fact that Dickinson should feel compelled to fabricate so convoluted a rationalization. If she had been more candid, she probably would have admitted that her attachment to the visible world eventually proved much stronger than she had expected or hoped. Disjunction between Dickinson's compensatory imagination and her ravenous hunger for sensory stimulation gave rise to a corresponding conflict in her poetry between the idealized realm of heaven and the sublunary, tangible realm of earth and sun, the source of her poetic imagery. Mediating between heaven and earth/sun was "Noon," a symbol so vital to understanding the interrelationships between Dickinson's idiosyncratic strain of Christianity, her poetry, and the symptoms of her illness that we should begin by examining its provenance.

Dickinson's fondness for "Noon" as a symbol (it appears no fewer than seventy-six times, according to Rosenbaum's *Concordance*) may be attributed chiefly to the midday sun's position in her private cosmography. At its zenith the sun became, in effect, a point of contact between the territories of heaven and earth, the infinite and the finite. Our "finite" eyes were ordinarily incapable, she believed, of seeing the workings of this "infinite" world except at revelatory times such as "Noon," when temporal beauty became so exalted as to approximate heavenly brilliance. She wrote, in poem no. 575,

> "Heaven" has different Signs—to me—
> Sometimes I think that Noon
> Is but a symbol of the Place—

The belief that earth *must* resemble heaven became a cornerstone of Dickinson's faith, for it reassured her that heaven would prove both familiar and hospitable. Similitude also implied physical proximity, permitting Dickinson to believe that heaven lay only as far away from her, metaphorically speaking, as the nearest town. Although undertaking to look for heaven might prove as hazardous as peering up with unshielded eyes at the noonday sun, a prospect of paradise was accessible, Dickinson believed, to the eyes of the worthy.

Yet her own worthiness was precisely what troubled Dickinson. Despite her well-known periodic refusals to attend church with the rest of her family or to proclaim herself a confirmed Christian while a student at Mount Holyoke Female Seminary, Dickinson wished desperately to believe that heaven existed and that it would admit her after her death. Thus her illness became an ill omen, a sign that she had somehow offended God. Sickroom confinement provided a chilling analog to being shut out of heaven, for during the peak of a June day when the sun was at its highest and brightest, Dickinson's doctor prohibited her from visiting the family garden, her own domestic, earthly paradise. Both "Noon" and heaven were therefore tantalizingly unattainable for Dickinson, who defined the latter by exclusion when she wrote "'Heaven' is what I cannot reach—."

In the wake of her attack Dickinson may well have concluded she had been punished for having seen something forbidden, like the noontime sun. Such, at least, would seem to be the assumption underlying the following poem, one critical to understanding Dickinson's interpretation of what had happened to her eyes (no. 327, written in about 1862):

> Before I got my eye put out
> I liked as well to see—
> As other Creatures, that have Eyes
> And know no other way—

But were it told to me—Today—
That I might have the sky
For mine—I tell you that my Heart
Would split, for size of me—

The Meadows—mine—
The Mountains—mine—
All Forests—Stintless Stars—
As much of Noon as I could take
Between my finite eyes—

The Motions of The Dipping Birds—
The Morning's Amber Road—
For mine—to look at when I liked—
The News would strike me dead—

So safer Guess—with just my soul
Upon the Window pane—
Where other Creatures put their eyes—
Incautious—of the Sun—

Interpreted literally, this poem narrates the consequences of Dickinson's failure to obey her doctor's command to shun direct sunlight.[12] Another reading of the poem is opened up, however, by her phrase, "I got my eye *put* out," which shifts the blame to an external agent. Although it is initially unclear who has injured the poet or why, the text provides a few clues. Her description of scenes she would look upon, were she to regain full use of her eyes, is so rapturous that we may infer her transgression had been to admire the visible world excessively. Despite her statement that, were she to recover her sight, her "Heart" would "split" with joy, it is actually her gluttonous eyes whose "size" would swell, having feasted upon the sensory world to the point of devouring even "Noon," the hour her doctors probably represented to her as being most dangerous to her sight.

Yet the potential metaphysical consequences of Dickinson's stealthy "consumption" of the visible world were much more serious than any physical injury. By finding the natural world transcendently beautiful, Dickinson had ventured too near the truth that earth *does* look like heaven. Further, her admiration for temporal beauty had become so great as to cause her to question, as she was prone to do from time to time, the biblical statement that "Eye hath not seen, nor ear heard, neither have entered into the heart of man, the things which God hath prepared for them that love him" (1 Cor. 2:9). In the darkest construction Dickinson put upon her illness, God attempted to teach her a lesson in humility by demonstrating the full consequences of comprehending the fact that earth resembles heaven, intensifying the splendor of the visible world until her eyes became afflicted by a premature glimpse of heaven they were utterly unequipped to assimilate.

Toward the end of "Before I got my eye put out," a chastened Dickinson professes her willingness to exercise a different mode of perception, turning from her eyes to her "soul," a term for which we can reasonably substitute, I think, "faith." Like the imagination, which can only "guess" about things the eyes actually see, faith is content to "guess" at what heaven will be like. As an organ of perception, faith offered Dickinson a twofold advantage over her eyes: first, should Dickinson be afforded another look at heaven, the incorporeal, less literal, less vulnerable "soul" could withstand the shock; second, because faith was divinely sanctioned, God might be placated and therefore less likely to punish her again with another "Heavenly Hurt" or "imperial affliction," as she says in "There's a certain Slant of light." Yet to renounce her eyesight was to forgo her need for ocular proof of heaven's existence, a deprivation that rankled Dickinson even more than the loss of her license to see. When we recall Dickinson's wry observation that "'Faith' is a fine invention / When Gentlemen can *see*—," her phrase "I got my eye *put* out" sounds fraught with resentment. Condemned without due process of law, Dickinson protests that other "Creatures," ignorant of the sun's latent destructive power, weren't compelled to learn another "way" of seeing, as she was. Dickinson's faith could not thrive in the absence of visual confirmation; it had to be supplemented by close, appreciative scrutiny of the same sort that had landed her in trouble in the first place. Thus Dickinson found herself caught in a cycle of transgression, repentance, and rebellion that played itself out, on a temporal level, in the weary repetition of exposure, pain, and restiveness that defined her everyday existence as a patient.

Dickinson's ambivalence about submitting to God's correction in "Before I got my eye put out" mirrors her reluctance to follow doctor's orders. Yet her only hope for recovering her eyesight evidently lay in shunning the visible world, and, because it must have been within her power to hasten or delay the progress of recovery, she had to exercise self-discipline and self-restraint on a daily basis. Her determination to accommodate herself to the realities of an extended convalescence may have provided the creative impetus for a second poem about eyes being "put out" (no. 745, written in about 1863):

Renunciation—is a piercing Virtue—
The letting go
A Presence—for an Expectation—
Not now—
The putting out of Eyes—
Just Sunrise—
Lest Day—
Day's Great Progenitor—
Outvie
Renunciation—is the Choosing
Against itself—
Itself to justify
Unto itself—
When larger function—
Make that appear—
Smaller—that Covered Vision—Here—   Covered / sated—

On the most literal of levels this poem may be interpreted as Dickinson's self-admonition to rebandage her eyes rather than expose them to morning's light.[13] Present sacrifices, she rather piously reminds herself, will ultimately be justified by recovery, the "larger function." Yet renunciation of the sensory world is "piercing," an adjective whose forcefulness is redoubled by its propinquity to "Eyes." So rigorous do Dickinson's efforts to rehabilitate herself become that she refers to herself as "Itself," a distancing that preserves the poem's façade of being an objective, dispassionate consideration of the importance of self-denial and not a descent into maudlin self-pity or, worse, self-recrimination. Because renunciation of temporal matters was one of the criteria for God's determination of who should enter heaven, or the "larger function," Dickinson forswears, or at least *says* she forswears, the tangible world. She reproves her hunger for visible things and tries to content herself with "Covered Vision," or a state of voluntary perceptual restraint. She promises to behave herself "Here," a word with dual significance: both the "here and now" of her own room, and temporal existence as a whole, which subsists in proportion to a life in heaven as bandaged sight does to 20–20 vision. That Dickinson interpreted "Covered Vision" as being the result of having over-exerted her eyes is also suggested by a manuscript variant, "sated," which reiterates the comparison Dickinson makes between consumption and perception in "Before I got my eye put out." Superficially, at least, this poem "answers" "Before I got my eye put out" by substituting adult self-discipline, dispassionate objectivity, and religious devotion for bewildered naïveté or smoldering resentment. Further, in this poem the narrator "puts out" her own eyes, rather than finding they've been put out for her, resigning herself to exercising a diminished form of perception. But this spare, virtually imageless poem's submissiveness may begin to seem disingenuous if we recall the poet's ecstatic catalog of earthly delights in "Before I got my eye put out." Correspondingly, "Renunciation—is a piercing Virtue—" completely deconstructs itself if we read it in the context of Dickinson's metaphysical explanation for her illness. The previous poem's barely suppressed anger toward God resurfaces in her subversive speculation that day—more precisely, sunrise—might "Outvie" day's "Great Progenitor," God. Even to raise the possibility that earthly beauty might compete successfully with heaven's interrogates the entire poem's ostensible mood of pious self-abnegation as well as her professed acceptance of a reduced or "Covered" mode of vision. As a consequence, this poem represents, I believe, a failed attempt by Dickinson to resolve her spiritual and perceptual crisis. Yet if she could not learn to defer until after death the pleasure she took in seeing the world, a different strategy she may have elected to pursue was to use her imagination to exchange the nighttime, which posed no threat to her eyes, for the proscribed day.

REVERSING THE CLOCK

As we have seen, the extended periods of treatment Dickinson endured in Boston resulted in an impression that she was out of synchrony with the rest of the world, so much so that she felt compelled to replace "June" with "November." Being deprived of light may have caused Dickinson to lose track, temporarily, of when day ended and night began; in contemporary terms, we might say her circadian rhythm had been disrupted. Quite possibly she responded to her disorientation by using the power or "option" of her imagination to adjust the clock, as she had already adjusted the calendar. In a handful of poems she explicitly exchanges day for night (no. 425):

Good Morning—Midnight—
I'm coming Home—
Day—got tired of Me—
How could I—of Him?

Sunshine was a sweet place—
I liked to stay—

But Morn—didn't want me—now—
So—Goodnight—Day!

I can look—can't I—
When the East is Red?
The Hills—have a way—then—
That puts the Heart—abroad—

You—are not so fair—Midnight—
I chose—Day—
But please take a little Girl—
He turned away!

Like a playmate who had grown too rambunctious at a neighbor's house, the narrator, who I think must represent the poet herself, has been sent home because day "got tired" of her, so that she must now court the favors of another, less desirable companion, Midnight. Dickinson's adoption of her "little Girl" persona in this poem indicates that she is being at least somewhat facetious, yet I think her childishness also reflects her feelings of helplessness as a patient. When the narrator asks in the third stanza still to be allowed to look upon the dawn, she leaves perhaps intentionally unclear which figure of authority is being addressed—a parent, a doctor, Midnight itself, or God. It is also significant, I think, that the narrator's exile in this poem is due at least in part to some failing of her own, as if her presence had become too exhausting for her playmate, day, to tolerate.[14] Thus the sense of having trespassed that lingers in some of Dickinson's poems recapitulating the story of how her eyes had been afflicted may be in evidence in this poem, as well.

But Dickinson's banishment from daytime was hardly child's play. The "unnaturalness" of her compulsory nocturnal schedule may have seemed to her a sign that the machinery of the entire cosmos had somehow slipped a cog (no. 415):

Sunset at Night—is natural—
But Sunset on the Dawn
Reverses Nature—Master—
So Midnight's—due—at Noon.

Eclipses be—predicted—
And Science bows them in—
But do one face us suddenly—
Jehovah's Watch—is wrong.

Dickinson's topsy-turvy schedule transforms "Noon" into "Midnight" because the meridian now marks the halfway point until "day" comes again for the poet at evening, when she could gaze out the window again. The metamorphosis of noon, the time of day she regarded most reverentially, into midnight's pitch blackness possesses an especially cruel irony for Dickinson. If she were somehow "closest" to heaven at that moment of the day when the sun reached its zenith, how much more distantly removed from God was she while ill? Her old sense of surety in the rightness and dependability of things now nullified, it seems to Dickinson as if the mainspring of "Jehovah's Watch" itself has broken, and the "eye" of the sun has been darkened by an unforetold eclipse. Thus the at least semivoluntary reversal of the clock that Dickinson had made with her imagination is suddenly converted or externalized into a frightening cosmic entropy.

In this poem Dickinson addresses a listening "Master" who evidently has no control or authority over what is happening to her, but functions instead as a kind of passive witness or chorus. Previous to reading the poem, "Master," who may or may not have been the same "Master" addressed in Dickinson's famous "Master" letters, had not understood the seriousness of her situation, and the argumentative tenor of the poem seems designed to persuade him (or her) that she deserves his understanding, or at least his respectful attention, rather than detached amusement. As she was to write in the second "Master" letter, "Chillon" (that is, the reality of being cooped up like François de Bonnivard, the hero of Byron's poem "The Prisoner of Chillon") was "not funny" (L374). Her experience as a sequestered invalid would continue to have a profound effect upon the carcerative images Dickinson used throughout her poetry, as well as in letters written late in life to Judge Otis Lord (discussed in chapters 3 and 7, respectively).

Dickinson's phrase "Sunset on the Dawn" verbally conflates two times of day that had already become perceptually indistinguishable from each other. Except that sunset occurred in the west and sunrise in the east, to Dickinson, who could no longer tell the difference between night and day, those two twilight hours had become virtually identical, because they were the only times she was permitted to look at the sun. Correspondingly, matutinal and crepuscular visions usually represent safe havens in her poems, zones of immunity that are bracketed by twin periods of "night," one natural and one generated by her bandages. And, because sunset and sunrise were the only remnants of day left to her, Dickinson clung to them. In "Good Morning—Midnight—," for ex-

ample, she asks some unspecified authority whether she will still be able
to look outside at dawn, "when the East is Red," and in "Renunciation—is a piercing Virtue—," she waits until "Just Sunrise" to rebandage her own eyes to protect them from the brilliance of broad daylight.
Being restricted to peering out her window only at such times must have
made Dickinson savor even more keenly two moments she had already
come to cherish both for their colorfulness and for the sense of imminence they imparted as precursors of day and night. Relishing each instant of her perceptual freedom, Dickinson could indeed tell readers "how
the sun rose" (no. 318), prolonging each minute until the sun's ascent
toward noon harried her away from her window.[15]

Perhaps because sunrise and sunset offered Dickinson temporary sanc-
tuaries from the visual monotonies of nighttime and blindness behind
her bandages, poems concerning those times of day often dwell upon
the nature of perception itself. Many of them also include an admoni-
tory component, as if Dickinson were trying to impress upon her readers the fragility and importance of *vision,* considered in both the physical and the metaphysical senses of that term. The following poem lays
out the simultaneous risks and rewards of vision extended beyond its
normal limits (no. 1018):

Who saw no Sunrise cannot say
The Countenance 'twould be.
Who guess at seeing, guess at loss
Of the Ability.

The Emigrant of Light, it is
Afflicted for the Day.
The Blindness that beheld and blest—
And could not find it's Eye.

The distinction we have seen Dickinson make before between "guessing" and "seeing" reappears in this poem's first stanza, when she says
that those who have never witnessed the "Countenance" of the sunrise
cannot even begin to picture it for themselves. Neither, however, can
those who are content to guess, rather than to look, viscerally comprehend what it would be like not to be able to see. Ironically, such people
essentially blind themselves by refusing to seek the testimonial their own
eyes could provide, a state of voluntary ignorance Dickinson transfers
in the second stanza to the "eye" of the sun, covered up by banks of
clouds soon after sunrise. The sun is an "Emigrant" on its sojourn from

the "country" of light, but it can proceed no further after being "blinded" by clouds near the horizon. Although the sun "blesses" those who see it rise, "beholding" them in turn like a gigantic eye, it abruptly loses its own way, caught in the predicament of the nearsighted person who has lost his spectacles and who then, to use Dickinson's powerful tautology from "I heard a Fly buzz—when I died—," could not "see to see."

Like a sightless beggar walking the streets, the sun blesses those it passes, yet cannot see itself being blessed. In this figure of the sun reduced to a wandering blind man we may perceive, I think, a projection of Dickinson's own situation as a "blind" person who looked, and then could not look again. Within that paradoxical phrase "The Blindness that beheld" is comprised an ingrained habit of perception that will inevitably aggravate her eyestrain still further: virtually "blind" to begin with, her eyes nevertheless turn toward the light to behold the world, and by seeing it, "bless" it; afterwards, of course, her eyes become exhausted, so that she is even worse off than before. Hazardous and self-defeating though this cycle of reexposure and relapse would be, it is still preferable to "guessing" exclusively about the world's appearance. Better to have looked and lost her eyes, Dickinson might have said, than never to have looked at all.

A "Stapled Song" in the Fascicles

Although Dickinson declares in "Renunciation—is a piercing Virtue—" and in her letters that the realm of the mind surpasses that of the senses, her exaltation of her own conceptual "Power" may have begun to seem more and more like empty bravado as the months of confinement wore on. Perhaps she concluded that the imagination, or "Expectation," is, in its most debased form, merely a lackluster imitation of primary experience, or "Presence," because the former derives virtually all of its images and contexts secondhand from the latter. Whether for this reason or some other, Dickinson did apparently finally admit to herself that "Covered" vision would always be intrinsically inferior to an unrestricted freedom to see.

Consequently, despite Dickinson's resolve to retreat within, she discovered she could not write in a perceptual vacuum after all, and the threat illness posed to her poetry may have proven even more frightening than the prospect of being shut up in her room or shut out of heaven. Denied the stimulus of perception, Dickinson's burgeoning creativity, which was driving her in 1862 to write at the rate of a poem a day, might slow down, wither, or even die. Such a waning may be alluded to in the following poem, which quite possibly chronicles one of the poet's flights from her sickroom to the brilliant, yet fatal, refuge of the family flower garden (no. 512):

The Soul has Bandaged moments—
When too appalled to stir—
She feels some ghastly Fright come up
And stop to look at her—

Salute her—with long fingers—
Caress her freezing hair—
Sip, Goblin, from the very lips
The Lover—hovered—o'er—
Unworthy, that a thought so mean
Accost a Theme—so—fair—

The soul has moments of Escape—
When bursting all the doors—
She dances like a Bomb, abroad,
And swings upon the Hours,

As do the Bee—delirious borne—
Long Dungeoned from his Rose—
Touch Liberty—then know no more,
But Noon, and Paradise—

The Soul's retaken moments—
When, Felon led along,
With shackles on the plumed feet,
And staples, in the Song,

The Horror welcomes her, again,
These, are not brayed of Tongue—

Although Dickinson's "jailbreak" narrative in this poem might seem initially melodramatic or even farcical, such escapes from the isolation of her sickroom must have been nerve-wracking for everyone involved. Not only did Dickinson suffer physical pain from having exposed her eyes to the sun, but also pangs of guilt for having made the task of her reluctant keepers (that is, her solicitous family) more difficult. Moreover, much of her suffering is done in private, for, except within the narrow limits of this very poem, Dickinson refuses to "bray" like a complaining ass to those entrusted with her care, who are already all too conscious of her plight. A note of stoicism is also present in her reference to herself as a "soul," a term that, like "itself" in "Renunciation—is a piercing Virtue—," distances Dickinson as narrator of the poem from Dickinson as participant.

Worst of all, perhaps, these flights exacerbated the slow deterioration of the narrator's creativity, for while her feet are "shackled" and her song "stapled," the bird, symbolic of Dickinson's identity as a poet, has no access to "Noon" or "Paradise," the sensory stimulation she needs in order to sing. R. W. Franklin, in his reconstruction of Dickinson's hand-sewn manuscripts, includes "The Soul has Bandaged moments—" in fascicle 17, where it appears to be the culmination of an extended recapitulation of the poet's various reactions to illness that begins in fascicle 15 and is sustained through fascicle 17. All three fascicles are among the twenty or so that Dickinson assembled during what Franklin rightly calls her *annus mirabilis* of 1862 (xii). Ironically, however, these poems collectively paint a portrait of someone deeply concerned that her creativity is being gradually destroyed.

Within fascicles 15, 16, and 17, Dickinson's ordering of her poems seems to have been chronological: first, the poet attempts to grapple with what was happening to her; then, she makes a temporary accommodation to being ill by exchanging day for night; then, she formulates various metaphysical explanations for what had happened to her; finally, in fascicle 17, she makes an abortive attempt to escape her condition of sensory deprivation. Fascicle 15 commences with "The first Day's Night had come—," a poem that succinctly dramatizes Dickinson's horror as the seriousness of her situation slowly dawns upon her and she realizes her creativity may be in jeopardy:

> The first Day's Night had come—
> And grateful that a thing
> So terrible—had been endured—
> I told my Soul to sing—
>
> She said her Strings were snapt—
> Her Bow—to Atoms blown—
> And so to mend her—gave me work
> Until another Morn
>
> And then—a Day as huge
> As Yesterdays in pairs,

Unrolled its horror in my face—
Until it blocked my eyes—

Fascicle 15 continues with "Sunset at Night—is natural" and "We grow accustomed to the Dark—," both of which may refer to the poet's new nocturnal regimen. They are followed in turn by "You'll know it—as you know 'tis Noon—":

You'll know it—as you know 'tis Noon—
By Glory—
As you do the Sun—
By Glory—
As you will in Heaven—
Know God the Father—and the Son.

By intuition, Mightiest Things
Assert themselves—and not by terms—
"I'm Midnight"—need the Midnight say—
"I'm Sunrise"—need the Majesty?

Omnipotence—had not a Tongue—
His lisp—is Lightning—and the Sun—
His Conversation—with the Sea—
"How shall you know"?
Consult your Eye!

In this poem Dickinson challenges the epistemological limits of rationalism and instead asserts the superiority of the sublime. The final line locates the authority for knowing that divinity is present in subjective experience, thereby validating her own belief that God's power was immanent in the light of the noonday sun. The first stanza's parallel structure emphasizes the duality of God the Father and God the Son/Sun, a play on words that Dickinson must have found especially provocative.

Fascicle 16 begins, portentously, with "Before I got my eye put out—," as Dickinson continues searching for a metaphysical explanation of why she had fallen ill. That poem is immediately followed by "Of nearness to her sundered Things," in which the narrator's depression, caused, perhaps, by having been "sundered" from the light or from books, is relieved by intermittent periods of lucidity:

Of nearness to her sundered Things
The Soul has special times—

When Dimness—looks the Oddity—
Distinctness—easy—seems—

Fascicle 16 also contains two poems concerning physical disorientation, "I felt a Funeral, in my Brain," of which I shall have more to say in chapter 4, and "When we stand on the tops of Things—," in which Dickinson distinguishes between "Sound" souls, who can see clearly, and "flawed" ones, such as, we may infer, her own:

When we stand on the tops of Things—
And like the Trees, look down—
The smoke all cleared away from it—
And Mirrorrs on the scene—

Just laying light—no soul will wink
Except it have the flaw—
The Sound ones, like the Hills—shall stand—
No Lightning, scares away—

The Perfect, nowhere be afraid—
They bear their dauntless Heads,
Where others, dare not walk at noon,
Protected by their deeds—

The Stars dare shine occasionally
Upon a spotted World—
And Suns, go surer, for their Proof,
As if an Axle, held—

Although other, "perfect" people might be capable of looking with unprotected eyes upon the various sources of bright light enumerated in the poem, including noon itself, the narrator wonders if she herself were "spotted," disqualified by some unspecified sin from ever being able to look upon eternity stripped of all artifice or impediment.

Fascicle 17 opens with "I dreaded that first Robin, so," in which Dickinson fears hearing the first sounds of a spring she will likely be forced to miss, prevented from seeing it, presumably, by her bandages. This grouping also includes the eerie "It was not Death, for I stood up," in which the narrator seems to be immobilized in some limitless and undefinable space, and the penultimate poem in the fascicle is "The Soul has Bandaged moments—," in which, as we have seen, the family flower garden may symbolize the entire visible world Dickinson had had to forswear. Concluding Fascicle 17 is "Like Flowers, that heard the news of Dews," which, although it makes no mention of blindness *per se,* ends with a list of distant, promised rewards for which the faithful must patiently wait:

> Like Flowers, that heard the news of Dews,
> But never deemed the dripping prize
> Awaited their—low Brows—
> Or bees—that thought the Summer's name
> Some rumor of Delirium,
> No Summer—could—for Them—

The garden, symbolic of the vegetative world Dickinson had been compelled to renounce as well as of the earthly Eden whose beauty competed with heaven's, provided the poet with an image of what she stood to regain by enduring the privation of being "imprisoned" indoors. Yet the garden also represented Dickinson's identity as a poet, that is, a person whose imagination could be stimulated from having seen "a sudden light on Orchards," creating a "palsy" that "the Verses just relieve—" (L408). In order to "bloom" herself, however, Dickinson needed to find a way of being "permitted" to stay outdoors, if only for a short time.

THE DICKINSONIAN INTERVAL

To continue functioning as a poet, Dickinson realized that she had to make some sort of accommodation with illness as well as a rapprochement with God. Being able to wield the "power" of her imagination was not enough; she needed the "glory" of the sensory world, as well. As the years passed and her eyesight did not seem to improve, Dickinson may have begun to appreciate intervals of days, weeks, or months during which her symptoms abated and she could walk in the garden, read books, and write as often as she wished. Seeing or being in an interval between twin areas or times of danger, as when she looked out the window at sunrise or sunset, is the characteristic Dickinsonian moment. Poetry itself was created within a zone of immunity, a margin of safety within which she and God observed a sort of détente. Like the intervals of the wood thrush's song to which Thoreau wished to migrate, the Dickinsonian interval is a place as well as a time, a platform from which the poet could safely regard both the pleasures of nature and a prospect of "noon," the portal to heaven.

Dickinson may have recognized that illness had helped foster this new attitude and given thanks for being able to exercise a modified, hybrid form of perception that combined conventional vision with poetic vision. To denote this "other way" of seeing I shall employ a term that Dickinson may or may not herself have used: "compound vision," which could be regarded as the antithesis of "covered vision," or seeing through faith only. The phrase "compound vision" appears in poem no. 906, "The Admirations—and Contempts—of Time," where it possesses, as I shall explain in the next chapter, specific associations with the sciences of both optics and astronomy. Nevertheless, "compound vision's" utility to Dickinson as a poetic methodology is perhaps most patently visible in the following poem, which may also include a condensed narrative of Dickinson's struggle with optical illness (no. 574, written in about 1862):

My first well Day—since many ill—
I asked to go abroad,
And take the Sunshine in my hands,
And see the things in Pod—

A'blossom just when I went in
To take my Chance with pain—
Uncertain if myself, or He,
Should prove the strongest One.

The Summer deepened, while we strove—
She put some flowers away—
And Redder cheeked Ones—in their stead—
A fond—illusive way—

To cheat Herself, it seemed she tried—
As if before a child
To fade—Tomorrow—Rainbows held
The Sepulchre, could hide.

She dealt a fashion to the Nut—
She tied the Hoods to Seeds—
She dropped bright scraps of Tint, about—
And left Brazilian Threads

On every shoulder that she met—
Then both her Hands of Haze
Put up—to hide her parting Grace
From our unfitted eyes.

> My loss, by sickness—Was it Loss?
> Or that Etherial Gain
> One earns by measuring the Grave—
> Then—measuring the Sun—

Permitted by her doctor to stroll in her garden again after a summer spent in semidarkness, Dickinson renews her pleasure in exposing her skin directly to the sun. While the poet walks, she compares her own declining health during the preceding spring to vegetative nature's descent into fall and winter. The poem's controlling simile comprises a miniature drama in which summer is personified as a "mother" who reluctantly abandons her "children" to winter's approach. In this desertion are projected Dickinson's own feelings of abandonment as summer passed her by during the "winter" of her confinement. Flower varieties bloom successively as the unseen summer unfolds, each more intensely colored than its predecessor, and this riot of color reaches a crescendo during early autumn, when she can finally walk about the yard once again. Yet all this hectic decoration is "fond," in the tandem senses of "foolish" and "loving," for winter will inevitably come, no matter how vividly each flower bed, tree, or hill ("shoulder") is dressed. Autumnal mists finally obscure all bright hues before the patient "fades" and winter's colorless reign is reinaugurated.

Dickinson quite possibly patterned the maternal "summer" upon her own mother, who nursed her at home, so that the juvenile patient of the fourth stanza who cannot be told the true gravity of her condition may be understood as representing the poet herself. Confusingly, however, the poet also plays the role of the adult "summer," but some of our perplexity may be dispelled if we realize that Dickinson has created a trope within a trope, so that mother and daughter resolve into a single figure representing the tacit conspiracy of silence engaged in by nurse and patient, parent and child, which becomes all the more painful if we recall that Emily Norcross Dickinson herself may have been an exotrope. The summer/mother tries repeatedly to distract her flower/child as well as herself with brilliant color, in much the same way, perhaps, as Mrs. Dickinson tried to maintain a brave face and cheer her sick daughter with bright sewing projects. Inevitably, however, her "Hands of Haze" have to perform their sad office of stretching the bandages once again over her daughter's "unfit" eyes. In the poem's analogical trope, winter's approach is similarly inevitable, a manifestation of Dickinson's internal winter or "Siberia," to which she is compelled to return whenever her eyes are covered over again.

The theme of this story-within-a-story is, nevertheless, one of spiritual and artistic rebirth, as a dawning appreciation for her own potential for self-renewal grows in Dickinson. Despite the imminence of winter's killing frosts, all of nature is "in Pod," as pregnant with new life as it had been during the spring, when everything was "A'blossom." This transferral of spring's fertility to fall represents another attempt by Dickinson to modify the calendar to suit her perceptions and her needs, although in this instance, her own experience remains synchronous with time in the natural world and receives visual confirmation in the redness of the surrounding leaves. Thus, the poet's transforming imagination no longer functions outside of experience, but in partnership with it, helping her to construct a "true" compensatory poetic interpretation of the summer she had missed, even as she denies the efficacy of the "false" compensatory strategy the summer/mother uses to soothe her sick child.

In the final stanza, Dickinson meditates upon the "Etherial Gain" she has won since her bout with illness. A consciousness of our proximity to the "Grave," Dickinson says, encourages us to "measure the sun," or to determine how much time remains to us so that we might more fully enjoy the present.[16] Yet Dickinson may have acquired her *carpe diem* attitude not so much from any reinvigorated sense of her own mortality, but from a more prosaic accommodation she had reached with the limits her doctors set upon the amount of time she spent outdoors. During her illness, Dickinson must literally have had to *measure the sun* each day, estimating the consequences of exposing her eyes to the noon sun or to the milder "slant light" of sunrise and sunset. The garden walk that inspired this poem was made after first consulting her doctor ("I *asked* to go abroad"), and then undertaken only with due caution and deliberation, in contrast to the desperate, headlong rush described in "The Soul has Bandaged moments—." But her obedience and self-restraint are finally rewarded: Dickinson wins the visual stimulus she needs to reflect upon her experience and write poetry, or more specifically, *this* poem.

ALTHOUGH HER optical illness never did threaten Dickinson with the "Sepulchre," it did bode the death of her creativity by raising the specter of near-perpetual sensory deprivation. The poet's outpouring of work during the difficult years of her illness is thus a tribute to her ability to mine a suddenly circumscribed world for new sources of inspiration, thereby solving the problem Robert Frost would later phrase as "what to make of a diminished thing." Afterwards, her renewed ability to write must have seemed, to Dickinson's way of thinking, a gift in the form of a reprieve granted by God. "Preceptor" in the ways of seeing "immortally," God occupied virtually the same role that her doctor did. Similarly, her poetry became the lens or set of spectacles Dickinson could look through to witness heaven and yet preserve her eyesight. Her poems might then successfully tap some of the dangerous energies that had been unwittingly unleashed before Dickinson had learned to exercise "compound vision." Indeed, a poem's ability to rerelease that power was one measure of its success to Dickinson, who wrote that a true poem should "pile like Thunder to it's close / . . . While Everything created hid" (no. 1247). Like love, the only other experience Dickinson thought comparable, the act of suddenly comprehending a poem was one that threatened to "consume" us, for in that moment we come face to face with divinity, and, as Dickinson reminds us, "None see God and live—." Thus we are both consumers and the consumed when we read, flirting with eternal meanings that can overwhelm our understanding as thoroughly as the noonday sun could scorch our unguarded eyes.

But poets should
Exert a double vision; should have eyes
To see near things as comprehensively
As if afar they took their point of sight,
And distant things as intimately deep
As if they touched them.

Elizabeth Barrett Browning, Aurora Leigh

The poet must be continually watching the
moods of his mind as the astronomer watches
the aspects of the heavens. What might we not
expect from a long life faithfully spent in this
wise—the humblest observer would see some
stars shoot.—A faithful description as by a dis-
interested person of the thoughts which visited
a certain mind in 3 score years & 10 as when
one reports the number & character of the vehicles which pass a particular point. As travel-
lers go round the world and report natural objects & phenomena—so faithfully let another
stay at home & report the phenomena of his
own life.

Thoreau, Journal, August 19, 1851

"COMPOUND VISION"

The Poet as Astronomer

DICKINSON'S FORMULATION OF "compound vision" as her primary artistic *modus operandi* arose out of a need to regard illness as having been a prescriptive, rather than punitive, experience. Initially, Dickinson wondered whether she had unknowingly committed some sort of perceptual sin for which God must be appeased. With the passage of time, however, she began trying to think of illness as a lesson that had been taught her, or, even more profitably, as a drastic form of therapy to which God had obliquely subjected her. Her optical ailment might then be a sign that God, like an attending physician, was building up the poet's tolerance to heaven's brilliance or "Noon" by exposing her eyes to ever-widening experiential "circumferences." Clearly, this "prescriptive" interpretation of her illness internalizes Dickinson's improving relationship with her actual physician; less obviously, it predicates for the poet a new role as exalted as her previous posture had been abject. In it she exchanged her role as God's victim for one in which she acted as his prophet.

Although her eyesight might never become so well "developed" or "infinite" as God's, Dickinson hoped that a measured combination of restrained vision and imaginative explorations made through the medium of poetry might safely reveal the insights into divinity she sought. By yoking perception to revelation, "compound vision" granted Dickinson insights inaccessible to more conventional modes of seeing. For example, at the conclusion of "My first well Day—since many ill—," compound vision enables Dickinson to interpret a natural phenomenon, the turning of the seasons, within the dual contexts of time, measured by the sun, and eternity, measured by the grave. By itself, neither of these perspectives would be sufficient to yield the imaginative material Dickinson needed in order to write, but together, they generate a powerful creative synergy. Tempered by the fire of illness, Dickinson's poetic vision became, to use her own analogy, like light that had been passed through double, or compound, lenses until it became more focused, more intensified. It was "Light—enabling Light," or a collaboration, not a competition, between herself and a higher authority.

In articulating "compound vision," Dickinson drew upon her conversations with doctors about the mechanics of vision and the properties of corrective lenses. Yet Dickinson's obvious interest in the principles of optics is contiguous with a more dominant and long-standing fascination with astronomy, especially the notion of being able to see across vast distances. In her poetry, "compound vision" became, in essence, a conceptual telescope Dickinson could use to bridge the gulf between herself and heaven. Furthermore, Dickinson appropriated from the astronomer not only the primary tool of his trade, but also his methods, and especially his terminology. She deploys her astronomical vocabulary with a high degree of sophistication reflective of the unusually thorough education she received in the natural sciences both at Amherst Academy and at Mount Holyoke Female Seminary. As Richard Sewall points out, when Dickinson uses such words as "parallax" or "perihelion" in her poems, we can be reasonably confident that she knows what she is talking about (*Life,* 354).[1] Moreover, Dickinson converted astronomical principles such as the parallax, planetary motion, and the solstice into paradigms to use in discussing her alienation from God, symbolized, in these poems, as physical distance.

COMPOUND LENSES

Careful scrutiny of those poems in which Dickinson describes lenses reveals the underlying theme of a supplemented vision that connects the optometrist's examination room to the astronomical observatory. In the following poem, God, to help the narrator (who I shall assume to be Dickinson herself) see as he does, fits her with a graduated series of corrective "lenses," each consisting of a lifetime's worth of comprehension:

> Time feels so vast that were it not
> For an Eternity—
> I fear me this Circumference
> Engross my Finity—
>
> To His exclusion, who prepare
> By Processes of Size
> For the Stupendous Vision
> Of His Diameters—

Evidently Dickinson is proposing here that the "size" of her ability to comprehend eternity, which illness had proven to be inadequate, could be adjusted by God over the course of eons until she, like a patient who has been fitted with the right pair of corrective lenses, could finally "see" clearly.[2] "Circumference," a major term in Dickinson's symbolic vocabulary, seems specifically intended here to designate a planetary circumference, which she equates with the limit of her understanding. "Diameters" has a threefold meaning: the diameter of God, or the largest "circumference" a mind can comprehend; God's own eyes, whose vision her own eyes must try to emulate; and the lenses of a pair of spectacles so "large" that they permit the viewer to see virtually everything. The theme of eyes being "strengthened" via a slow progression of exposures to ever brighter sources of light appears as well in poem no. 63:

> If night stands first—*then* noon
> To gird us for the sun,
> What gaze!
>
> When from a thousand skies
> On our *developed* eyes
> Noons blaze!

The comparison Dickinson is making to her own spiritual "development" is, I think, clear: spiritual ignorance, or night, is followed by consciousness, or "noon," followed by revelation, or a look at the naked light of the sun. The dreary "night" to which Dickinson's eyes had been consigned during her convalescence is translated in the final stanza to the astronomer's majestic panoply of stars, each of which, Dickinson speculates in a final, exponential leap of the imagination, could shine as brightly as the sun.

Yet Dickinson customarily uses compound vision's augmentation of her eyes' ability to withstand brighter light primarily as a metaphor for an improved comprehension of time. Coming to terms with time may have accrued particular importance for Dickinson during her long convalescences indoors, when she probably learned more about patience and renunciation than she had ever wished to know, and during those brief intervals when she could explore the family garden and orchard. Although she could not accept the idea of vision deferred until after death, "covered vision," she did learn to take a longer view of her situation that helped her look across the span not just of a year, but of entire lifetimes. Her most succinct expression of this idea is to be found in the poem explicitly setting forth the mechanics of "compound vision," "The Admirations—and Contempts—of time—" (no. 906, written probably in about 1864):

> The Admirations—and Contempts—of time—
> Show justest—through an Open Tomb—
> The Dying—as it were a Hight
> Reorganizes Estimate
> And what We saw not
> We distinguish clear—
> And mostly—see not
> What We saw before—

'Tis Compound Vision—
Light—enabling Light—
The Finite—furnished
With the Infinite—
Convex—and Concave Witness—
Back—toward Time—
And forward—
Toward the God of Him—

The final stanza of this poem echoes Dickinson's observation at the end of "My first well Day—since many ill," in which the poet uses both the grave and the sun to "measure" the time available to her in which to look upon the world. As she did on that other occasion, Dickinson uses the prospect of death to achieve a wider perspective, but in this instance, she sees all the way through eternity to the "God of Him—," the Father of Christ. A consciousness of death permits us, she suggests, to achieve a new "height" from which she, and we, may "distinguish clear" what we could not see before. In the second stanza this improvement to our vision is effected through the use of twin corrective lenses: our mortal lives bulge forward toward eternity like a convex lens, Dickinson suggests, while God's presence recedes away from us like the surface of a concave lens, the combination of the two producing a heightened form of perception, or "Light—enabling Light."[3]

Although the optical details of Dickinson's trope are not technically correct, clearly she is referring to a refracting telescope's compound lenses. The telescopic sight that Dickinson has achieved by exercising compound vision permits her vision to traverse time as well as space, foreshortening the "distance" between her and God without actually requiring her to die as a precondition. Yet Dickinson did not ascend the heights of "compound vision" merely for the sake of the view it afforded. Instead, she used it to mount an active search for heaven, of which she had been disenfranchised by illness, by her religious unorthodoxy, and by science itself, which had deprived all Christians of the comfortably familiar heaven in which they had been taught, as children, to believe. In its place, science had substituted a new, material universe that could be mapped, charted, and even photographed.

Astronomy in Amherst

Although most of Dickinson's contemporaries would have acknowledged the scientific validity of discoveries made centuries before by Copernicus and Galileo, it could be argued that the full spiritual significance of the

Copernican revolution did not make itself widely felt in America until the first decades of the nineteenth century. Some Christians who read their astronomy textbooks as thoroughly as they did their theological tracts found their faiths to have been irrevocably altered. Emerson, for example, decided in 1832 after reading John Herschel's *Preliminary Discourse on the Study of Natural Philosophy* that he could no longer continue administering communion, the tangible symbol of Christ's sacrifice, to his Unitarian congregation, saying, "I regard it as the irresistible effect of the Copernican astronomy to have made the theological scheme of redemption absolutely incredible" (*Journal,* May 27, 1832). Later, in "Historic Notes of Life and Letters in New England," he wrote:

> But I think the paramount source of the religious revolution was Modern Science; beginning with Copernicus, who destroyed the pagan fictions of the Church, by showing mankind that the earth on which we live was not the centre of the Universe, around which the sun and stars revolved every day, and thus fitted to be the platform on which the Drama of the Divine Judgment was played before the assembled Angels of Heaven—"the scaffold of the divine vengeance," Saurin called it,—but a little scrap of a planet, rushing around the sun in our system, which in turn was too minute to be seen at the distance of many stars which we behold. Astronomy taught us our insignificance in Nature; showed that our sacred as our profane history had been written in gross ignorance of the laws, which were far grander than we knew; and compelled a certain extension and uplifting of our views of the Deity and his Providence. (600)

Perhaps because, paradoxically, astronomical knowledge *did* challenge the faith of educated nineteenth-century Christians, some embraced it with a fervor unparalleled in the history of science. Colleges and universities in Britain and America competed to build observatories, fund positions for astronomy faculty, and publish scholarly papers. This flurry of investigation yielded several important discoveries. Much was learned, for example, about the activity and periodicity of sunspots, the composition and structure of Saturn's rings, and the number and positions of Jupiter's moons and those of Mars. Because astronomers' instruments had yet to attain the high levels of resolution that would become available at the century's end, during the early and middle decades of the century observers capitalized whenever possible upon unusual celestial phenomena such as total eclipses, cometary visits, and planetary oppositions. Expeditions were dispatched to Spain and India in 1860 and 1868 to witness total solar eclipses, while others voyaged to India and

California in 1874 and 1882 to photograph Transits of Venus. Halley's comet, aside from bringing Mark Twain into this world in 1835 and taking him back out again in 1910, was also intensively studied and photographed. In 1846 the sensational news of the discovery of Neptune, first planet to be found since Uranus in 1781, signaled to the public mind once again that the sky was much larger, and human beings much smaller, than had been previously believed.

To comparatively isolated rural communities such as Amherst the concurrent scientific and religious revolutions Emerson describes came late, and with a correspondingly greater shock. Yet rather than attempting to suppress them, Amherst's village elders confronted astronomers' new ideas head on. For example, the trustees of Amherst College—founded, ironically, to help counteract the spread of liberalism and Unitarianism from Boston—assembled one of the better astronomy faculties in all of New England. Many of these young professors were recruited by the Reverend Edward Hitchcock, president of the college from 1845 to 1854. A strong believer in the ultimate compatibility of science and Christianity, Hitchcock exerted an influence that extended beyond the college to Amherst Academy, the town's secondary school, where Dickinson received an unusually thorough preparation in astronomy, geology, chemistry, and botany (Sewall, *Life*, 338).[4] Astronomy was incorporated in the curriculum at Mount Holyoke Female Seminary as well, and Dickinson finished a course in it there during her final term as a student.[5]

Dickinson's reaction to the information she learned in her astronomy classes was, as might be expected of someone whose formal education conflicted with the faith of her fathers, profoundly ambivalent. In her poems, she combines a romantic's distrust of science's motives, especially its urge to quantify and classify, with a progressive Victorian's admiration for scientists' discoveries and persevering spirit. This synthesis produces what Daniel J. Orsini calls a distinctively romantic use of science, in which the poet applies the objective methods of science to her metaphysical quests, making use of it "both as counter to her spiritual ideals and as proof of their validity" (63). Such a strategy is very much in evidence in an early[6] poem which I believe is central to understanding Dickinson's underlying attitude toward astronomy and toward science in general, "'Arcturus'—is his other name—." Frankly speaking, it is not one of the poet's better efforts. Before she acquired confidence in her poetic voice, Dickinson often affected a girlish, highly self-conscious poetic persona whose giddy tone can discourage readers from taking her seriously (perhaps because she did not yet *wish* to be taken very seriously). For us, however, despite its flaws, the poem yields important insights into Dickinson's fundamental discomfort both with science and with orthodox Christianity (no. 70):

"Arcturus" is his other name—
I'd rather call him "Star."
It's very mean of Science
To go and interfere!

I slew a worm the other day—
A "Savan" passing by
Murmured "Resurgam"—"Centipede"!
"Oh Lord—how frail are we"!

I pull a flower from the woods—
A monster with a glass
Computes the stamens in a breath—
And has her in a "class"!

Whereas I took the Butterfly
Aforetime in my hat—
He sits erect in "Cabinets"—
The Clover bells forgot.

What once was "Heaven"
Is "*Zenith*" now—
Where I proposed to go
When Time's brief masquerade was done
Is mapped and charted too.

What if the poles sh'd frisk about
And stand upon their heads!
I hope I'm ready for "the worst"—
Whatever prank betides!

Perhaps the "Kingdom of Heaven's" changed—
I hope the "Children" there
Wont be "new fashioned" when I come—
And laugh at me—and stare—

I hope the Father in the skies
Will lift his little girl—
Old fashioned—naughty—everything—
Over the stile of "Pearl."

Throughout this poem Dickinson wittily mocks science's condescending arrogance and its preoccupation with taxonomy, which she dismisses as mere taxidermy. Scientists collect plucked flowers and netted butterflies not to admire them, as she does, but rather to exhibit them in museum display cases. Dickinson also unfavorably compares science's macabre version of "resurrection" with Christianity's. When the narrator herself capriciously kills a worm, presumably by slicing it in half, a passing professor not only classifies it, but confidently predicts ("Resurgam!") that it will regenerate itself, a profanation of Christ's promise to his disciples that Dickinson disparages in the second stanza's fourth line.[7]

But now that heaven has been rechristened "Zenith," Dickinson wonders if it too has become so infected with science's mania for categories and nomenclature that it will no longer preserve a niche for someone as "old fashioned" as she. Such a self-appellation may sound peculiar at first blush, especially in light of the poet's well-known refusals to attend church with the rest of her family, yet Dickinson's lifelong apostasy should be understood as being as reactionary as it was revolutionary. In a letter to Thomas Higginson, Dickinson reported that her family was "religious—except me—and address an Eclipse, every morning—whom they call their 'Father'" (L404), and although this dark, paternalistic deity repelled Dickinson, she could discover no refuge in the more liberal doctrines that had found favor in Boston. Despite her friendship with Higginson and admiration for Emerson, Dickinson found their Unitarian and Transcendental ideologies too peripheral to her own experience. Instead, she perceived herself as believing with a fervor more reminiscent of her Puritan forebears'. This conservatism reveals itself indirectly in "'Arcturus' is his other name—" through Dickinson's speculation that any new-fangled or "new fashioned" heaven, as unprecedented as the next astonishing scientific discovery, might imitate science's imposition of taxonomies by making absolute distinctions between the saved and the damned—thereby exhibiting a divine narrowness of mind more in the spirit of Calvinistic Puritanism than of her parents' conventional Trinitarian Congregationalism.

Therefore, despite the overly sentimental wistfulness of the narrator's voice in the final two stanzas of the poem, the question of whether the "Father" would still recognize his "naughty" unorthodox daughter and admit her to heaven just as she was, *sui generis,* held profound importance for Dickinson. An anachronism marooned between a virtually extinct Puritan past and Victorian scientific positivism, an "orphan" with no "place" reserved for her in heaven, Dickinson was acutely conscious of her isolated position. The poet's alienation is underscored in "'Arcturus' is his other name—" by her ubiquitous quotation marks, which subtly impugn terms and certainties of all kinds, scientific or religious. If no epistemology could be subscribed to with any degree of real confidence, perhaps the answer was to be found in heaven itself. But science had confiscated heaven, or at least the literal heaven of Dickinson's girlhood. Where had it gone?

THE SEARCH FOR HEAVEN

If Dickinson could determine *where* heaven was, she might determine *what* it was and assess a heretic's chances of admittance. Consequently, with a scientist's methodicalness, yet a romantic's distrust of science's short-sighted goals and reductionist techniques, Dickinson mounted her own search for heaven.[8] In the process she emulated astronomers, exploring her own inner spaces with the same zeal they brought to the task of mapping outer space. In the following modest poem, her only explicit portrait of an astronomer, Dickinson honors him above all for his perseverance (no. 851):

When the Astronomer stops seeking
For his Pleiad's Face—
When the lone British Lady
Forsakes the Arctic Race

When to his Covenant Needle
The Sailor doubting turns—
It will be amply early
To ask what treason means.

Dickinson's reference to the Pleiades is technically accurate. Only six of the "Seven Sisters" are normally visible to the unaided eye; to see the seventh star (or an eighth) requires either unusually favorable viewing conditions or a telescope. In searching for the elusive seventh, the astronomer serves as one of Dickinson's three exemplars of faithfulness, the others being Lady Jane Franklin, who sought her husband Sir John for ten years after he disappeared during an Arctic expedition, and the sailor's compass. Intriguingly, this entire poem is "aligned" toward the north: the Pleiades is a constellation of the northern sky, and the sailor's compass needle points northwards, toward the Arctic, where Franklin had disappeared. The poem therefore serves as a kind of "compass" in its own right, pointing the reader toward the polestar of the speaker's fidelity.

Yet sending the light of introspection down to such depths or out to such distances required the poet to redefine the concept of distance itself, as she had already used compound vision to redefine the notion of time. In the following poem she experiments with the inherent spatial contradictions of what she was attempting to do (no. 370):

Heaven is so far of the Mind
That were the Mind dissolved—
The Site—of it—by Architect
Could not again be proved—

'Tis vast—as our Capacity—
As fair—as our idea—
To Him of adequate desire
No further 'tis, than Here—

Dickinson's use of "so far" in the first line is purposefully misleading. Rather than saying that heaven lies distant from the mind, she declares the two to be so intimately related that if the mind were ever to collapse, heaven's site could never again be reconstructed. Rather than "far" from the mind, heaven is "Here," if we are willing to exert the mental effort necessary to imagine it. More commonly, however, Dickinson represented heaven as being discoverable not within the mind, but rather wherever the sun was. As we have seen in previous poems, Dickinson believed the sun and heaven were "closest" to her at noon, an association that may have been a vestige of the poet's childhood "map" of the sky, in which heaven lay directly overhead, at the zenith. Moreover, as we have also seen, the noon sun was simultaneously desirable yet potentially hazardous for Dickinson, making it a peculiarly appropriate surrogate for heaven, which might either welcome her or turn her away.[9] In considering how far distant heaven might be from her, Dickinson may well have borne in mind contemporary astronomers' own efforts to determine the earth's distance from the sun. At midcentury, virtually the only means of doing so was to estimate the solar parallax, which Dickinson adopted as one paradigm for her own metaphysical quest.

Parallaxes are found essentially through a process of triangulation, or calculating the position of an indeterminately far point by taking bearings on it from two locations a known distance apart from each other. Astronomical parallaxes are determined by two widely separated investigators observing the same object by sighting along a common point of reference, such as the disk of the moon or of Venus.[10] The angle of difference between the two observations may then be used to calculate the object's distance from earth. In 1873 astronomers of several nations were looking forward to the next year's Transit of Venus, one of only two that century, as an opportunity to determine the solar parallax.[11] In probably that same year, Dickinson wrote the following poem (no. 1286):

I thought that nature was enough
Till Human nature came
But that the other did absorb
As Parallax a Flame—

Of Human nature just aware
There added the Divine
Brief struggle for capacity
The power to contain

Is always as the contents
But give a Giant room
And you will lodge a Giant
And not a smaller man.

The tripartite alignment necessary for determining the solar parallax is present as well in this poem, save that Dickinson substitutes nature, human nature, and divinity for earth, moon/Venus, and sun. In addition, rather than revealing the distance between herself and divinity, Dickinson's model of the parallax replicates the universe's inherent hierarchy, its nested shells of "circumference." As she matured, Dickinson says in this poem, her grasp of nature's complexity was supplanted first by an awareness of human complexity, which was then dwarfed in its own turn by awe in the face of divinity. Questions of distance for Dickinson were always subordinate to, even determined by, measurements of relative degrees of importance, expressed in terms of size, and as the poet's intellectual sophistication grows, one "flame" of comprehension blots out another.[12]

"We see—Comparatively—" Dickinson said, and comparison became an important intellectual strategy she could employ in attempting to determine heaven's "distance" from her. But even this approach was subject to error, as shown by another poem referring to the parallax (no. 949):

Under the Light, yet under,
Under the Grass and the Dirt,
Under the Beetle's Cellar
Under the Clover's Root

Further than Arm could stretch
Were it Giant long,
Further than Sunshine could
Were the Day Year long,

Over the Light, yet over,
Over the Arc of the Bird—
Over the Comet's chimney—
Over the Cubit's Head,

Further than Guess can gallop
Further than Riddle ride—
Oh for a Disc to the Distance
Between Ourselves and the Dead!

A riddle about the riddle of death, this poem concludes with Dickinson wishing for a "Disc to the Distance" between herself and heaven, the same lunar or planetary disk astronomers needed to establish the solar parallax. Even as this poem expresses a desire for a method of measuring distances, however, its logical contradictions subvert all our preconceived notions of directionality and three-dimensional space. The way to the dead is under, yet over, as familiar and concrete as the beetle in our backyard, yet abstract and intangible as a guess or a riddle. The question of how far away from us heaven lies finally cannot be answered by making comparisons, Dickinson says, for the simple reason that none of our comparisons are up to the task. Our imaginations remain circumscribed by the limitations of our senses. Without a standard gauge of measure to go by, Dickinson's efforts to contrive a spiritual "parallax" to use in finding heaven's location would inevitably be doomed.

A Revolution in Locality

Among the most speculative of sciences, astronomy also lent itself well to Dickinson's discussions about looking for heaven in the "wrong" place.[13] While Dickinson's other primary scientific interests, botany and geology, provide relatively reliable empirical data upon which to base hypotheses, astronomy often requires an observer either to disregard the evidence of his own eyes or else to forgo all forms of visual confirmation whatsoever. Perhaps because the process of conceptual restructuring to which Dickinson voluntarily subjected herself in searching for heaven also demanded that she disabuse herself of perceptual errors, she developed an interest in the various illusions engendered by apparent planetary motion. For example, the visual confusion caused by the presence of two suns in the following poem gives Dickinson a metaphor for discussing anticipation's illusory relationship to fulfillment (no. 1299):

Delight's Despair at setting
Is that Delight is less
Than the sufficing Longing
That so impoverish.

Enchantment's Perihelion
Mistaken oft has been
For the Authentic orbit
Of it's Anterior Sun.

Here, delight and longing comprise dual suns, one proximal and one distal, or "anterior." Dickinson proposes that our despair at delight's "premature" departure stems from a mistaken belief that delight is both equivalent to and opposite from longing. On the contrary, the "sun" of longing may merely have receded to its "aphelion," or most distant point, thereby producing, by its absence, only a temporary impression of delight. Actually, the "sun" of delight "orbits" independently from longing—the two are unrelated. Thus Dickinson uses an error of perception to characterize what is really an error of understanding.

Descriptions of planetary movement are also apt to appear in poems equating the idea of "place" with particular states of mind. For example, Dickinson often portrays new realizations about the universe's underlying order as a shifting of the ground underfoot. In "'Arcturus' is his other name—," for example, science's confiscation of intellectual territory previously reserved for religious considerations confounded Dickinson's impression of where she "stood" as much as would a sudden reversal of the earth's poles. Confronted by science's new worldview, she experienced a wooziness resembling the sense of disorientation she had felt during periods of religious doubt, as in the following (no. 972):

Unfulfilled to Observation—
Incomplete—to Eye—
But to Faith—a Revolution
In Locality—

Unto Us—the Suns extinguish—
To our Opposite—
New Horizons—they embellish—
Fronting Us—with Night.

Dickinson uses "revolution" here in a twofold sense. First, the earth "revolves" (or more properly, rotates) upon its axis, producing night and day. While to a naïve observer, day appears to end with sunset, actually the earth has merely turned a new face to the sun, creating "New Horizons." Science tells us this is so, despite our eyes' "Incomplete" evidence. Similarly, faith tells us heaven exists, even though we cannot *see* it. Believing in heaven requires us to refute the erroneous evidence submitted by our own eyes, says Dickinson, as much as when we learned, during childhood, to accept the disturbing concept that it is we and the earth that turn, not the sky. Then too, during times when her illness required her to wear bandages, Dickinson may have needed to reassure herself continually that the sun still shone despite being, for her, "Unfulfilled to Observation."

The "error" in observation Dickinson makes in searching for heaven could be corrected only during the summer solstice, a moment in which all motion, and indeed all time, came to a full stop (*sol* + *status*, past participle of *sistere*, to come to a halt). The solstice held a special significance for the poet because it seemed to her the best simulacrum the temporal world could offer of life in eternity. She pictured heaven as resembling the year's longest day drawn out to an infinite length (no. 1056):

> There is a Zone whose even Years
> No Solstice interrupt—
> Whose Sun constructs perpetual Noon
> Whose perfect Seasons wait—
>
> Whose Summer set in Summer, till
> The Centuries of June
> And Centuries of August cease
> And Consciousness—is Noon.

Without even mentioning the word "heaven," Dickinson nevertheless paints a portrait of the immutable, timeless summer which she hoped paradise would resemble. There, June would succeed June and August succeed August for entire centuries, until summer could whirl on autonomously as a gyroscope. Night would cease to exist. Without days and seasons to demarcate its passage, time itself would come to an end. Then, finally, outer space would become indistinguishable from inner space: "Consciousness" becomes "Noon," and we would assume the sun's position in the cosmos.

Dickinson's term "Zone" in this poem is shorthand for "tropic zone," or the latitude in which the length of the day varies least, year-round. This is the locational equivalent of a peak perceptual moment maintained in perpetuity, a "noon" that lasts forever. In New England's rigorous climate, the closest physical approximation of this "tropical" state Dickinson would ever know was summer, and poets, we will remember her declaring in "I reckon—when I count at all—," are enabled by their imaginations to have summers lasting "a Solid Year." Yet aside from poetry, only love, Dickinson's poems asseverate, can defeat mutability. An association of love with the solstice is apparent in the following poem (no. 646):

I think To Live—may be a Bliss
To those who dare to try—
Beyond my limit to conceive—
My lip—to testify—

I think the Heart I former wore
Could widen—till to me
The Other, like the little Bank
Appear—unto the Sea—

I think the Days—could every one
In Ordination stand—
And Majesty—be easier—
Than an inferior kind—

No numb alarm—lest Difference come—
No Goblin—on the Bloom—
No start in Apprehension's Ear,
No Bankruptcy—no Doom—

But Certainties of Sun—
Midsummer—in the Mind—
A steadfast South—upon the Soul—
Her Polar time—behind—

The Vision—pondered long—
So plausible becomes
That I esteem the fiction—real—
The Real—fictitious seems—

> How bountiful the Dream—
> What Plenty—it would be—
> Had all my Life but been Mistake
> Just rectified—in Thee

The poem's fourth stanza constitutes a virtual catalog of Dickinson's worst private fears: unwanted change, the annual death of her cherished garden, sudden appalling news.[14] But all such fears, large and small, would be banished from the changeless, timeless perfection of Dickinson's imaginary heaven, "Midsummer" of the mind. "Midsummer" in the fifth stanza's second line specifically denotes the summer solstice, the pre-Christian festival celebrated in *A Midsummer Night's Dream,* and something of the same pagan spirit adheres to her use of the word. Additionally, a manuscript variant for "Midsummer," "Meridian," suggests that Dickinson's imagined emotional equivalent for heaven conflates time *and* space, existing both as a moment precisely in the "middle" of the year and as a palpable site resting squarely upon the equator. The poet is frustrated that her heaven-solstice exists so tantalizingly near, its presence being contingent upon a mere change of attitude or point of view. The one hope she has of rectifying her geographical "mistake" of living the wrong existence rests in the transforming power of love, which could allow her to relive life in a more emotionally rewarding "South" antipodal to the soul's former "Polar time."

That hope is fulfilled in another poem concerning the solstice, "There came a Day at Summer's full" (no. 322). In that poem's description of what may have been an actual event, love succeeds in halting the sun to create a new time and place from which the lovers may finally achieve a preview of heaven (no. 322):

> There came a Day at Summer's full,
> Entirely for me—
> I thought that such were for the Saints,
> Where Resurrections—be—
>
> The Sun, as common, went abroad,
> The flowers, accustomed, blew,
> As if no soul the solstice passed
> That maketh all things new—
>
> The time was scarce profaned, by speech—
> The symbol of a word

Was needless, as at Sacrament,
The Wardrobe—of our Lord—

Each was to each The Sealed Church,
Permitted to commune this—time—
Lest we too awkward show
At Supper of the Lamb.

The Hours slid fast—as Hours will,
Clutched tight, by greedy hands—
So faces on two Decks, look back,
Bound to opposing lands—

And so when all the time had leaked,
Without external sound
Each bound the Other's Crucifix—
We gave no other Bond—

Sufficient troth, that we shall rise—
Deposed—at length, the Grave—
To that new Marriage,
Justified—through Calvaries of Love—

Although the speaker (who I will assume once again to be Dickinson herself) narrates the events of an ostensibly ordinary day, the symbolism used here is clearly eschatological, and the poem must be read in the context of its multiple references to the Book of Revelation, one of Dickinson's favorite sections of the Bible.[15] Correspondingly, this particular summer day heralds the end of the old world and the beginning of the new: she describes the solstice as making "all things new," as God declares he has done following the Second Coming (Rev. 21:5). The solstice is "Summer's full" because on that day the entirety of summer has yet to come, so that the solstice is as replete with potential as the private ceremony of betrothal celebrated by Dickinson and her lover. The midsummer marriage the lovers anticipate, whether in this life or the next, derives significance from its similarity to the mystic marriage between the Lamb, or Christ, and the new Jerusalem (Rev. 21:9).[16] In Revelation, an angel explains to John that once that marriage has been consecrated, night will cease to exist in the new Jerusalem, nor will there be any sun, for God will Himself be the light continuously illuminating all (22:5). Similarly, the new Jerusalem will require no temples, for God will live

there among mortal men forever (21:3). Therefore, God's dwelling place
will no longer be removed from mankind; place and divinity will finally
be united.

Yet even though Dickinson probably discovered her original inspiration for a vision of the new Jerusalem among the pages of Revelation,
she may very well have also had in mind another Revelation-influenced
scene, at the conclusion of Barrett Browning's *Aurora Leigh:*

> My Romney!—Lifting up my hand in his,
> As wheeled by Seeing spirits toward the east,
> He turned instinctively, where, faint and far,
> Along the tingling desert of the sky,
> Beyond the circle of the conscious hills,
> Were laid in jasper-stone as clear as glass
> The first foundations of that new, near Day
> Which should be builded out of heaven to God.
> He stood a moment with erected brows
> In silence, as a creature might who gazed,—
> Stood calm, and fed his blind, majestic eyes
> Upon the thought of perfect noon: and when
> I saw his soul saw,—"Jasper first," I said,
> "And second, sapphire; third, chalcedony;
> The rest in order,—last, an amethyst."

On the day of the solstice, "perfect noon" of the entire year, Dickinson
and her lover are enabled, like Aurora and Romney, to anticipate the
existences they will lead once summer collapses in upon itself and eternity, having reached critical mass, becomes the rule rather than an exception.

For Dickinson, the solstice's efficacy as a symbol for expressing the
latent presence of heaven within temporal existence derives chiefly from
its sacramental aspect. The solstice stands, synecdochically, not just for
the remainder of the summer, but for the totality of eternity, as well.
Ironically, however, Dickinson is also projecting in this poem an end to
the need for using symbols of any kind, including language. The lovers
need no longer resort to expressing themselves in words, linguistical acts
having been rendered superfluous by the presence of absolute meaning.
Similarly, if the spirit of Christ is truly present during communion, the
"wardrobe" of his body and blood becomes completely unnecessary.[17]
Further, because Dickinson's imagined betrothal to her lover prefigures
the ultimate marriage between God and Jerusalem, divinity and place,
heaven has, at least for the moment, been found. The poet need no longer

rely upon compound vision to "measure the sun," for love has helped her withstand the brilliance of a heaven fully revealed on earth.

ALTHOUGH DICKINSON adopted the terms, and to some extent the methods, of science, her goals were utterly foreign to what we would normally think of as the purposes of scientific inquiry. Seeking neither to reconcile her philosophy to the evidence of her own senses nor, despite a keen interest in nature, to understand the world's physical laws any better, she assembled from the raw materials of science a set of symbols and concepts with which to record her cognitive growth. Dickinson came to believe that her ability to perceive metaphysical realities already immanent within the temporal world had been "compounded" by illness, and she described what she saw in the same authoritative language the physical sciences used to describe empirical phenomena. Moreover, astronomy provided Dickinson with a paradigm for vision stretched beyond its corporeal limit, and perhaps because plumbing the "circumferences" of eternity and of her own mind demanded the most strenuous of mental gymnastics, Dickinson displays an affinity with the astronomer and for the steadfast attitude with which he approaches his work. It was he who stood at the very edge of space and time, looking outward, and each new astronomical finding rendered all previous estimations of space's size and complexity instantly obsolete in a manner reminiscent of the poet's outward-rippling "circumferences" and "parallax" flames. Dickinson converted the shock of understanding space's enormousness (still reverberating today, of course) into a metaphor for the change in outlook she believed illness had forced upon her.

It is a final historical irony that in 1886, the year in which Dickinson died, astronomer Sir David Gill proposed organizing an international effort to photograph, for the first time, the entire night sky. Thus, as Dickinson had predicted, "Heaven" was indeed to be "mapped and charted." In her own way, however, Dickinson had already used her art to achieve a vision the astronomers' cameras could never capture. Above all, she may have come to believe that her vocation as poet might yet help her to discover heaven's portal, once her "mistakes" of incomprehension had been corrected and time's "brief masquerade" was ended. Rather than trying to use her poems to curry favor from God or win redemption, Dickinson appears to have regarded them as mental exercises, or as opportunities to expand her consciousness by "circumferences." Writing poems therefore rehearsed Dickinson's mind for admittance to heaven, a final act of the imagination that would ultimately surpass any form of expression.

Not less excellent . . . was the charm, last evening, of a January sunset. The western clouds divided and subdivided themselves into pink flakes modulated with tints of unspeakable softness; and the air had so much life and sweetness, that it was a pain to come within doors. What was it that nature would say? Was there no meaning in the live repose of the valley behind the mill, and which Homer or Shakspeare could not re-form for me in words? The leafless trees become spires of flame in the sunset, with the blue east for their background, and the stars of the dead calices of flowers, and every withered stem and stubble rimed with frost, contribute something to the mute music.

Emerson, Nature

THE "SCIENTIST OF FAITH"

Overcoming the Obstacles to Perception

"COMPOUND VISION" assumed a crucial role in Emily Dickinson's meta-poetics, giving her the analytical tool she needed to determine the heavenly significance of earthly events as well as a means of aggrandizing her own role as witness, revelator, translator. On a more fundamental level, however, compound vision must also be recognized as the poet's desperate attempt to salvage what she could in the wake of a profound personal crisis. Dickinson adopted the imagination as an organ of perception not by choice, but out of necessity; thus the ambivalence she displays about her sensory deprivation, alternately glorying in the power of her imagination to supplement conventional vision or mourning the loss of unrestricted eyesight. One concomitant of this uncertainty was, as we have also seen, an equally equivocal attitude toward heaven, as Dickinson veered between counting herself lucky that God had selected her to learn about the larger "circumferences" of the divine perspective, or wondering whether she was being chastised for having discovered that earth's beauty rivals heaven's. Evidently, rather than allowing her eyes to be surprised and stunned again by another sudden encounter with revelation, she resolved to preserve her sight in the future by integrating an eternal perspective in the perceptions that became grist for her poems.

To pursue her avocation in safety, Dickinson required the tacit approval of God, whom she continued to regard with wary respect. As teacher, exemplar, and enabler of compound vision, God exerted a near-total control over Dickinson's perceptual freedom, and therefore her identity as poet, as well. Some poems even seem to be suffused by a panic verging upon incipient paranoia as Dickinson imagines God, whose vision was as omniscient as her own was "finite," to be monitoring her every movement. Like a watchful parent, God was prone, Dickinson believed, to use compound vision to keep a close eye on his "children," as in the last two stanzas of poem no. 413, "I never felt at Home— Below—":

If God could make a visit—
Or ever took a Nap—
So not to see us—but they say
Himself—a Telescope

Perennial beholds us—
Myself would run away
From Him—and Holy Ghost—and All—
But there's the "Judgment Day"!

Because God does not go away to make visits, nor are his immense "eyes" ever closed by sleep, his "telescopic" attention would inevitably follow Dickinson wherever she fled. Dickinson's use of her childish persona in these lines serves to make God's vigilance seem only more ponderous, while simultaneously resurrecting, for an adult reader's consideration, the truism taught to children that nothing they did would escape God's attention. In this subjection of the individual life to an invasive scrutiny that was microscopically or telescopically keen, even the conscious self could become complicitous (no. 894):

Of Consciousness, her awful Mate
The Soul cannot be rid—
As easy the secreting her
Behind the Eyes of God.

The deepest hid is sighted first
And scant to Him the Crowd—
What triple Lenses burn upon
The Escapade from God—

Here, although the "triple Lenses" of God's compound vision are enfolded within a trope, they still possess the terrible capacity to ferret out the presence of any "Soul" who tries to escape his attention. Significantly, the "Soul," who is as much a victim, in this poem, as was the "Soul" in "The Soul has Bandaged moments—," makes a desperate attempt to conceal herself "Behind the Eyes of God," as if by adopting his perspective, she could somehow escape his notice.

Constrained by God's unceasing vigilance, Dickinson restricted herself to a comparatively narrow range of poetic activity, while nevertheless continually testing the limits of her perceptual and artistic freedom. Her approach to the subjects of her poems typically blends close, nearly microscopic, empirical observations of phenomena with speculations about the significance of what she is seeing. This ability to shift her attention almost cinematically from a close-up shot to a panoramic view qualified Dickinson to call herself a "scientist of faith," an apparent oxymoron that captures Dickinson's determination to hybridize the scientist's intense observation with an amateur theologian's insights. Although her adoption of this "compound" role affected several facets of her poetics, in this chapter I will address four: her strategies for making close observations; her conversion of those observations into metaphors and "apprehensions"; her determination to overcome the physical barriers circumscribing her vision; and finally, her use of irony to "shield" herself from God's surveillance.

The Scientist of Faith

In attempting to integrate a scientific worldview with her religious beliefs, Dickinson could emulate the example set by Amherst's own "scientist of faith," Dr. Edward Hitchcock, of whom I spoke in the previous chapter. In his biography of Dickinson, Richard Sewall characterizes Hitchcock as a "man of God and man of Science, who inspired a whole generation with a love of nature that combined a sense of its sublimity with an accurate knowledge of its parts and processes, as far as the natural sciences of the day knew them," while nevertheless remaining "a devout apologist for revealed religion" (342–43). Hitchcock's approach to the natural sciences was both eclectic and inclusive. Although his official title, by the time he became president of Amherst College, was "Professor of Natural Theology and Geology," Hitchcock was also knowledgeable about chemistry, biology, and astronomy. Moreover, as Sewall observes, Hitchcock was a bit of a poet himself, and his descriptions of nature inclined toward the rhapsodic (343–44).

Dickinson's "romantic" use of science, to which I earlier alluded, may have originated as a sort of imitation of Hitchcock's paradoxical blending of progressive thought with reactionary piety. In her poems, Dickinson combined keen naturalistic observations of the sort a scientist might make with intimations of meaning that simultaneously remove the subject from the purview of conventional scientific discourse. In "The Lilac is an ancient shrub," for example, Dickinson employs her by-now familiar strategy of appropriating the tools and concepts of science—in this case, astronomy and botany—to contradict both scientific dispassionateness as well as religion's insistence upon deferred gratification (no. 1241):

> The Lilac is an ancient shrub
> But ancienter than that
> The Firmamental Lilac
> Upon the Hill tonight—
> The Sun subsiding on his Course
> Bequeathes this final Plant
> To Contemplation—not to Touch—
> The Flower of Occident.
> Of one Corolla is the West—

The Calyx is the Earth—
The Capsules burnished Seeds the Stars—
The Scientist of Faith
His research has but just begun—
Above his synthesis
The Flora unimpeachable
To Time's Analysis—
"Eye hath not seen" may possibly
Be current with the Blind
But let not Revelation
By theses be detained—

The depth of Dickinson's botanical background is indicated not only by
the presence of specialized terms in the poem, but also by her observation that the lilac is an "ancient" shrub, for the genus *Syringa* is indeed
a very old one. The poem's movement through time is complemented by
as vast a movement through space: the poet's scrutiny rapidly shifts from
a microscopic viewpoint to a telescopic one as she characterizes earth as
the "Calyx," or external fringe, of an immense "flower" whose brilliant
center, or "Corolla," is the setting sun. This titanic blossom has expelled
its "seeds" into space as stars, and Dickinson's trope echoes Emerson's
language in the passage from "Nature" that serves as an epigraph to
this chapter. Stipulating to a kind of transcendence of her own in this
poem, Dickinson asserts that the type of vision she has just had does not
properly belong to any field of science, despite her appropriation of the
botanist's and the astronomer's points of view. Rather, it is the business
of the "Scientist of Faith," or poet such as Dickinson, whose "research"
has just begun as she exercises her own "synthesis" of faith and close
observation "outside" of present time. Her use of the term "Flora" mocks
scientists' obsessive need to classify phenomena, even though the vesper-
tinal "lilac" she describes surpasses her own powers of analysis, being,
literally, over her head.[1]

The biblical quotation rebutted in this poem is 1 Cor. 2:9, part of
a Pauline discourse contrasting intellectual wisdom with the power of
the spirit, which stores up emoluments for the faithful surpassing mens'
descriptive powers: "But as it is written, Eye hath not seen nor ear heard,
neither have entered into the heart of man, the things which God hath
prepared for them that love him." The poem's witty ending contends
that we *can* perceive a "Revelation" of heaven right here on earth, if we
will only refrain from depending on "theses," whether scientific or doc-
trinal. Although the Book of Revelation was, as we have seen, one of

Dickinson's favorite parts of the Bible, her use of the word here is emphatically not eschatological, for "revelation" is both immediate and tangible, as "proven" by the twilight vision she has just witnessed. In her office as poet, Dickinson could study heaven and God like any other kind of phenomena, and construct hypotheses to be proved or disproved either in this life or after death.[2]

While either poets or scientists could observe and theorize, their methods, of course, differed radically from each other. Preparatory to offering their "syntheses," or unifying explanations, scientists dissected specimens by "touch," while poets, to justify their own theories, offered metaphors based upon their impressions and intuitions. In the following poem, Dickinson explicitly associates metaphor with "faith" and observation with "definition," the taxonomic, narrow-minded approach to experience she habitually rejected (no. 797):

By my Window have I for Scenery
Just a Sea—with a Stem—
If the Bird and the Farmer—deem it a "Pine"—
The Opinion will do—for them—

It has no Port, nor a "Line"—but the Jays—
That split their route to the Sky—
Or a Squirrel, whose giddy Peninsula
May be easier reached—this way—

For Inlands—the Earth is the under side—
And the upper side—is the Sun—
And it's Commerce—if Commerce it have—
Of Spice—I infer from the Odors borne—

Of it's Voice—to affirm—when the Wind is within—
Can the Dumb—define the Divine?
The Definition of Melody—is—
That Definition is none—

It—suggests to our Faith—
They—suggest to our Sight—
When the latter—is put away
I shall meet with Conviction I somewhere met
That Immortality—

Was the Pine at my Window a "Fellow
Of the Royal" Infinity?

Apprehensions—are God's introductions—
To be hallowed—accordingly—

Dickinson's playful substitution of "Royal Infinity" for (Royal) "Academy" in the final stanza's second line clearly demarcates the boundary between her activity as a poet and that of the scientist. Her conceit about the tree being a "sea" is offered as evidence of the pine tree's complexity, summarized in the word "Melody," which is sophisticated enough to qualify the tree for admittance to that most select and learned circle of all, heaven.[3] "Melody" is the pronominal referent for "It" in the seventeenth line, so that "melody" suggests to our faith by harnessing it as a kind of sixth sense. "They" in the line following refers elliptically to "Definition[s]," or the imposition of taxonomies that Dickinson resisted as being both passionless and reductive.

Dickinson's contrasting of "Melody" to definition points up the differences between the imagination's impression of a pine tree and the tree's simple visual appearance by implicitly comparing language to music, or the literal to the figurative. The pine tree's distinctive "melody" is not discernible to sight alone, but only to sight used in conjunction with the senses of smell and hearing. Dickinson's metaphors, products of her imagination, can at least approximate "melody," or an interweaving of the multilayered contexts of existence revealed by perceiving with all the senses aided by faith. Yet in the poem's fourteenth line, Dickinson dramatizes the limits even of metaphor, coming to an abrupt halt and throwing up her hands in frustration, having been rendered "dumb" by her dependence upon sight. Only after her sight has been "put away" after death, Dickinson says, will she be able to understand the tree in its truest light, as an "Immortality." Dickinson also conveys the limitations of sight in the way she uses the term "Apprehensions" in the penultimate line. There are some objects, she avers, like the tree, which we do not merely see, but rather *apprehend,* or grasp suddenly and intuitively, as if "meeting" them for the first time. Such special introductions are endorsed, or even precipitated, by God, as part of a divine plan to help us understand the interconnectedness of the things of this world before moving on to the next.

Dickinson's emphasis upon employing all of her senses would logically derive from having used them, while she was ill, to compensate for her curtailed eyesight. Yet although sharing out the burden of perception among her several senses would undoubtedly have relieved the pressure exerted upon her eyes, Dickinson's holistic approach to the objects of her vision is also indicative of the "compound" strategies she adopted

overall. Her distinction between exercising one's faculties in the context
of faith and using them unaided is finally similar to the one Emerson
makes (by way of Coleridge) between Reason and the Understanding.
Dickinson italicizes the difference for her readers in the following poem
(no. 733):

> The Spirit is the Conscious Ear.
> We actually Hear
> When We inspect—that's audible—
> That is admitted—Here—
>
> For other Services—as Sound—
> There hangs a smaller Ear
> Outside the Castle—that Contain—
> The other—only—Hear—

In this poem Dickinson makes a distinction between the spoken and the
written word that could serve well as an illustration of Derridean *dif-
férance.* The poet says that when we "inspect" something we "listen" to
it with a spiritual ear capable of detecting an object's "audible" significance, and she makes her point with a pun: the inferior ear, the one
outside the "Castle" of the head, cannot distinguish between "hear"
and "here," while the "Conscious Ear" can, capable as it is of differen-
tiating between insignificant and eternally significant things as easily as
the reading eye can differentiate between homophones. Dickinson might
just as easily have said "The *mind* is the Conscious Ear," but the sense of
hearing described in the first stanza has behind it the controlling presence not of the intellect, but of the spirit or soul, which compounds the
powers manifested by the senses working in isolation. Calling the reader's
attention to the existence of unsuspected new levels of meaning was an
integral part of the poet's office, Dickinson believed, and she adroitly
uses another pun to say as much in the following poem (no. 448):

> This was a Poet—It is That
> Distills amazing sense
> From ordinary Meanings—
> And Attar so immense
> From the familiar species
> That perished by the Door
> We wonder it was not Ourselves
> Arrested it—before—

The presence of the extraordinary within the ordinary is revealed by the "sense"/"scents" distilled by the poet, who is enabled by a talent for integrating sharpened powers of perception, such as smell, with heightened powers of comprehension and expression. Within the alembic of poetry, close analysis concentrates meaning into "sense," while close observation discloses the rare "Attar" concealed within the most familiar of objects.

Dickinson's obvious delight in puns reflects an abiding fondness for figures of speech of all sorts, which is based, in turn, upon her intense curiosity about metaphorical language's ability to generate new meanings. Persuaded that her vision must bridge the gap between earth and heaven by being able to occupy either perceptual standpoint simultaneously, Dickinson used metaphor as a means of shuttling back and forth between the two. At the highest levels of meaning, metaphors (and even words themselves) became virtually sacramental for Dickinson, vessels with the potential for conveying huge quantities of significance. This sacramental quality emerges from the peculiarly "compound" quality of metaphor itself, that is, its capacity for uncovering new reservoirs of meaning by comparing objects ordinarily thought of as being utterly unrelated.

It is in this metapoetic treatment of metaphor that Dickinson borders most closely upon resembling a mystic, for even though she frequently asserts, like Whitman, the accessibility and universality of her poetic vision, she is equally as likely to distinguish between her own construction of tropes and more conventional means, tacitly demanding that her particular creative methods be privileged. In effect, Dickinson stakes a claim for the extraliterariness of her metaphors, the tangible form her "apprehensions" have taken. To adopt a distinction originally made several years ago by Albert Gelpi in *Emily Dickinson: the Mind of the Poet,* the Dickinsonian metaphor is not exactly a trope, for it indicates a dimension beyond language where direct correspondences exist between the terrestrial and the celestial. Neither, however, is it a Puritan typology of the sort her ancestors had drawn from experience, because the correspondences are essentially subjectively determined, and the degree of relatedness between the mundane and the miraculous depends upon an individual's ability to discover points of similitude (153–56). Nevertheless, in some of these poems describing compound vision, Dickinson treats her culminating "revelation" as the final step in a kind of objective correlative that will ideally reproduce the same feelings of awe in her readers that she had felt, and consequently a good deal of manipulation may go on in Dickinson's poems as she cajoles or browbeats her readers into assenting to the validity of her vision.

Whether because exercising her eyes invited further injury, or because her metaphors possessed the "sacramental" quality of containing divine significance, Dickinson associated the writing of poetry with incurring considerable personal risk. Even the physical act of writing may have imperiled her eyesight to some degree: she apologized to Higginson during one of her treatments in Boston for writing to him in pencil, saying that the physician had "taken away [her] Pen" (L431). Dickinson interpreted the threat to her eyes as a portent of the danger writing poetry might pose to her immortal soul, and this attitude infuses Dickinson's poetics with a Promethean spirit. Although it is light, not fire, that she steals, Dickinson's poems make forays into a place where it is always "noon," and the consequences of her trespass are the same as would be suffered by anyone who had stared too long at the sustaining, menacing sun.

A BARRIER OF GAUZE

Dickinson universalized the idea of blindness, using it to represent an obstinate refusal to credit what the eyes reveal. Ordinarily, Dickinson exempted herself from the "blind" or the misguided, compound vision having given her a new form of vision which was, ironically, more acute than the eyesight of those whose eyes had never been stricken. Her illness "blinded" Dickinson only involuntarily, and, having become, perforce, acutely conscious that the senses could be overstimulated to the point of exhaustion, Dickinson wondered whether other people refused to recognize the beauty around them simply out of a sense of self-preservation (no. 1284):

> Had we our senses
> But perhaps 'tis well they're not at Home
> So intimate with Madness
> He's liable with them
>
> Had we the eyes within our Head—
> How well that we are Blind—
> We could not look upon the Earth—
> So utterly unmoved—

That serious repercussions might result from extending the range of one's senses Dickinson does not deny, for extreme sensitivity to beauty makes the beholder vulnerable to madness, but the attempt is worthwhile none-theless, Dickinson concludes, and her irony in this poem approaches sarcasm as she reproves readers so intimidated by the prospect of "taking leave of their senses" that they remain unmoved in the midst of temporal pleasures once forbidden to her by her physician-God.

As a "scientist of faith," Dickinson drove her senses, and her sensibilities, to the limits of their endurance. To increase our capacities for awareness, Dickinson proposed, we must demolish the barriers separating us from the visible world, for if we do not, we have no hope of overcoming the even more formidable intellectual obstacles potentially barring us from realizing heaven. Knowing that her own time was limited both by her doctor's orders and by mortality, Dickinson capitalized upon every opportunity that presented itself to see and hear the rapidly receding physical world. This effort to see more and see farther continued in parallel with her search for heaven, and her contrasting phrase "covered vision" in "Renunciation—is a piercing Virtue—" consolidates the impediments to both her faith and her sight. A sequestered convalescent, she described herself as living in a "soft prison" with walls of "gauze" that separated her not only from light but from God.

As Dickinson appropriated the sensory deprivation she had suffered during illness as a metaphor for the self-imposed blindness suffered by all people who cannot or will not recognize the presence of divinity within the world, so she also used the experience of having been blindfolded as an analogy for humankind's separation from godhead. To understand the connection more clearly, let us begin by considering the concrete realities of having one's eyes bandaged. Dickinson's blindfold almost certainly did not shut out daylight entirely, but rather let in a diffuse light dim enough not to tax her eyesight. Furthermore, her eyes beneath her bandages would have been open rather than shut, although all she could have seen would have been a white, hazy monotony, with perhaps a few shapes looming up from the unfathomable distance or else receding into it, like figures swallowed up in fog. Thus, in "My first well Day—since many ill—," the "hands of haze" put up before the convalescent's eyes externalize the subjective reality for Dickinson of having her eyes covered. The allied terms "haze," "veil," "film," and "gauze" accrue a particular significance in Dickinson's poems as images for the barrier separating the poet from heaven, whose temporal equivalent was the visible world from which she was similarly excluded.

The image of "gauze" should also be understood as having been derived in part from Dickinson's juvenile, stereotypic heaven, which co-

cooned the blessed in fleecy clouds. For example, in poem no. 273, "He put the Belt around my life—," she looks forward to becoming "A Member of the Cloud," and in poem no. 293, "I got so I could take his name—," she describes prayer as "My Business, with the Cloud," harkening back to the biblical description of God's mode of address to Moses. As cloud, God was both the revealer and concealer of heaven beneath and heaven above, a deity perceived by Dickinson from below as an intangible, yet impenetrable barrier interposing itself/himself between her and the sun she wanted so desperately to see. Dickinson was probably familiar with Emerson's assertion in *Nature* that "The axis of vision is not coincident with the axis of things, and so they appear not transparent, but opake" (55), and when Dickinson refers to God as "the Gauze," he embodies the very essence of opacity (no. 263):

A single Screw of Flesh
Is all that pins the Soul
That stands for Deity, to Mine,
Upon my side the Vail—

Once witnessed of the Gauze—
Its name is put away
As far from mine as if no plight
Had printed yesterday,

In tender—solemn Alphabet,
My eyes just turned to see,
When it was smuggled by my sight
Into Eternity—

More Hands—to hold—These are but Two—
One more new-mailed Nerve
Just granted, for the Peril's sake—
Some striding—Giant—Love—

So greater than the Gods can show,
They slink before the Clay,
That not for all their Heaven can boast
Will let it's Keepsake—go

The copula joining God's universal soul to the narrator's is her own body, a "Screw" piercing the veil of gauze separating her from heaven.[4] By returning the individual to a kind of Oversoul, death effectively wipes out the deceased's name, which, while she lived, had been printed carnally in "tender—Solemn Alphabet." Significantly, the speaker cannot see her own body being repossessed, although God, who has "witnessed" the new soul's entry into heaven, can, and this sense that things are taking place outside of the speaker's field of vision derives, I think, from Dickinson's experience of sitting bandaged in her room. Dickinson goes on in the poem to anticipate the replacement of her own soul with another, "new-mailed" in flesh, to take its chances in the world for the sake of love, the "striding—Giant" of whom even God, or the gods, are afraid. Love holds fast to its "keepsake" of clay, refusing to relinquish it despite both the fragility of the "screw" pinning the soul to earth and the blandishments proffered by heaven. Thus in this poem the simmering rivalry between heaven and earth that animates several Dickinsonian poems addressing the limits of perception threatens to boil over once more.

Although faith was an important adjunct to perception, God himself could become an impediment, if, Dickinson postulated, we permitted ourselves to become too easily discouraged by his seeming opaqueness. As I mentioned, Dickinson usually dismissed a deliberate turning away from perceptual challenges as an act of intellectual and perceptual cowardice that she scorned in herself and in others (no. 105):

> To hang our head—ostensibly—
> And subsequent, to find
> That such was not the posture
> Of our immortal mind—
>
> Affords the sly presumption
> That in so dense a fuzz—
> You—too—take Cobweb attitudes
> Upon a plane of Gauze!

Instead, barriers to our perception should, and often do, stimulate our curiosity, motivating us to exert our powers of observation more strenuously to see what lay behind the curtain (no. 210):

> The thought beneath so slight a film—
> Is more distinctly seen—
> As laces just reveal the surge—
> Or Mists—the Apennine

Like a woman's intentional, partial revelation of her bust beneath a lacy blouse, echoed in the equally mammarian image of mountain peaks half-

shrouded by mist, God's concealment of himself behind his semitrans-
parent wall of gauze could be interpreted as an act of flirtation, not
obfuscation. Correspondingly, bandages in Dickinson's poems sometimes
function as playful, deliberate goads to investigation and pursuit, rather
like the grass in Whitman's "Song of Myself":

> . . . I guess it is the handkerchief of the Lord,
> A scented gift and remembrancer designedly dropped,
> Bearing the owner's name someway in the corners, that we may
> see and remark, and say Whose?

A corresponding erotic tension invests many of Dickinson's poems about
blindfolds and barriers, as if the object concealed from her were hiding
by its own volition, as a form of sexual teasing. That teasing could assume either a positive role, as in poem no. 421:

> A Charm invests a face
> Imperfectly beheld—
> The Lady dare not lift her Vail
> For fear it be dispelled—
>
> But peers beyond her mesh—
> And wishes—and denies—
> Lest Interview—annul a want
> That Image—satisfies—

or a negative one, as was the case in "The Soul has Bandaged moments—,"
in which the narrator describes the horrifying experience of being "Salute[d]" and "Caress[ed]" by some unseen hand while she sits, blindfolded and helpless. Dickinson despairingly recognizes the eroticizing
power of her own concealing, misrepresenting imagination in the following poem (no. 253):

> You see I cannot see—your lifetime—
> I must guess—
> How many times it ache for me—today—Confess—
> How many times for my far sake
> The brave eyes film—
> But I guess guessing hurts—
> Mine—get so dim!
>
> Too vague—the face—
> My own—so patient—covets—
> Too far—the strength—

My timidness enfolds—
Haunting the Heart—
Like her translated faces—
Teazing the want—
It—only—can suffice!

Here, rather than the hands of her mother or some other nurse, Dickinson's own imagination performs the function of blindfolding her, its "timidness enfold[ing]" the image of her missing lover so that it shows through imperfectly, a "translated face" that teases her into missing, even more keenly, the face itself. Unable to see, she has to "guess" as she did in "Before I got my eye put out," but, as her redundancy aptly demonstrates, guessing "hurts" after a while, because the image of the beloved inevitably fades, imperfectly retained within the memory. This poem thus stands in direct contradiction to the following, more widely known lyric (no. 939):

What I see not, I better see—
Through Faith—my Hazel Eye
Has periods of shutting—
But, No lid has Memory—

For frequent, all my sense obscured
I equally behold
As someone held a light unto
The Features so beloved—

And I arise—and in my Dream—
Do Thee distinguished Grace—
Till jealous Daylight interrupt—
And mar thy perfectness—

Perhaps better than any other, this poem demonstrates why Dickinson equated "faith" with memory and the imagination, dual compensatory perceptual strategies she could rely upon following the failure of her eyesight. Although the speaker of this poem describes the features of the beloved as revealed to her in a dream, the phrase "periods of shutting" would connote for Dickinson more than just the time during which she slept, because during the long hours while she wore her bandages, faith could still represent the world "faithfully" to her.

In addition to the religious and erotic significance of gauzy barriers in Dickinson's poems, a heroic dimension also attaches to her character-

izations of a soul restrained against its will by bandages. As we saw in
"The Soul has Bandaged moments—," Dickinson could be resolutely
silent on the topic of her own infirmity, whether because she feared to
burden her family any more than she already had or because a pride in
her own stoicism prevented her from complaining overmuch. The idea
of keeping a "bandaged secret" reappears in the famous and puzzling
poem "Rearrange a 'Wife's' affection!" (no. 1737), in which Dickinson
may be comparing her appearance, while bandaged, with that of injured
soldiers, a suggestion which gains credibility through a close examination of the poem's possible provenance:

> Rearrange a "Wife's" affection!
> When they dislocate my Brain!
> Amputate my freckled Bosom!
> Make me bearded like a man!
>
> Blush, my spirit, in thy Fastness—
> Blush, my unacknowledged clay—
> Seven years of troth have taught thee
> More than Wifehood ever may!
>
> Love that never leaped its socket—
> Trust entrenched in narrow pain—
> Constancy thro' fire—awarded—
> Anguish—bare of anodyne!
>
> Burden—borne so far triumphant
> None suspect me of the crown,
> For I wear the "Thorns" till *Sunset*—
> Then—my Diadem put on.
>
> Big my Secret but it's *bandaged*—
> It will never get away
> Till the Day its Weary Keeper
> Leads it through the Grave to thee.

In his variorum edition Thomas Johnson located this poem among other
poems and fragments without ascertainable dates of composition, but
R. W. Franklin, in his reconstruction of Dickinson's packets, placed it in
fascicle 11 and assigned it a date of about 1861 (*Manuscripts*, 284). The
martial tone of the poem certainly supports the inference that it was
written during the Civil War, and its description of a fortress under bom-

bardment is strongly reminiscent of the shelling of Fort Sumter on April 12, 1861. Furthermore, if we recall Dickinson's statement to Higginson in April 1862 that she had had a "terror since September"—a terror, perhaps, of blindness or of near-constant confinement—we might reasonably conclude that her optical problems may have undergone a progressive worsening during the spring and summer of 1861. Moreover, in a letter probably sent to her Norcross cousins in spring 1861, Dickinson reports that "The seeing pain one can't relieve makes a demon of one" and concludes with the rhetorical question "When did the war really begin?" (L375–76). For all these reasons, I think we are justified in assuming that the narrator of this poem is indeed Dickinson herself and that she is writing it during wartime.

Dickinson's characterization of her body as a fortress under attack suggests that she imbricated newspaper accounts of Sumter's bombardment with a description of the mental and emotional strain concomitant to keeping two secrets—that of an imagined "betrothal" to an unnamed fiancé and that of her optical illness. Even though an awareness of Dickinson's susceptibility to eye problems does not shed much light on the identity of the unknown beloved to whom she has been engaged for seven years,[5] it can, like the provisional assignment of a Civil-War era date to the poem's composition, provide a basis, at least, for understanding why she chose tropes grounded in physical injury and endurance of pain. The primary lesson taught to Dickinson by prolonged, perhaps voluntary, secrecy is courage under fire, and her adoption of a military idiom appears designed to permit her to claim a man's prerogative of physical courage without having to renounce her femininity, which she combatively asserts in the poem's first stanza. The effort of preserving the "fastness" of her own body in its virginal, prenuptial state for seven years, despite possible temptations from without, has been every bit as psychologically and physically taxing as any conventional married couple's adherence to their vows of fidelity. Unacknowledged love is the "secret" which, like a soldier forbidden to bolt from his position under fire, must not be permitted to leap "its socket" (not a foxhole, perhaps, but rather an eyesocket?) by being confided to anyone; furthermore, because the secret is "Big" it must be "bandaged," in the dual senses of being tied up and blindfolded, to prevent it from "getting away" and being made public. Yet using the term "bandaged" suggests that the secret itself is wounded as well, setting up an identity between captive and captor which is entirely fitting for Dickinson's trope of civil conflict. It is she herself whom Dickinson must guard, an agonizing paradox not to be resolved until her own death would liberate both the secret and its "Weary Keeper." While the poet remains alive, her only relief comes at night, when, freed temporarily from her bandages, she can achieve some catharsis by writing poetry.[6] Then the bandage that had been a "crown of thorns" for her during the day is exchanged for the royal crown or "Diadem" that emblematizes her role as poet. Save for those few moments of regal splendor, however, she continued, while ill, to serve involuntarily as her own censor, jailer, torturer.

THE PRISONER OF CHILLON

Aside from the bandages Dickinson wore as a "prisoner," the other instrument of torture used against her was, of course, the cell or sickroom itself. Dickinson's figurative presentations of imprisonings and subsequent escapes in her poems may have participated in a larger discourse she had absorbed from her readings in romantic literature. Even though prison narratives were a staple of the nineteenth-century literary diet, stories about liberation after long confinement appear to have possessed a special resonance for women writers. As Sandra Gilbert and Susan Gubar point out, "Dramatizations of imprisonment and escape are so all-pervasive in nineteenth-century literature by women" that they seem to represent "a uniquely female tradition in this period" (85).[7] Nevertheless, Dickinson's frequent employment of carcerative images in her poems should, I think, also be recognized as another by-product of her experience as a patient. This inference is borne out by the appearance of prison imagery in correspondence written during her convalescence. For example, in 1864, during her first treatment in Boston, she wrote to Colonel Higginson: "He [her physician] does not let me go, yet I work in my Prison, and make Guests for myself—Carlo [her dog] did not come, because that he would die, in Jail" (L431). During July of the same year she wrote to Lavinia, in anticipation of her return to Amherst, "You remember the Prisoner of Chillon did not know Liberty when it came, and asked to go back to Jail" (L432).

Dickinson's comparison of her experience to that of the narrator of Byron's "The Prisoner of Chillon" warrants closer examination. We will recall that in one of the "Master" letters she wrote, "when I do not see . . . 'Chillon' is not funny," and "Chillon" was, of course, anything *but* "funny"; Dickinson probably means that during her illness, Byron's poem lost its literariness, having come too close to her own experience to be read objectively or for pleasure. The chief similarities between her own experience and that of the prisoner François de Bonnivard were their isolation from the sun and their eventual paradoxical fondness for their places of confinement (no. 652):

A Prison gets to be a friend—
Between its Ponderous face
And Our's—A Kinsmanship express—
And in it's narrow Eyes—

We come to look with gratitude
For the appointed Beam
It deal us—stated as our food—
And hungered for—the same—

We learn to know the Planks—
That answer to Our feet—
So miserable a sound—at first—
Nor ever now—so sweet—

As plashing in the Pools—
When Memory was a Boy—
But a Demurer Circuit—
A Geometric Joy—

The Posture of the Key
That interrupt the Day
To Our Endeavor—Not so real
The Cheek of Liberty—

As this Phantasm Steel—
Whose features—Day and Night—
Are present to us—as Our Own—
And as escapeless—quite—

The narrow Round—the Stint—
The slow exchange of Hope—
For something passiver—Content
Too steep for looking up—

The Liberty we knew
Avoided—like a Dream—
Too wide for any Night but Heaven—
If That—indeed—redeem—

Immured within her own room to protect her eyes from daylight, Dickinson hungers for her "appointed Beam," the scanty jailhouse ration of light permitted her. The "kinsmanship" she feels with her confinement derives from the realization that she is, in fact, a voluntary prisoner, so that her jailer is none other than herself. Her room mimics and externalizes her predicament, its windows becoming "narrow Eyes" squinted almost shut to keep out the light. Thus the prison's features become as "present" to her as her own, and just as inescapable. Dickinson's bandages could make of her head a little "room" "outside" of which she could see virtually nothing, whether of God, or of a lover—or even of her face, reflected in a mirror. The theme of kinship raised in Dickinson's carcerative poems may owe its existence to her awareness that she was her own prison, prisoner, and imprisoner, as well as fellow-sufferer and potential liberator. Like de Bonnivard, she slowly accommodates herself to her limitations, pacing in a "Demurer Circuit" around her "cell" until she finds in it a "Geometric Joy" she can sustain as long as she resists the impulse to think about freedom.[8] Only at night, when she could use her eyes more freely, can she even "dream" of escaping the conceptual prison confining her, but her dream appears to her to be so impossibly ambitious or "wide" that only heaven can redeem it.[9]

While Dickinson was recovering at home, her movements may have been restricted to her bedroom, so that a place which had once served as a refuge was transformed into her "dungeon." The irony of this was not lost on the poet, who knew that the "Phantasm Steel" enclosing her was a phantasm indeed, her room actually being a "soft prison" of feather pillows, quilts, and counterpanes (no. 1334):

How soft this Prison is
How sweet these sullen bars
No Despot but the King of Down
Invented this repose

Of Fate if this is All
Has he no added Realm
A Dungeon but a Kinsman is
Incarceration—Home.[10]

Her prison is her "Kinsman" in part because she is at home, put there by no "Despot" other than her doctor or her own free will. This voluntary self-incarceration left Dickinson with no external agency to blame and no one with whom she could share the experience. Unlike de Bonnivard, whose brother died beside him, she had no siblings "imprisoned" alongside her, so that she was forced to invent a proximal "other" that externalized her own situation, thereby rendering it more bearable as well as more susceptible to rational, dispassionate analysis. Correspondingly, in the following romantic prison-escape narrative, Dickinson may be playing the dual role of lady in distress and knight-errant (no. 398):

> I had not minded—Walls—
> Were Universe—one Rock—
> And far I heard his silver Call
> The other side the Block—
>
> I'd tunnel—till my Groove
> Pushed sudden thro' to his—
> Then my face take her Recompense—
> The looking in his Eyes—
>
> But 'tis a single Hair—
> A filament—a law—
> A Cobweb—wove in Adamant—
> A Battlement—of Straw—
>
> A limit like the Vail
> Unto the Lady's face—
> But every Mesh—a Citadel—
> And Dragons—in the Crease—

Several commentators have assumed that this poem depicts Dickinson chafing under some moral stricture or "law" (the commandment forbidding adultery, perhaps) preventing her from joining her unknown lover.[11] Instead, however, the poem may be Dickinson's dramatization to herself of her twofold predicament as convalescent and as supplicant to heaven. The "Cobweb" and "Vail" separating her from her unnamed correspondent are versions of the "gauze" restricting her vision, and even though it is "his" eyes the speaker wishes she could look into once more, that masculine possessive pronoun would apply equally as well to a twin brother as it would to a lover. A suggestion of kinship or twinship is present as well in the symmetry of "his" situation and hers: the speaker would tunnel until her own "Groove" met his, and their projected reconciliation scene, when they look into each others' eyes, resembles a face gazing into a mirror. The "wall" between them is compared to "the

Vail / Unto the Lady's face," as if lifting that veil were equally the object of the hero-narrator's quest, so that each twin could see and be seen. The "law" proscribing their meeting could reasonably refer to a doctor's orders to keep her bandages on, which Dickinson has willed herself to obey. Such a "law" would, in its susceptibility to being instantly violated, indeed resemble a hair, a filament, a cobweb, or a flimsy veil. Furthermore, at point-blank range, every "mesh" or "crease" in the patient's bandage would look very much like a "Citadel" surrounded by "Dragons"—objectivized symbols, respectively, of the restrictions Dickinson had to impose upon herself and of the consequences of defying those restrictions.

In the sense that recovery of her previous freedom to see and be seen became Dickinson's goal in continuing to wear her bandages, the "other" or "kinsman" she sought behind the wall of confinement was herself, or at least, the person she had been before her illness and might yet be, again.[12] A corresponding symmetry invests many of the poems describing the beloved concealed either behind the "gauze" or prison walls. For example, the same film of tears that covers the speaker's eyes in "You see I cannot see—your lifetime—" simultaneously covers the beloved's, and the "Soul" in "A single Screw of Flesh" is pinned to its twin, Deity, in an embrace as intimate as Whitman's depiction in "Song of Myself" of the body's fellation by the soul. "Banish Air from Air—," said Dickinson in poem no. 854, "Divide Light if you dare—/ They'll meet," as if she and the beloved constituted a single unit which, if divided, would not or could not rest until its pieces were reunited. On a secondary level, Dickinson's separation from the beloved may even symbolize her separation from light itself, as in poem no. 1556:

> Image of Light, Adieu—
> Thanks for the interview—
> So long—so short—
> Preceptor of the whole—
> Coeval Cardinal—
> Impart—Depart—

Dickinson is separated from her "Coeval Cardinal" by a barrier of gauze as adamantine as the dressed rock walls of a prison. In "I had not minded—Walls—" she does not hear, or at least hearken to, the siren song or "silver Call" of self-liberation because she has forbidden herself to do so, primarily to improve her chances of recovery. To explain to herself why she had renounced the sun and light itself she constructed a

compensatory romantic fiction of imprisonment that is articulated in
the following poem (no. 474):

> They put Us far apart—
> As separate as Sea
> And Her unsown Peninsula—
> We signified "These see"—
>
> They took away our Eyes—
> They thwarted Us with Guns—
> "I see Thee" each responded straight
> Through Telegraphic Signs—
>
> With Dungeons—They devised—
> But through their thickest skill—
> And their opaquest Adamant—
> Our Souls saw—just as well—
>
> They summoned Us to die—
> With sweet alacrity
> We stood upon our stapled feet—
> Condemned—but just—to see—
>
> Permission to recant—
> Permission to forget—
> We turned our backs upon the Sun
> For perjury of that—
>
> Not Either—noticed Death—
> Of Paradise—aware—
> Each other's Face—was all the Disc
> Each other's setting—saw—

Dickinson and her complementary lover/other manage to communicate
despite having been deprived of their vision by some unnamed mutual
enemy. In the style of prison melodrama the fellow inmates resort to
using "Telegraphic signs," but they also rely upon their "Souls" to see,
as the narrator of "Before I got my eye put out" was compelled to do,
and when about to be "executed," the two companions hoist themselves
erect upon feet that are "stapled," like the "Soul['s]" song in "The Soul
has Bandaged moments—." Ironically, their sentence consists of being
forced to see, in the conventional sense, which they refuse to do, boldly
turning their backs upon the sun. At their deaths, they appropriate the

sun's role to create a private, alternative "Paradise" of their own, becoming a composite "Disc" that sees only itself as it "sets" into death. In this poem Dickinson explains that she turned inward and developed the compensatory strategy of compound vision as a defensive measure against the allied inimical forces of God and sun. A major drawback of such a rationalization was, however, that in it she would be eternally cast as a victim, passive as a prisoner bullied from prison cell to the headsman's block as she dodged the noon sun's rays or monitored herself for signs of perceptual backsliding. Dickinson may have begun to explore the possibilities of carving out a more positive role for herself in her own psychodrama, while simultaneously using liberal doses of irony in her poems to protect herself from becoming excessively—or even dangerously—foolhardy.

A GALLOWS HUMOR

Dickinson generalized from her experience of sitting solitary and almost sightless within the narrow precincts of her room to create poems with existential themes such as the following, written only two years before her death (no. 1601):

> Of God we ask one favor,
> That we may be forgiven—
> For what, he is presumed to know—
> The Crime, from us, is hidden—
> Immured the whole of Life
> Within a magic Prison
> We reprimand the Happiness
> That too competes with Heaven.

Many of the elements of which I have spoken previously are clearly present here: the sense that God had punished Dickinson for an unidentified crime, which had somehow involved a rivalry between temporal and heavenly beauty; the necessity of exerting self-control and self-discipline; a concealment of activity or of evidence from the narrator's eyes; and the characterization of life on earth as a "magic Prison" that has become, over time, a haven, if not a heaven. Although her father's house was the most tangible manifestation of the prison/sanctuary enclosing her, her art also inscribed a pentagram of safety or "magic Prison" about her while she experimented as a "scientist of faith," borrowing eclectically from the best facts, terms, and ideas that natural science and religion had to offer. To continue her investigations, however, she had to shield herself from the very knowledge she uncovered as it broke in upon her consciousness whenever she discovered another particle's role in the whole. Compound vision therefore describes not only the compromise Dickinson struck between her injured eyes and her robust imagination, but also the position she occupied as a poet, a vantage point from which she could descry glimpses of divinity without approaching too closely or being compelled to invest precious perceptual resources that she realized, after her initial brush with illness, had to be conserved.

It was a perilous undertaking, and to avoid courting disaster a second time, Dickinson employed such "slant" tools as her poetic personae, metaphor, symbolism, and occasionally irony to approach heaven indirectly, rather than mounting a frontal assault. Consider, for example, how irony functions in the following poem (no. 766):

> My Faith is larger than the Hills—
> So when the Hills decay—
> My Faith must take the Purple Wheel
> To show the Sun the way—
>
> 'Tis first He steps upon the Vane—
> And then—upon the Hill—
> And then abroad the World He go
> To do His Golden Will—
>
> And if His Yellow feet should miss—
> The Bird would not arise—
> The Flowers would slumber on their Stems—
> No Bells have Paradise—
>
> How dare I, therefore, stint a faith
> On which so vast depends—
> Lest Firmament should fail for me—
> The Rivet in the Bands.

In this poem Dickinson describes compound vision's utility to heaven, that is, what benefits her service as revelator or "scientist of faith" might offer to God. Essentially, her existence as poet guarantees nothing less than the continued existence of all creation. Although Dickinson's description of her faith as being "larger than the Hills" is more than a little facetious, I think her description of herself assisting at the sun's rising represents a strategy for regaining the sun without jeopardizing her eyesight. Otherwise, the world would be placed in the same sort of predicament she faced: deprived of light, birds would remain silent, drooping flowers could not straighten themselves, and "Paradise," or at least the earthly paradise, would have no "Bells," that is, birds or flowers, to celebrate creation's existence. Then the "Firmament" itself might fall, bringing down heaven with it. As poet, Dickinson is the "Rivet in the Bands" linking earth to heaven through an image borrowed, probably, from the smithy: in the hoop or "circumference" binding the temporal to the eternal, the poet becomes the rivet holding the entire system together, like the "screw of flesh" connecting Dickinson's soul to God's parent soul.

For us as readers, however, Dickinson's irony is more saliently the "rivet" joining the various levels at which she evidently intends for this poem to be read, or rather, heard. Dickinson's poetic voice is often a highly ironic one, and sometimes it is difficult to know precisely where her irony begins and ends. For example, how serious is Dickinson being in the last line of this poem, where she describes herself performing the Christlike role of fastening heaven to earth?[13] How much self-satire should we read into the statement, "How dare I, therefore, stint a faith / On which so vast depends"? Quite a bit, I would argue, for her irony performs the same office as her "child" persona or any of her other methods of misdirection by relieving her of some of the responsibility for what she is saying. Dickinson implicitly demands that her readers be not only sensitive to verbal irony, but also familiar enough with her as a person to understand that her words are often tinged by a second level of irony predicated upon a fundamental incongruity between the magnificence of her imagination and the provincial obscurity in which she lived. There is, however, yet a third level of irony discernible in some poems, one directly related to her conviction that God monitored her: by telling the truth "slant," Dickinson attempts to conceal her motives from God.

That Dickinson should use irony for such a purpose accords well with irony's origins as a rhetorical strategy for representing the actions of men controlled by the whims of the gods. For her, however, a suspicion that she was intermittently the object of divine scrutiny led her to adopt irony in her poems as a principal means of obscuring her true motivation for writing. In the third essay of his book *Anatomy of Criticism,* "Archetypal Criticism," Northrop Frye identifies this obscuring characteristic about irony as one of the features distinguishing it from satire. "[W]henever a reader is not sure what the author's attitude is or what his own is supposed to be," says Frye, irony is present rather than satire, which requires a "relatively clear" moral standard (223). Because God is omniscient, the irony in "My faith is larger than the Hills—" resembles Frye's sixth phase of irony, which depicts life, he suggests, "in terms of largely unrelieved bondage. Its settings feature prisons, madhouses, lynching mobs, and places of execution . . . ," and it has a corresponding tragic theme, Frye continues, in the "humiliation of being constantly watched by a hostile or derisive eye" (238). Is it any wonder, then, that the irony in some of Dickinson's poems resembles that which underlies jokes prisoners make to each other in the turnkey's presence, surreptitiously twitting him, then appeasing him in the next breath?

But in "My Faith is larger than the Hills—," Dickinson also covertly "competes" with heaven as a creator, for although she says it is her "Faith" which must take the "Purple Wheel" and pilot the sun after the hills "decay," she is clearly using the term "faith" once again to refer to her own imagination. Unable to look out her window and watch the sun ascending over the neighboring Pelham Hills, the poet reconstructs the landscape in her mind, embellishing it with each visual detail withheld from her. Dickinson has "faith" that this scene is being reenacted every morning on the other side of the gauze barrier blocking her eyes, and she could use this particular brand of faith as a means of practicing to have faith in heaven, itself equally invisible. As someone who was denied the palpable reality of place on a daily basis, Dickinson imaginatively re-created the landscape every morning from memory, and if her imagination could do that, perhaps it and her poetry might even be equal to the task of constructing the landscape of heaven.

The god of bounds,
Who sets to seas a shore,
Came to me in his fatal rounds,
And said: "No more!
No farther shoot
Thy broad ambitious branches, and thy root.
Fancy departs: no more invent;
Contract thy firmament
To compass of a tent."

Emerson, "Terminus"

POETRY AS PLACE

*Heaven, Ill/locality, and
Continents of Light*

ONE STRATEGY Dickinson adopted as part of her campaign to determine heaven's location was to replicate heaven in her mind. Her confinement during illness offered an "opportunity" she could exploit by trying to remove every vestige of the visible world from her imagination; any residue left behind, severed from all connections to the temporal world, simply *had* to be heaven, she reasoned. This concept of a completely nonmaterialistic heaven stimulated her poetically by providing one more barrier to be conquered, a center of resistance upon which she could push, another truth to be wrested from a reluctant God. Yet Dickinson's idealized heaven also participates in her larger poetic project of radically redefining the entire concept of physical space, which she treats in her poems with a distinctive subversiveness. Paradoxical phrases such as "Latitudeless Place," "Acres of Perhaps," and "A nearness to Tremendousness" can contest our preexisting ideas about location so aggressively that even we as readers may be left feeling momentarily dizzy or disoriented.

Dickinson's tropes redefine the notion of place according to states of being rather than sense evidence, a practice in keeping not only with her determination to realize heaven, but also with her experience as a person with injured eyes. Although commentators have written about the equivocal nature of place in Dickinson's poetry, her vagueness having been interpreted as a symptom of existential dread[1] or terror in the face of romantic sublimity,[2] strangely, it has not generally been associated with her optical problems, which may have impaired both her ability to focus and her depth perception. If they did, the characteristic ambiguousness of figure and ground in Dickinson's poems was probably rooted in experience. Thus, when she wrote "Doubt Me! My Dim Companion!" in poem no. 275, the dimness her eyes registered may have been all too actual, and when she wrote, in poem no. 1187, "Oh Shadow on the Grass, / Art thou a Step or not?," she may simply have been describing the precariousness, for her, of walking across the untrustworthy space of her own lawn. Similarly, her poetic personae "Step lightly" or "softer tread" over narrow piers, planks, or bridges spanning bottomless pits or unfathomed seas. Frequently they topple off, and the sensations of falling, floating, or crashing to earth are described in excruciating detail. So treacherous and ephemeral is the ground underfoot that the most dependably "real" places available to Dickinson's personae are often the poems themselves, intellectual and artistic constructs capable of reclaiming, if only for a brief time, the physical spaces of which both their protagonists and their author have been dispossessed. More than most writers, Dickinson depended upon her art to create an alternative reality, a "here" that was constantly imperiled by a "wilderness" of spatial and conceptual chaos. Her dual intellectual projects of establishing a world of her own and of apprehending the "placeless place" which was heaven should be interpreted in the context of her optical illness because both seek to establish the primacy of the imagination over the realm of sensory evidence.

As part of her efforts to reimagine heaven, Dickinson did succeed, to some degree, in disabusing herself of some of the stereotypes about heaven she had imbibed in Sunday school. Yet she found it virtually impossible to stop thinking of heaven as an Eden of sensuous pleasures, one somewhat similar, perhaps, to that described in the Koran. Thus Dickinson came to stipulate two contradictory requirements for heaven: it had to be familiar enough to be comfortable, yet different enough to inspire awe. To Dickinson, "familiar" meant "like Amherst," her birthplace remaining as central to her consciousness as Concord did for Thoreau, and being "lost" in her poems is equivalent to being unable to find one's way back to Amherst. Drawing upon the realities of growing up in her native village, Dickinson even assigned various thematic qualities to the points of the compass. The west itself, for example, represents both wilderness and frontier, the land beyond the Berkshires where the sun disappears and where the soul migrates after death. The sparsely settled north is the abode of God—capricious, elementally powerful, cold and remote. The "torrid" south, besides providing a refuge for birds in wintertime, is both exotic and erotic. The east, Dickinson's preferred direction, is old, yet eternally self-renewing; passionate, yet calm. Although many of these directional associations are certainly not unique to Dickinson, they possess specific connotations in her poems that arose autochthonously out of Amherst's soil.

VISIONS AND VERSIONS OF HEAVEN

"Heaven" became synonymous in Dickinson's poetry with the farthest limits of consciousness, experience, or vision—what Wallace Stevens called, in "Of Mere Being," "The palm at the end of the mind." Dickinson's own statement that "'Heaven'—is what I cannot reach!" (no. 239) was made in perhaps unconscious paraphrase of Browning's lines in "Andrea Del Sarto," "Ah, but a man's reach should exceed his grasp, / Or what's a heaven for?" In this regard, heaven is symbolic of the imagination itself, which continually transcends its surroundings. Nevertheless, Dickinson's poems are simultaneously infused with a highly materialistic urge to "own" heaven, to possess it like a piece of real estate that could not be confiscated.

In seeking to understand why Dickinson's mental construct of heaven wavered between the physical and the ideal, we may begin with Barton Levi St. Armand's thorough and insightful treatment of the topic in the fourth chapter of his book *Emily Dickinson and Her Culture*, "Paradise Deferred: Dickinson, Phelps, and the Image of Heaven." St. Armand describes how Dickinson modified, without entirely rejecting, the sometimes absurdly literal paradise popularized in sentimental Victorian literature such as Elizabeth Stuart Phelps's 1868 novel *The Gates Ajar*, which Mark Twain was to parody so memorably in his story "Extract from Captain Stormfield's Visit to Heaven." This materialistic heaven of the Victorians, which helped assuage the entire nation's need for consolation in the years following the Civil War, is a direct descendant of the old-fashioned "Sunday school heaven" productive of most of the stereotypes that progressive early-nineteenth-century Christians began to find so ridiculous: harps, wings, halos, and so forth.[3] Although St. Armand says that Dickinson rejected the Sunday school heaven "because it was all too silly when subjected to a pragmatic commonsense scrutiny" (131), in her youth and young adulthood she clung persistently to her emphatically literal childhood conception of heaven.[4] While still probably in her twenties, she wrote to Mrs. J. G. Holland:

My only sketch, profile of Heaven is a large, blue sky, bluer and larger than the *biggest* I have seen in June, and in it are my friends—all of them—every one of them—those who are with me now, and those who were "parted" as we walked, and "snatched up to Heaven."

If roses had not faded, and frost had never come, and one had not fallen here and there whom I could not waken, there were no need of other Heaven than the one below—and if God had been here this summer, and seen the things that *I* have seen—I guess that He would think His Paradise superfluous. (L329)

This passage concisely delineates the internal contradictions endemic to Dickinson's thinking about heaven: it was a palpable "place" floating in the air above her head; it was a compensatory reward, or, as St. Armand says, a paradise "of personal fulfillment" (151); and sometimes it was the earthly paradise, which became, especially during the summer, so beautiful that it could rival—ominously—heaven itself.

The most signal advantage of believing that the earthly paradise was a sort of rehearsal for, or preliminary draft of, the "further Heaven" was that she could tell herself she lived in heaven *now*, rather than having to wait until after death. By experiencing temporal life as intensely as possible, or by knitting together a series of peak moments during which the mundane world was illuminated so brightly that it approximated heaven, Dickinson hoped not only to prepare herself for revelations to come, but to "possess" a slice of heaven in the here and now. She wrote, in poem no. 1544:

Who has not found the Heaven—below—
Will fail of it above—
For Angels rent the House next our's,
Wherever we remove—

Dickinson's characterization of heaven in this poem as a property to be rented, as an item of *real estate*, is typical of many of her poems about eternity, and indicative of her belief that it was, indeed, susceptible to being possessed. Similarly, in one of the more wittily concise poems in all our national literature, she wrote (no. 1069):

Paradise is of the option.
Whosoever will
Own in Eden notwithstanding
Adam and Repeal.

Paradise is "optional" in two regards: it is the terrestrial Eden we may readily apprehend if only we are willing to make the imaginative effort necessary to perceive it, and, unlike the celestial, Calvinistic heaven Dickinson had inherited from her Puritan ancestors, it is available to anyone who petitions for "ownership," notwithstanding Original Sin and Adam's expulsion from Eden. Yet this poem also represents itself as the terms of a legal contract, an option to sell being tendered to the world at large. Those who can grasp the "Fact that Earth is Heaven," as Dickinson says, "whether Heaven is Heaven or not" (no. 1408) effectively "own" a chunk of paradise, with or without God's approbation. Because Dickinson was the daughter of a prominent local attorney, it is only to be expected, perhaps, that she would be highly attuned to the rights and privileges entailed in property ownership (and even as those rights applied to her own carnal body, as we shall see in chapter 7). Yet her campaign to persuade herself into believing, with the same degree of certitude and finality that attends legal disposals of chattel, that she already dwelled in heaven was doomed to end in failure, chiefly as a result of contradictions implicit in her own thinking.

One of Dickinson's metaphysical explanations for why she had fallen ill was, we may recall, that God was admonishing her for having insufficient confidence in the superiority of the world to come. Such a rationalization also involves, however, a self-imputation of intellectual and religious immaturity, for no "adult" heaven, the poet told herself, would submit to being confirmed by sense evidence. I agree with St. Armand that Dickinson, in conceiving of heaven as the imagination shorn, ironically, of its images, appears to have been following the lead of the Reverend Charles Wadsworth, the Presbyterian minister she idolized. St. Armand uses the following excerpt from Wadsworth's sermon "The Ceasing of the Manna" as an epigraph to "Paradise Deferred: Dickinson, Phelps, and the Image of Heaven":

> And all those descriptions and word-paintings of heaven with which ambitious poetry and oratory so often strive to interest and astonish us are as pitiful caricatures of the ineffable reality as a child's notion of the universe—a flat, earthly plane a score of miles in circumference, and a firmament above it a little greater in altitude. The heaven they describe is but the poor, flitting phantasms of man's childish fancy. But heaven, as it is, is the perfect realization of the infinite and transcendent imagination of God. (202)

If she read or heard Wadsworth's sermon, Dickinson might well have taken this particular passage directly to heart as an uncannily clairvoyant insight into the fairy-tale version of heaven she had harbored, somewhat guiltily, since girlhood. Furthermore, Wadsworth's comments about the imagination possess implications about Dickinson's understanding of how the poetic faculty worked. Wadsworth allocates the fancy to childhood, because it is a mere secondhand rendering of sensory impressions. Only the imagination, unfettered by empirical experience, can approximate the scope and grandeur of God's creative will. Heaven is an idea in the mind of God, Wadsworth says, a realm that lies perhaps beyond language's power to articulate.

Although Dickinson strove to embrace this "adult" version of heaven, she never entirely succeeded, betrayed by her own inextirpable fondness for the things of this world, which continued to provide the foundations for her "childish" view of heaven (the "blue sky" bigger than any she had seen in June, for example). Anchored to Amherst, Dickinson was prone to continue conceiving of heaven in insistently materialistic terms, a habit of mind that she was nevertheless fully capable of poking fun at, as in the following poem (no. 374):

I went to Heaven—
'Twas a small Town—
Lit—with a Ruby—
Lathed—with Down—

Stiller—than the fields
At the full Dew—
Beautiful—as Pictures—
No Man drew.
People—like the Moth—
Of Mechlin—frames—
Duties—of Gossamer—
And Eider—names—
Almost—contented—
I—could be—
'Mong such unique
Society—

The landscape of heaven Dickinson paints here is almost laughably literal, and she undermines her own ostensible ingenuousness by repeatedly contradicting both her own and a reader's expectations of heaven. Rather than finding spacious Elysian fields, she discovers a "small Town," albeit one more beautiful than pictures "No Man drew." She calls heaven's inhabitants not "angels," but rather "People" who are insubstantial as moths, with names and responsibilities that are similarly lightweight. At the end of the poem she declares that she could "Almost" be contented in this alternative Amherst, this pocket paradise, yet the very materiality of its ephemerality, represented by pairings of the concrete with the intangible in such phrases as "Lathed—with Down—," "Mechlin frames," and "Eider—names," is somehow dissatisfying. The direction Dickinson's thinking takes in this poem would appear to indicate that she finally decided she needed a "higher" heaven, one stripped of clichés and capable of instilling in her the requisite feeling of awe.

Heaven and Ill/locality

Dickinson strove to believe as confidently in a heaven she could not see as she did in the continued existence of a tangible reality beyond the curtain imposed by her bandages. In reconstructing her confiscated visual world, the poet at least enjoyed the advantage of being able to remember what it had looked like, but she possessed no empirical evidence whatsoever to help her picture heaven (no. 696):

Their Hight in Heaven comforts not—
Their Glory—nought to me—
'Twas best imperfect—as it was—
I'm finite—I cant see—

The House of Supposition—
The Glimmering Frontier that
skirts the Acres of Perhaps—
To Me—shows insecure—

The Wealth I had—contented me—
If 'twas a meaner size—
Then I had counted it until
It pleased my narrow Eyes—

Better than larger values—
That show however true—
This timid life of Evidence
Keeps pleading—"I don't know."

Dickinson's three spatial tropes for heaven's borders in the second stanza proceed farther and farther afield from her circumscribed perspective, moving from a nearby supposititious house, to a hazy frontier, to the lands beyond that frontier, the "Acres of Perhaps" which are as indistinct to her as an antique map's *terra incognita*. That even a nearby house should be so dimly defined makes it highly unlikely that she would ever be able to "see" as far as heaven's "Acres of Perhaps," however. Moreover, because being persuaded of heaven's existence is a form of security, she is "insecure," possessing only the lesser sureties of living in the sensory world. Dickinson's sources of spiritual "wealth" are emphatically local in this poem, and it is only after she had been told of the existence of other unvisited lands such as heaven that she becomes dissatisfied with her current temporal values.[5]

To envision heaven, Dickinson told herself, she would have to learn to think purely conceptually, severing her bonds with sensory experience as she had done while enduring periods of enforced blindness. Her primary rhetorical tool for doing this was paradox, which she could use to turn earthly imagery back upon itself until it was obliterated by logical contradiction. For example, as she said of illness itself (no. 963),

[It] cannot stay
In Acres—It's Location
Is Illocality—

"Ill/locality" was precisely where Dickinson was situated while afflicted with her optical ailment. Her sickroom, a scene without dimensions, constricted her sphere of activity virtually to nonexistence, yet, for all that she could tell beneath her bandages, the room might be "wider than the Sky." The sole advantage of living in such a "place" was that it trained Dickinson to think without images, as she imagined the blessed dead might be able to do (no. 489):

We pray—to Heaven—
We prate—of Heaven—
Relate—when Neighbors die—
At what o'clock to heaven—they fled—
Who saw them—Wherefore fly?

Is Heaven a Place—a Sky—a Tree?
Location's narrow way is for Ourselves—
Unto the Dead
There's no Geography—

But State—Endowal—Focus—
Where—Omnipresence—fly?

The living know only "location's way" because they require points of reference, circumscribed areas, and an orientation, all of which are limitations imposed on them by the possession of corporeal bodies. For the dead, however, conventional ideas of space no longer apply, nor do ordinary measurements of time, the "o'clock" at which they "fled." The poem's scrupulously symmetrical structure reinforces Dickinson's argument, which refutes point for point, as if in scholastic debate, conventional ideas about location. "Place," "Sky," and "Tree" are contrasted, one by one, with "State," "Endowal," "Focus," Dickinson's own focus moving from close-up to wide-angle, from specific to general. "State," a condition of being (with a collateral pun upon the political entity), involves possession of concrete value, or "Endowal," which in turn produces a sense of being concentrated in one spot, or "Focus." Similarly, in the poem's first three lines, the parallelism created by consonance and assonance in "pray," "prate," and "Relate," unobtrusively supports, by implying an equivalency between those verbs, the poet's assault upon the entire notion of conventional prayer on the dual grounds that it is self-serving as well as logically absurd, for we are praying *to* an omnidirectional, omnipresent God. Unlike Emerson, who declared in "Self-Reliance" that "Prayer . . . crav[ing] a particular commodity—anything less than all good, is vicious," Dickinson takes prayer to task as an implicit form of intellectual "provincialism." Prayer finally provides merely one more illustration of the way the living see narrowly or locationally, as opposed to the broader "vision" of the dead.

Dickinson's statement "Unto the Dead / There's no Geography—" also possesses dual meanings: not only do the dead no longer recognize the validity of physical space, there's simply no way to travel toward them—no chart exists. The only "route" to the dead was through death itself, or at least thinking "as if" one were already dead. Through a projection of her thoughts "westward" via compound vision, Dickinson could hope to arrive at death, and by so doing, achieve the preview she needed to imagine heaven's featureless landscape. Yet just as often, Dickinson represents herself as having first to negotiate an intervening "wilderness" in which all "sizes," including that of both her body and of her identity as a poet, would be precipitated into chaos.

Going West

In many of her poems Dickinson proves, of course, to be as provincial in her thinking about heaven as the neighbors she berates in "We pray—to Heaven—," fervently desiring a paradise equipped with skies and trees, familiar objects she could use to gauge the scale of things around her in importance, if not in size. "The Fact that Earth is Heaven," Dickinson wrote, confirms that it would "affront" us to exist anywhere else, and often her pictured heaven does indeed closely resemble earth, with the significant difference that heaven is immutable. Dickinson sent the following poem, accompanied by a gift of apples, to Susan Dickinson (no. 1067):

> Except the smaller size
> No lives are round—
> These—hurry to a sphere
> And show and end—
> The larger—slower grow
> And later hang—
> The Summers of Hesperides
> Are long.

It is only while we remain mortal that our lives are finite, hurrying toward "ripeness" or closure, but our later, larger lives in eternity, Dickinson predicts, will resemble the golden apples of the western Hesperides, taking so long to "ripen" that they appear to be everlasting. Dickinson usually followed classical tradition in allocating the afterlife to the west (no. 336):[6]

> The face I carry with me—last—
> When I go out of Time—
> To take my Rank—by—in the West—
> That face—will just be thine—....

or no. 726:

> We thirst at first—'tis Nature's Act—
> And later—when we die—
> A little Water supplicate—
> Of fingers going by—
>
> It intimates the finer want—
> Whose adequate supply
> Is that Great Water in the West—
> Termed Immortality—

but she could also exhibit a distinctly *American* sense of the West as a sanctuary for the refugee from civilization, as in no. 1033:

> Said Death to Passion
> "Give of thine an Acre unto me."
> Said Passion, through contracting Breaths,
> "A Thousand Times Thee Nay."
>
> Bore Death from Passion
> All His East
> He—sovreign as the Sun
> Resituated in the West
> And the Debate was done.

In this last poem, Passion, like a settler removing to the more untrammeled West, accompanies the individual soul into eternity, beyond the reach of Death. The West preserved for Dickinson, as it did and does for most Americans, connotations of open spaces, of land to be categorized either as wilderness or as acreage that could cleared and tilled. In making this connection Dickinson spoke not from personal experience, but out of the context of Amherst's accumulated pioneer lore. She very likely never saw true wilderness herself, the Connecticut Valley having been thoroughly cultivated since long before her birth; yet memories of the frontier lay only so far back in the past as her grandfather Samuel Dickinson's generation. In poems such as "I've known a Heaven, like a Tent" Dickinson does betray an awareness of America's wide-open spaces, but her sedentary way of life prevented her from imbuing the word "wilderness" with anything more than an abstract meaning. For Dickinson, wilderness or "wildness" did not usually offer the "Preservation of the World" that it did for Thoreau in "Walking," but rather represented a potential threat to that world, or else betokened a scene of exile or alienation like the wilderness Moses or Elijah wandered in. Thus Dickinson wrote to Lavinia from her Cambridgeport sickroom, "It is a very sober thing not to have any Vinnie, and to keep my Summer in strange Towns, what I have not told—but I have found friends in the Wilderness" (L433).

"Wilderness" can also signify in Dickinson's poems not *the* frontier but *a* frontier, a boundary beyond which the scale of physical objects increased dramatically, even incomprehensibly. In this sense, wilderness is a prelude to compound vision, a preliminary state of disorientation to be endured before objects and events may be correctly gauged (no. 856):

> There is a finished feeling
> Experienced at Graves—
> A leisure of the Future—
> A Wilderness of Size.
>
> By Death's bold Exhibition
> Preciser what we are
> And the Eternal function
> Enabled to infer.

The word "Size," as used in this poem, conflates space and time, for the future has the "leisure" to expand, or to become more drawn out, like the lives Dickinson characterized as Hesperian apples. In a wilderness, all sense of proportion vanishes, and the viewer feels herself to be lost, dis/*oriented*, literally deprived of the east or of the sun. On the other hand, intermittent exposure to the sun could generate its own brand of wilderness (no. 1233):

> Had I not seen the Sun
> I could have borne the shade
> But Light a newer Wilderness
> My Wilderness has made—

If Dickinson had been blind from birth, she says in this poem, she could have borne her illness better; however, because she can remember what it was like to see, and because her bandages permit a diffuse light to pass through, she is tormented by the knowledge that the sun and the rest of the visible world remain tantalizingly just beyond her reach. Brief respites during which she could doff her bandages only served to sharpen her sense of deprivation when she returned to the "wilderness" of interdicted sight (no. 430):

It would never be Common—more—I said—
Difference—had begun—
Many a bitterness—had been—
But that old sort—was done—

Or—if it sometime—showed—as 'twill—
Upon the Downiest—Morn—
Such bliss—had I—for all the years—
'Twould give an Easier—pain—

I'd so much joy—I told it—Red—
Upon my simple Cheek—
I felt it publish—in my Eye—
'Twas needless—any speak—

I walked—as wings—my body bore—
The feet—I former used—
Unnecessary—now to me—
As boots—would be—to Birds

I put my Pleasure all abroad—
I dealt a word of Gold
To every Creature—that I met—
And Dowered—all the World—

When—suddenly—my Riches shrank—
A Goblin—drank my Dew—
My Palaces—dropped tenantless—
Myself—was beggared—too—

I clutched at sounds—
I groped at shapes—
I touched the tops of Films—
I felt the Wilderness roll back
Along my Golden lines—

The Sackcloth—hangs upon the nail—
The Frock I used to wear—

But where my moment of Brocade—
My—drop—of India?

This poem will demonstrate as well as any other how an awareness of her experience as a convalescent can pleasurably complicate and deepen our readings of Dickinson rather than diminish the significance of her achievement. As in poems discussed previously, Dickinson incorporates her sensations as a person temporarily deprived of sight to construct a poem with a theme much broader than simple physical suffering. Instead, the poem records a kind of imaginative collapse following the failure of her eyes, as if the license she had been granted to acquire new "territory" through being able to see and to write poetry had been suddenly rescinded. "Films" of opacity return and cut her off from sources of poetic stimulation, symbolized by images of wealth. The poem's initial pronoun refers to her world formerly enriched by being a poet, an "aristocratic" way of life that stands in contrast to the "Common" life she might have led. As a poet, she enjoys an imaginative freedom and a physical liberty comprised in her image of the bird, her preferred symbol for herself as poet. The pleasure she has felt following her liberation from her sickroom is so great that it overflows, "Dower[ing]" the rest of the world with poetry, the "word[s] of Gold" she freely distributes. When her freedom is annulled once again, however, both she and the world she had enriched as a poet are simultaneously impoverished.

Clearly, Dickinson's economic imagery in "It would never be Common" denotes a change of attitude, and not a change of material condition. The luxurious frock she had worn is diminished in her eyes to sackcloth, and from that state of emotional wealth she summarizes with the metonym "India" she is transported back to the bleak confines of what might be a convent. Her former unhappiness and frustration, ever present beyond the limits of her joy as the wilderness is beyond civilization's boundaries, roll back to their previous positions as easily as jungle foliage reclaiming the ruins of a richer antiquity. Not only are the "riches" of her creativity taken away, but her physical space is curtailed as well, as depicted by the sixth and seventh stanzas, which show the "land" upon which she stands progressively shrinking until she is left in midair, clutching at sounds and groping at shapes as she resumes her despised existence as a patient.

Dickinson's panic in "It would never be Common" is driven home by the seventh stanza's breathless repetition, its extra line, and its minimal rhyme. Her orderliness and control as a poet contrasts dramatically with the state of emotional and intellectual chaos the poem describes, an indication of poetry's importance to Dickinson as a refuge from disorder. A poem was a rock of stability for Dickinson, a perch from which she could assess events in their eternal contexts. Yet being a poet also helped her by giving her an elevated or "aristocratic" stature, a dignity that permitted her to maintain a sense of self in the face of reversals.[7] Dickinson sometimes used size in her poems to indicate merit, and she derives a comic effect by disingenuously confusing physical size with literary reputation (no. 738):

> You said that I "was Great"—one Day—
> Then "Great" it be—if that please Thee—
> Or Small—or any size at all—
> Nay—I'm the size suit Thee—. . . .

More frequently, however, "size" simply means "ratio," or the proportion between Dickinson and eternity. Only in her poems, perhaps, could Dickinson achieve the golden mean she sought between herself and God that permitted her to witness the presence of eternity safely, without hazarding either her eyesight or her immortal soul (no. 756):

> One Blessing had I than the rest
> So larger to my Eyes
> That I stopped guaging—satisfied—
> For this enchanted size—
>
> It was the limit of my Dream—
> The focus of my Prayer—
> A perfect—paralyzing Bliss—
> Contented as Despair—
>
> I knew no more of Want—or Cold—
> Phantasms both become
> For this new Value in the Soul—
> Supremest Earthly Sum—
>
> The Heaven below the Heaven above—
> Obscured with ruddier Blue—
> Life's Latitudes leant over—full—
> The Judgment perished—too—
>
> Why Bliss so scantily disburse—
> Why Paradise defer—

> Why Floods be served to Us—in Bowls—
> I speculate no more—

Now that she has discovered the "enchanted size," or the optimal ratio between temporal and eternal existence, Dickinson declares her perceptual "hunger" to have been satisfied. Her compensation has been to see the world illuminated against a backdrop of eternal verities: deeper understanding has substituted for a wider, more liberal range of vision. Life suddenly possesses a more manifold meaning, and her terrene heaven swells up until it eclipses the heaven overhead. Her heaven is a "ruddier Blue," a chromatic oxymoron that anticipates the final stanza's references to being well fed. In a sense, Dickinson has achieved the ideal weight for her size. Neither obese nor emaciated, she has struck the perfect median between the incomprehensibly huge "Bliss" of heaven and the irresistible attractions of earthly life. Now that what had before seemed to her a "wilderness of size" may be viewed in perspective, she can reclaim the world of which she had been deprived by illness. Because "Judgment" has perished, she need no longer fear punishment or retribution for having stolen a premature glimpse of heaven.

PURGATORY

The converse of either "greatness" or the "enchanted size" that permitted Dickinson to write was sudden diminution, the equivalent of a fall in Dickinson's poetry, or of compound vision's antithesis, "covered vision." Again her imagery draws upon her experience as a convalescent: Dickinson saw her sphere of activity steadily shrink within the narrow confines of her sickroom, where, if she did not stay constantly upon her guard, she might trip and fall over obstacles unseen or imperfectly seen. In conjunction with descriptions of a "wilderness of size," Dickinson's falling imagery represents not just a physical body but a soul or an entire world in chaos. The directionless, purgatorial condition in which the soul was condemned to remain for some unspecified time until she could regain her "proper" size was a ghastly parody of the "paralyzing bliss" Dickinson describes in "One Blessing had I than the rest," a negative form of stasis in which no more comprehension, the rational equivalent of salvation, may be hoped for.

The narrators of Dickinson's poems frequently describe themselves as falling, as having just fallen, or living in fear of falling. To protect herself, the poet may have had to remain immobile for long periods. In her poems she contrasts the virtually motionless woman she had become since the advent of her illness with the woman she once had been, one who had had a greater range of imaginative and physical freedom, or what Dickinson called "Instincts for Dance" and "An Aptitude for Bird" (no. 1046). To translate the mundane realities of falling into spiritual terms, Dickinson occasionally characterized the soul's failure to gain admittance to heaven as a "crash" or a "fall," and the soul's subsequent stranding in purgatory as another form of paralysis. In the following poem the grave becomes a door or a window whose handle the narrator, who I shall assume to be Dickinson herself, cannot grasp to gain "entry" to the house of eternity (no. 1503):

> More than the Grave is closed to me—
> The Grave and that Eternity
> To which the Grave adheres—
> I cling to nowhere till I fall—
> The Crash of nothing, yet of all—
> How similar appears—

Here Dickinson expresses a fear that her ignorance about the afterlife, the "Grave" that is "closed" to her, is a harbinger of her future spiritual banishment from heaven for religious unorthodoxy. Her skepticism and her shaky faith in heaven have left her no metaphorical "purchase" from which to hang, so that she clings to "nowhere"; moreover, lacking support from heaven, she herself is "nothing," a nonperson whose fall is a nonevent, despite being "all" to Dickinson. Nevertheless, the narrator remains coolly detached as she watches, in the poem's last line, her world ending with both a bang and a whimper.

But from what vantage point, precisely, is the narrator addressing us at the poem's end? Readers have often noted Dickinson's habit of having her personae speak proleptically from beyond the grave or from some other liminal condition giving them a unique perspective both upon the lives they have led and upon the eternity stretching out before them.[8] Perhaps her most famous poem in this vein is no. 280:

> I felt a Funeral, in my Brain,
> And Mourners to and fro
> Kept treading—treading—till it seemed
> That Sense was breaking through—
>
> And when they all were seated,
> A Service, like a Drum—
> Kept beating—beating—till I thought
> My Mind was going numb—

And then I heard them lift a Box
And creak across my Soul
With those same Boots of Lead, again,
Then Space—began to toll,

As all the Heavens were a Bell,
And Being, but an Ear,
And I, and Silence, some strange Race
Wrecked, solitary, here—

And then a Plank in Reason, broke,
And I dropped down, and down—
And hit a World, at every plunge,
And Finished knowing—then—

In the first three stanzas Dickinson carefully erects a plausible physical setting, which she then demolishes in the last two stanzas. The poem itself functions as a house with a "cellar" in which the narrator listens to the mourners carrying a coffin, perhaps her own, across the floor "above" her head; then, in the fourth stanza, the word "here" suddenly becomes problematic, immediately before the narrator drops, first, through the cellar floor, then through her own grave, and then through the last line of the poem—multiple levels of reality or "World[s]" that her body and consciousness pierce, at every "Plunge." The "here" at the end of the poem, or the point of view from which the narrator describes the action, is finally a very different "here" from that in the fourth stanza, the place where the speaker stands as she listens to the heavens tolling like an immense bell. Because the poem replicates the disappearance or appropriation of a physical space, it can inspire in readers a sensation of bodily and intellectual disorientation that may begin to approximate Dickinson's own confusion as she made her way around the Dickinson household. Furthermore, the narrator's "unconsciousness" resulting from her "fall" in the poem's last line becomes a metaphor not only for the cessation of consciousness that is death but for the soul shut out of heaven, condemned to pass from world to world, existence to existence, without ever achieving the physical stability which is analogous to spiritual salvation.

Another fine poem describing a sense of physical disorientation attendant upon imagining one's own funeral is "It was not Death, for I stood up," which is so similar to "I felt a Funeral, in my Brain" that it might be considered a sequel (no. 510):

It was not Death, for I stood up,
And all the Dead, lie down—
It was not Night, for all the Bells
Put out their Tongues, for Noon.

It was not Frost, for on my Flesh
I felt Siroccos—crawl—
Nor Fire—for just my Marble feet
Could keep a Chancel, cool—

And yet, it tasted, like them all,
The Figures I have seen
Set orderly, for Burial,
Reminded me, of mine—

As if my life were shaven,
And fitted to a frame,
And could not breathe without a key,
And 'twas like Midnight, some—

When everything that ticked—has stopped—
And Space stares all around—
Or Grisly frosts—first Autumn morns,
Repeal the Beating Ground—

But, most, like Chaos—Stopless—cool—
Without a Chance, or Spar—
Or even a Report of Land—
To justify—Despair.

Here the individual soul is trapped in the "wilderness of size" or a physical chaos containing not a single landmark or report of "Land," symbolic here of heaven's shores. Chronological chaos prevails as well, for time has stopped, and the whole world is comparable to "Space" staring sightlessly "all around" or to the extinction of vegetative life during fall's first hard freeze, which "repeals" the earth's "Beating" heart. The narrator defines her condition by a series of negations, so that she is neither cold nor hot, neither dead nor alive, existing instead in that bland, featureless compromise state of "covered vision." In *Dickinson: Strategies of Limitation,* Jane Donahue Eberwein links such negatively defined landscapes to lines appearing in section 9 of "The Prisoner of Chillon," wherein de Bonnivard recalls that in his dungeon cell he had lost all track of both time and space (87):

It was not night—it was not day,
It was not even the dungeon-light
So hateful to my heavy sight,
But vacancy absorbing space,
And fixedness—without a place;
There were no stars, no earth, no time,
No check, no change, no good, no crime—
But silence, and a stirless breath
Which neither was of life nor death;
A sea of stagnant idleness,
Blind, boundless, mute, and motionless.

The appearance of Dickinson's anti-landscape could indeed be used to confirm the notion that, after a sufficiently long period of time, a place of confinement seems to an "imprisoned" person to have lost all its boundaries. A very small space is thus subjectively experienced, paradoxically, as being without limits. Yet Dickinson's strategy of defining through negation also works to associate the body's ambiguous position in space with the soul's uncertain status in a continuum stretching from life into eternity. By dismissing, one by one, the various conventional explanations for why she feels the way she does, Dickinson's speaker induces in herself a barely suppressed sense of physical and metaphysical panic that readily communicates itself to the reader. The narrator of "It was not Death" leaves open the possibility that she is in fact already dead, having mistaken her own funeral bell for noon chimes; consequently, readers will find themselves compelled to wonder whether the poem implicitly begs to be read from the perspective, or "here," of the already dead, in which they themselves may be standing as a sort of spectral chorus. Furthermore, we as readers may also feel somewhat discomfited when we arrive at the poem's ending, which defeats our expectations by placing "Despair" where we might reasonably anticipate seeing "Hope." In the featureless monotony of "covered vision," not even the option of despair presents itself, so that the soul is left floating in limbo, constantly threatened, nonetheless, with destruction by "drowning."

A number of Dickinson's poems concern themselves with drowning, a fate that is parallel, I think, to the poet's fear of falling for the reason that water, like empty air, has no "amplitude" or "axis" (as she says in poem no. 1428), that is, nothing to cling to. Then too, Dickinson's vision impeded by her bandages may have caused her to feel as if she were *seeing* the world from under water. Dickinson prefaced one of the letters

she sent to her sister-in-law during the first of her summer-long confine-
ments with a remark that it was being written "At Centre of the Sea—"
(L434).[9] In some poems, the distinction between water and land becomes
so blurred that the narrator appears to be floating in both or neither, at
the very center of the compass (no. 721):

Behind Me—dips Eternity—
Before Me—Immortality—
Myself—the Term between—
Death but the Drift of Eastern Gray—
Dissolving into Dawn away,
Before the West begin—

'Tis Kingdoms—afterward—they say—
In perfect—pauseless Monarchy—
Whose Prince—is Son of None—
Himself—His Dateless Dynasty—
Himself—Himself diversify—
In Duplicate divine—

'Tis Miracle before Me—then—
'Tis Miracle behind—between—
A Crescent in the Sea—
With Midnight to the North of Her—
And Midnight to the South of Her—
And Maelstrom—in the Sky—

Here Dickinson is a "Term"—in both the lexical and the chronological
senses—riding the crest of a wave dividing the twin troughs of Eternity
and Immortality. Belonging to neither, she is instead a transient "Crescent" in the sea, a moment in time, a spot on the map. The profound
loneliness of the Dickinsonian interval contrasts with the society of "His"
kingdom, where God can manifest himself as Son or Father as he pleases,
a "monarchy" that continues unbroken because prince and king are one
and the same. This miracle is one of many about which Dickinson
has heard, including the miracle of heavenly redemption, yet all she can
see is enveloping "Midnight," which the poem's symmetry opposes to
"Miracle[s]." A further note of insecurity intrudes with the addition of
"they say" in the seventh line, raising the possibility that the dynastic
succession and all other Christian miracles are legends only, pretty fictions held out to encourage the believer like a carrot before a horse.
Finally, the heaven she had heard about does not resemble the heaven

she sees overhead, which looks more like an inverted "maelstrom" that threatens to suck her up like a tornado. Thus, on her journey from east to west, from eternity to immortality, the suspended soul is threatened from virtually every other direction: up and down, north and south. Straying even slightly from her obscure course would plunge her back into physical and spiritual chaos, where she could expect to receive no assistance from a distant, perhaps even mocking, God.

CONTINENT OF LIGHT

Yet the soul's free fall through space could constitute an alternative mode of existence in its own right, an embracing of skepticism as a way of life. If the path to heaven proved almost too narrow for Dickinson's feet to negotiate, and if faith had to be maintained even in the absence of ocular proof, the poet may have found herself wondering, from time to time, whether her fears of being banned from heaven were justified to begin with. Such, at least, may be the tenor of the following poem (no. 1712):

A Pit—but Heaven over it—
And Heaven beside, and Heaven abroad;
And yet a Pit—
With Heaven over it.

To stir would be to slip—
To look would be to drop—
To dream—to sap the Prop
That holds my chances up.
Ah! Pit! With Heaven over it!

The depth is all my thought—
I dare not ask my feet—
'Twould start us where we sit
So straight you'd scarce suspect
It was a Pit—with fathoms under it
Its Circuit just the same
Seed—summer—tomb—
Whose Doom to whom[10]

The narrator cannot even dream for fear of diminishing her chances for admission to the heaven hovering, somewhat threateningly, all around her. The straightness with which she sits belies her anxiety about the potential consequences of falling into the "pit," which is not the hell into which Jonathan Edwards prophesied the damned would tumble, but rather the abyss of unknowing, an existential void. But the narrator asks herself what kind of existence "falling" would be, conjecturing that the pit's "circuit" is just the same as that of life on earth, proceeding from birth ("Seed"), to maturity ("summer"), to death; perhaps she could move, or drop, after all, and by so doing, discover an alternate, less procrustean form of eternity. "Whose Doom to whom?" she asks, implicitly challenging heaven's absolute authority over her immortal soul. Notably, the poem could be read equally as validly as a contemplation of rebellion against her doctor's orders, as Dickinson wonders just how serious the consequences of removing her bandages could actually be.

Freed from the constraints of space and time, the "fallen" Dickinson might be able to establish a new territory for herself, one conforming to her own requirements and desires.[11] Above all else, in such a place nothing would be "hidden" from her, no answers denied her. As she wrote in a letter to Joseph Lyman, to whom she also described the fear instilled in her by her optical troubles, "So I conclude that space & time are things of the body & have little or nothing to do with our selves. My country is Truth" (Sewall, *Lyman Letters*, 71). At its height, her confidence that she could establish a "new world" of her own was such that she seems to have been determined to strike out immediately, as in the following poem, in which she pilots a sort of private planet *away* from heaven (no. 378):

> I saw no Way—The Heavens were stitched—
> I felt the Columns close—
> The Earth reversed her Hemispheres—
> I touched the Universe—
>
> And back it slid—and I alone—
> A Speck upon a Ball—
> Went out upon Circumference—
> Beyond the Dip of Bell—

Rebuffed by God, Dickinson takes her own world out upon the sea of "Circumference," choosing the "Universe" rather than heaven because it politely slides open for her like an observatory dome. Death is not mentioned as an intrinsic part of the experience, and the final line may even indicate that Dickinson, occupying once again the role of astronomer or space explorer, has journeyed beyond death's bailiwick, symbolized by the sexton's bell audible in both "I felt a Funeral, in my Brain" and "It was not Death, for I stood up."

In other poems, however, Dickinson's success in constructing a new "place" depends more visibly upon her skill in exercising her art. Consider, for example, the following poem about a spider, another of Dickinson's foremost symbols for the artist (no. 605):

> The Spider holds a Silver Ball
> In unperceived Hands —
> And dancing softly to Himself
> His Yarn of Pearl — unwinds —
>
> He plies from Nought to Nought —
> In unsubstantial Trade —
> Supplants our Tapestries with His —
> In half the period —
>
> An Hour to rear supreme
> His Continents of Light —
> Then dangle from the Housewife's Broom —
> His Boundaries — forgot —

The spider in this poem embodies a few of Dickinson's own more prominent qualities as an artist in that he is covert ("unperceived"), industrious, domestic yet "supreme" within his own realm of the imagination as the poet was within hers. Even though his "Continents of Light," like the "Golden lines" Dickinson used to hold back the wilderness in "It would never be Common — more — I said —," are invisibly anchored in "Nought," they do make a temporary stay against confusion. Finally, however, the "Housewife's Broom" puts an end to the spider-artist's newfound territory, so that he winds up falling prey to forces beyond his ken.[12] Like the spider, the artist can be supreme in the world he creates, but the very fact that he has created it out of himself, that is, out of "nothing," means that his new "territory" will inevitably crumble away. A variant of the poem further emphasizes the fraudulent nature of the spider's creation by substituting "Theories" for "Continent" and "Sophistries" for "Boundaries." When these variants are transposed, the poem may be seen as describing the spider as a mendacious geometer who weaves false equations into his web. In either draft of the poem the spider has created something that is not true, and it is the truth that brings about his defeat; however, in the first version the spider is merely dispossessed, while in the second he is destroyed, for line 11's variant substitutes "perish by" for "dangle from." Although the poem's ironical humor derives from the insignificance of the spider and the banality of the broom, that domestic article nevertheless represents an arbitrary force potent enough to demolish the artist's "continent" or invalidate the "physicist's" theories. The artist figure in this poem suffers because he either does not comprehend or will not acknowledge the scale of his universe, and what he believes to be a "continent" is actually a minuscule construction of gossamer.[13]

In "I saw no Way" the poet's revolt against heaven is complete and successful because she assumes the role of explorer rather than of victim. Like the astronomer with his telescope, she extends her grasp by wielding compound vision. But the new world she discovers between earth and heaven could prove to be an unsustainable fiction, a temporary platform she had erected by sheer force of will in order to gain a perspective of eternity. Poetry's very fictitiousness put it at risk, and the stability and consistency of Dickinson's customary, exceedingly regular hymn-form quatrains may finally have contributed little toward making her life as a patient either more harmonious or more comfortingly predictable. Moreover, unlike faith, which was, Dickinson decided, perhaps equally fictitious itself, poetry enjoyed no divine sanction, and therefore had to be practiced with God's approval—if she could secure it.

Stepping upon the North

Ultimately, Dickinson needed God's approbation to maintain the mediating vision that was the cornerstone of her personal poetics, but the "route" to his throne was hedged all about with dangers, not the least of which was the intellectual strain of imagining a heaven where her supplicating voice might be heard. In Dickinson's poems, the road to God's house usually leads northwards. From the north the most powerful storms came to Amherst; the north was also the site of the aurora borealis, which wavered on the nighttime horizon like a drawn curtain. Then, too, popular interest in the Far North ran high during Dickinson's lifetime, which coincided with the first great age of polar exploration. Fancying herself something of an explorer, Dickinson paid close attention, as we saw in chapter 2, to the exploits of Sir John Franklin, whose ship disappeared in arctic waters while she was still in her teens. Finally, the north also stood in her mind for something true, if not for truth itself, because all compass needles (at least, those in the Northern Hemisphere) swing northwards, and the North Star provides a trustworthy guide for the wayward or the lost.

Although the north was preeminently the province of God for Dickinson, she could also exhibit a New Englander's pride in her own northern austerity, as in the following poem (no. 525):

> I think the Hemlock likes to stand
> Upon a Marge of Snow—
> It suits his own Austerity—
> And satisfies an awe
>
> That men, must slake in Wilderness—
> And in the Desert—cloy—
> An instinct for the Hoar, the Bald—
> Lapland's—necessity—
>
> The Hemlock's nature thrives—on cold—
> The Gnash of Northern winds
> Is sweetest nutriment—to him—
> His best Norwegian Wines—
>
> To satin Races—he is nought—
> But Children on the Don,
> Beneath his Tabernacles, play,
> And Dnieper Wrestlers, run.

To satisfy our hunger for "awe" we need the "Wilderness" Dickinson says, and here, at least, her definition of that word would seem to agree with Thoreau's of "wildness" in his essay "Walking." The wild northern chill imposes a kind of salubrious rigor that spurs Dickinson's creativity by establishing clearly defined boundaries she knew she could not exceed. Like the hemlock, Dickinson always preferred to dwell on the margins or in the verge, her best poems elicited from her by the onrush of time, by crisis, or by the presence of death. Correspondingly, an image she returned to often in her poems was that of a garden threatened by northern frost, and in the following poem (no. 442), the positional "verge" in which the hemlock thrives has its temporal counterpart in the brief blooming season of the gentian:

> God made a little Gentian—
> It tried—to be a Rose—
> And failed—and all the Summer laughed—
> But just before the Snows

There rose a Purple Creature—
That ravished all the Hill—
And Summer hid her Forehead—
And Mockery—was still—

The Frosts were her condition—
The Tyrian would not come
Until the North—invoke it—
Creator—Shall I—bloom?

Like the gentian, Dickinson may have envisioned herself as a late bloomer
who did not "flower" until the autumn of adulthood, perhaps because
she had lacked the necessary mental preparation in youth or, more pe-
destrianly, because she had been sequestered indoors until she reached
her midthirties, prevented by her weakened eyes from emerging, like the
rose, during the summer of her youth. Northern winds are the catalyst
that "invoke[s]" her bloom, and they fall somehow within the jurisdiction of God, whom Dickinson importunes in the poem's final line as if
he himself were the frost. Yet the north is often explicitly unapproach-
able in Dickinson's poems, a zone so remote from human concerns that
its isolation assumes a kind of grandeur, like that of the aurora borealis
(no. 290):

Of Bronze—and Blaze—
The North—Tonight—
So adequate—it forms—
So preconcerted with itself—
So distant—to alarms—
An Unconcern so sovreign
To Universe, or me—
Infects my simple spirit
With Taints of Majesty—
Till I take vaster attitudes—
And strut upon my stem—
Disdaining Men, and Oxygen,
For Arrogance of them—

My splendors, are Menagerie—
But their Competeless Show
Will entertain the Centuries

When I, am long ago,
An Island in dishonored Grass—
Whom none but Daisies—know.

In this poem the northern lights constitute a work of art in their own right, one with which Dickinson's own poetic "splendors" cannot compete, having been reduced by comparison to the status of circus sideshows. The poet wishes she could emulate the self-sufficiency and immunity from public opinion that the artist who created the lights apparently enjoys, but whenever she assumes "vaster attitudes," she soon realizes that she is actually as "small" in size or as insignificant as a flower trampled underfoot. As an artist, Dickinson probably could not help being stung by the public's indifference when she "strut[ted]" upon her "stem"; like the gentian, she had to endure others' disdain in hopes of one day receiving the recognition she knew she deserved.

Dickinson's sense of alienation as an artist parallels her alienation from God the creator, the "sculptor" of the northern lights who is utterly unconcerned not just with the "reception" of his art by the public, but with the public's entire existence. Such perfect insularity simultaneously attracted and repelled Dickinson, who knew, from having been closed up in her room, both solitude's consolations and its drawbacks— or as she put it, "Captivity is Consciousness / So's Liberty." In trying to conceive of someone as isolated and as estranged from heaven as she, the only personage she could envision was "Horror's Twin," the semblance of herself we saw her tunneling toward in poems about "imprisonment" (no. 532):

I tried to think a lonelier Thing
Than any I had seen—
Some Polar Expiation—An Omen in the Bone
Of Death's tremendous nearness—

I probed Retrieveless things
My Duplicate—to borrow—
A Haggard Comfort springs

From the belief that Somewhere—
Within the Clutch of Thought—
There dwells one other Creature
Of Heavenly Love—forgot—

> I plucked at our Partition
> As One should pry the Walls—
> Between Himself—and Horror's Twin—
> Within Opposing Cells—
>
> I almost strove to clasp his Hand,
> Such Luxury—it grew—
> That as Myself—could pity Him—
> Perhaps he—pitied me—

Within the desolate polar landscape of Dickinson's intentionally imageless imagination, the poet encounters the final wall of resistance separating her from her alienated "twin," who might be her complementary lover/ brother, or light, or God himself, as distant from the temporal world as Dickinson thought heaven was from her, yet as "near" as death. The poet pauses at the moment of direct encounter before their "hands" can meet, preserving the symmetry that allows her to pity her "other," as she imagines it pities her. Recontextualized within the framework of the illness "imprisoning" Dickinson, however, the poem may also be seen as documenting the blindfolded poet's almost aggressive attempt to reciprocate the pity her visitors felt for her, a project doomed to fail as soon as she admits to herself once again that there is, in fact, no one so isolated as she. Immured within the polar whiteness of her bandages, the poet cannot go anywhere but more deeply within, and her introspection carries her only farther and farther away from human contact. The "Expiation" described in the first stanza may be the same plea for forgiveness she refers to indirectly in "Renunciation—is a piercing Virtue," an atonement to God for whatever unspecified crime she had committed against him.

Although Dickinson could resort to using prayer to petition God for redress directly, she believed him to be so far removed from human concerns that prayer was reduced, as she said in poem no. 437, to "the little implement / Through which Men reach / Where Presence—is denied them." More pertinent to the present discussion, however, is another description of failed prayer (no. 564):

> My period had come for Prayer—
> No other Art—would do—
> My Tactics missed a rudiment—
> Creator—Was it you?

God grows above—so those who pray
Horizons—must ascend—
And so I stepped upon the North
To see this Curious Friend—

His House was not—no sign had He—
By Chimney—nor by Door
Could I infer his Residence—
Vast Prairies of Air

Unbroken by a Settler—
Were all that I could see—
Infinitude—Had'st Thou no Face
That I might look on thee?

The Silence condescended—
Creation stopped—for Me—
But awed beyond my errand
I worshipped—did not "pray"—

At this poem's outset, the narrator, who I will assume to be Dickinson herself, addresses God in the second person as if speaking to a casual acquaintance, but he does not respond, and by the end of the second stanza he has become the "curious friend," a hermit or eccentric so unconventional as to own neither house nor inn. What she is naïvely expecting to see when she "steps" upon the north is a kind of hyperborean farmer tending his "crop" in the immense plains of heaven as Amherst farmers do on earth, but she gradually realizes that he will reveal no human aspect to her. To see God's "Face" had been the fundamental goal of Dickinson's religious and artistic "Tactics," but her mistake had lain in expecting him to be phenomenal rather than noumenal. Thus she commits the same error she accuses her neighbors of in "We pray—to Heaven," that of permitting her imagination to be circumscribed by whatever is familiar and tangible.

By "other art" in the second line Dickinson must surely be referring to her skills as a writer. The purpose of either "art" (prayer or poetry) is to communicate with God, but the imaginative effort required for prayer is of an entirely different order. Dickinson says that those who pray must ascend "horizons"; that is, they must attempt to perceive on a titanic scale if they wish to comprehend God's magnitude. The poem essentially records an attempt to imagine the unimaginable, a feat of mental gymnastics for which the poet had prepared herself by employing paradoxical spatial tropes. When God does grant her an audience, however, he is so decidedly nonanthropomorphic that he is better described as a quality—silence—or as a process—creation. Creation itself (or "Heavens," in a variant) stops in midcareer for Dickinson as the sun did for Joshua, revealing the solstitial moment we have seen previously, the moment when heaven on earth is temporarily realized. In this poem eternity itself becomes frozen rather than she, and for an instant Dickinson occupies the "enchanted size" she needed to discern heaven's lineaments.

The narrator is initially alarmed by the fact that the "prairie" is unbroken by a single settler, making it a "Wilderness" just as much as a forest or a mountain range would be, but more specifically it is the "wilderness of size" that had intimidated her before, the measureless expanse with no familiar landmarks with which she might estimate scale or proportion, particularly her own proportion to heaven. The narrator has overstepped her "boundaries" and received more revelation—what she elsewhere calls "floods"—than she had bargained for. She had not been prepared by "processes of size" to apprehend divinity's real magnitude, and he is truly a colossus. As she says in poem no. 350:

> They leave us with the Infinite.
> But He—is not a man—
> His fingers are the size of fists—
> His fists, the size of men—. . . .

In the final stanza of "My period had come for Prayer—" the size of God is made clear to the narrator, disconcerting her so profoundly that she finds herself unable to pray. Fittingly, that stanza is the only one in the poem without a comparatively regular rhyme, as if the shock of her discovery had somehow "unbalanced" her. In the last two stanzas she assumes a tone of abject humility that contrasts sharply with the flippancy of the first three, addressing God more formally as "Thou" and "thee," as if her respect for him had increased in proportion to her comprehension of his inaccessibility.

Quotation marks enclose the last word in "My period had come for Prayer—" to signify an important discovery the narrator has made in the course of her adventure: prayer is as ineffective a "tactic" as poetry because it, too, circumscribes the imagination. Poetry could give Dickinson a glimpse of the infinite, but the fact that poetic imagery is predicated upon fictions engendered by the mind means that the revelations it grants are necessarily transient and unreliable. Prayer is ineffectual as well because it is directed *at* something which by its very nature does away with either directionality or personality. Images of place, for heaven, or face, for God, were characteristic of "location's way," and in order to realize the "circumferences" native to God more accurately, Dickinson would have to learn to "ascend horizons" in her own mind and forgo the urge merely to acquire "new territory" from which to observe God more minutely. To prevent her poem-prayers from falling impotently short of God's throne, she needed to ensure that divinity was present in the substance of language itself.

In the woods, is perpetual youth. Within these plantations of God, a decorum and sanctity reign, a perennial festival is dressed, and the guest sees not how he should tire of them in a thousand years. In the woods, we return to reason and faith. There I feel that nothing can befal me in life,—no disgrace, no calamity, (leaving me my eyes,) which nature cannot repair. Standing on the bare ground,—my head bathed by the blithe air and uplifted into infinite space,—all mean egotism vanishes. I become a transparent eyeball; I am nothing; I see all; the currents of the Universal Being circulate through me; I am part or parcel of God.

Emerson, Nature

THE "CONSENT OF LANGUAGE"

Symbolism in Nature, Mathematics, and the Sacrament

PERHAPS BECAUSE she believed her identity as a poet was maintained through God's sufferance, it became virtually an article of faith with Dickinson that she was not entirely responsible for what she wrote. "It was given to me by the Gods—/ When I was a little Girl—" she affirmed of her talent for writing, having received, like Pandora, "Presents" when she was "new—and small" (no. 454). Such utter self-abnegation might be expected of an "automatic" writer or some other species of mystic, yet Dickinson usually resists being placed in such categories; indeed, her worksheet drafts show her to have been a meticulous craftsperson, striking out phrase after phrase in search of the most expressive word. Thus we are confronted with the paradoxical spectacle of a poet who, at least in the major phase of her artistic career, attributed both the fact of her own existence as a poet and even the text that revealed itself upon the page to forces largely beyond her control, despite doing virtually everything within her power to set a personal stamp upon her work.

The hallmark of Dickinson's poetic style is her conciseness, that is, her knack for cramming as much meaning as possible into the space of a few words. In essence, Dickinson "compounded" her meanings in a manner analogous to the way she "compounded" the range and acuity of her perceiving imagination. She increased the semantic density of her poems by doing away with superfluous grammatical structures, by using paronomasia and other forms of polysemy to inject ever greater quantities of signification into single words, and by building up cumulative layers of meaning through the use of recurring archetypal images such as "Noon," "Immortality," and "Circumference."[1] Above all, however, she made an intensive use of literary symbolism, in which the boundaries of meaning are stretched by invoking sources of authority from outside the actual text. Dickinson's symbolism, like all the rest of her strategies for "compounding" meaning, may finally be viewed as an extension of an underlying, essentially sacramental, paradigm for writing and for being a poet.

Dickinson understood virtually all language to be symbolic, and for this idea, as well as for many of her other opinions about how words worked, she had Emerson largely to thank. Nevertheless, Dickinson disagreed sharply with Emerson over the nature of language as a phenomenon. To him, language was a closed system—a tool, at best, albeit a highly evolved one. Therefore, even though, as he famously put it in *Nature*,

1. Words are signs of natural facts,
2. Particular natural facts are symbols of particular spiritual facts,
3. Nature is the symbol of spirit,

words are *not* symbols of the spirit. Nature was the necessary middle term in Emerson's equation linking mankind with deity. For Dickinson, on the other hand, language was at least partially autonomous, even volitional, because God was as immanent in words as he was in nature. Dickinson used her poems to explore the similarities between nature and language as symbolic systems, yet always with a view toward understanding how either could serve as a conduit for "bulletins" sent to her by "Immortality."[2]

Dickinson interpreted her entire function as a poet symbolically as she, the "Rivet in the Bands," interceded or mediated between heaven and the temporal world, "translating" those urgent messages from forces larger than herself to a mortal audience. This second aspect of her symbolism was intimately related to the first: that is, her role as a poet impinged heavily upon the way she used words.[3] Because her employment of symbolism transcends the conventional milieu of literary technique to become a statement of identity, I want to explore in this chapter the possibility that Dickinson approached literary symbolism from a perspective that was considerably more literal than that of any other nineteenth-century poet writing in English (with the possible exception of Blake). I will begin by looking among Emerson's pronouncements about language, nature, and symbolism to discover possible points of origin for Dickinson's thinking on those topics, and I will treat statements she makes in her poems either as continuations of or divagations from currents of thought already established at Concord. Although I will pay particular attention to what Dickinson has to say about nature and language, I will also look at two other types of symbolic transaction in which the visible is confirmed and validated by the invisible — mathematics and the eucharist.

Conjugating Nature

More than a few observers have commented upon how well the following lines from "The Poet," marked for emphasis in the Dickinson family copy of *Essays*, Second Series,[4] apply to Dickinson's resolutely domestic existence:

> Day and night, house and garden, a few books, a few actions, serve us well as would all trades and all spectacles. We are far from having exhausted the significance of the few symbols we use. We can come to use them yet with a terrible simplicity. It does not need that a poem be long. Every word was once a poem. Every new relation is a new word.

As a provincial artist, Dickinson would have received considerable assurance from reading these words, in that her relatively circumscribed existence could yet become a life of consequence, and a comparatively limited vocabulary could yet be used to describe the entire scope of human experience. The passage also justified Dickinson's strategy of condensation: if every word had once been a poem, the language was already packed with significance—as it had to be, to be commensurate with the task of describing a world which, as Dickinson saw it, was a tremendously complex phenomenon made up of both the great number of things she could see and the much greater number of things she couldn't. A few words could serve the purpose if they were used with "terrible simplicity," that is, in full consciousness of their potential symbolic meanings, or what Dickinson called their "freight," rather than for their solely denotative meanings.

For Emerson the degree of sublimity or "terror" instilled by a poem was determined by the skill of the poet, and not by any property generic to the words themselves. To him language was "dead," or rather, simply inanimate; "fossil poetry," he called it in "The Poet," suggesting that words should be most rightly regarded as artifacts left over from an almost prelapsarian era in which humankind could translate empirical experience directly into perfectly symbolic language. Since that time, words have lost most of their distinct connection with nature and the rest of the tangible world, so that, like the fossil record of an extinct species, they hold the shapes of their original meanings without preserving their rich content. Although words are "signs of natural facts," they remain *signs* only, not quite, as Saussure would go on to say, arbitrarily assigned ones, but certainly largely disconnected from their ancient poetical significations. Nature, and not language, therefore became, for Emerson, the primary symbolic vehicle for conveying meaning from deity to humanity.

Considered strictly as symbolic entities, however, language and nature may be thought of as having a good deal in common. Multiplicity in nature, for example, is countervalenced by the presence of consistent architectures of form; in language, this office is performed by such features as syntax, grammar, and the rules of orthography. Moreover, because every linguistic element contributes toward the expression of meaning, language exhibits a homogeneity similar to that in nature, which is, as Emerson declared, "a symbol in the whole, and in every part." Finally, language, like nature, follows an evolutionary pattern of development as new meanings or new organisms struggle into being. Thus, in nature, the impulse that will ultimately manifest itself as man is latent within the primitive worm:

> A subtle change of countless rings
> The next unto the farthest brings
> The eye reads omens where it goes,
> And speaks all languages the rose;
> And, striving to be man, the worm
> Mounts through all the spires of form.[5]

In these lines on the first page of *Nature*, Emerson emphasizes the sanctity or self-sufficiency of nature's protean power, which itself will not submit, despite having the polyglot ability of speaking "all languages," to being described by language. "What we call nature," Emerson says in "The Poet," "is a certain self-regulated motion, or change; and nature does all things by her own hands, and does not leave another to baptise her, but baptises herself; and this through the metamorphosis again."

Dickinson recasts Emerson's spiraling, evolutionary trope into her own terms in the following poem, denying, like Emerson, language's competency to "capture" nature, while asserting, simultaneously, language's ability to imitate nature (no. 811):

> The Veins of other Flowers
> The Scarlet Flowers are
> Till Nature leisure has for Terms
> As "Branch," and "Jugular."
>
> We pass, and she abides.
> We conjugate Her Skill
> While She creates and federates
> Without a syllable.

Nature's evolutionary, teleological impulse demonstrates itself here through the progressive articulation of a single, homogeneous "body." Primitive nature employs scarlet flowers as "veins" for other flowers until it can develop specialized botanical and anatomical channels, such as veins and arteries, for all that "redness" to flow through. Moreover, the vegetable kingdom is contiguous with the animal, the architecture of the tree branch smoothly metamorphosing, over time, into the circulatory system.[6] The second stanza contrasts our transitoriness with nature's constancy, representing language as a symbolic system that can only "conjugate" nature's mute ability to generate new forms with terms such as "Branch" and "Jugular" in the first stanza. Nature, meanwhile, remains pure process, pure verb, continually "baptising" herself into being while we, with a language that seems to consist only of static, unconjugatable nouns, can only aspire to represent her at second hand. Yet language itself is not hopelessly out of touch with nature, for such botanical and anatomical features as "Branch" and "Jugular" are nature's own "Terms," the "words" she herself concocts succeeding a period of raw, "prelexical" creativity. Thus, even though Dickinson asserts language's difference from nature in this poem, the example she provides could be used just as easily to justify a belief that language and nature shared an "occult relation" of their own. Significantly, Dickinson's style here displays an exuberance reminiscent of nature's, as her internal rhymes in lines 3 and 7 rather adroitly capture the speed with which organic forms proliferate. Then too, nature's creative method, as described in that poem, bears a marked resemblance to her own, as a preliminary period of inspiration is followed by one of inscription during which the poet "federates" her thoughts (recollecting her emotions in tranquility?) in her lists of alternatives and variants.

Unlike Emerson, who saw our dependence upon language as a corollary of humankind's separation from nature, Dickinson interpreted language's vestigial similarity to nature as a clear sign of a common bond between us and it. She also took it upon herself to occupy a position as "reporter" or "interpreter" of meanings nature wished to communicate to us. Poised on the threshold between nature and human consciousness, she converted the former's kinetic, wordless creative process into the more accessible medium of language—primarily, she would have us believe, for our benefit (no. 441):

> This is my letter to the World
> That never wrote to Me—
> The simple News that Nature told—
> With tender Majesty
>
> Her message is committed
> To Hands I cannot see—
> For love of Her—Sweet—countrymen—
> Judge tenderly—of Me.

In this poem Dickinson implicitly compares her function as a poet to that of a go-between, writing at a friend's behest to a complete stranger.[7] Although Dickinson is purportedly asking the "letter's" intended recipient to excuse, for the sake of their mutual friend Nature, any inaccuracies or infelicities of expression that may be found within her version of the "News," the poem is really an apology for her art. The unknown recipient of the "letter" is, of course, us, the readers of this poem-letter, whom Dickinson addresses as directly as Whitman does the readers of "Crossing Brooklyn Ferry," and she asks us to judge her poetry tenderly by imputing any failings to the difficulty of her task as translator rather than to her own ineptness. Nature's "simple" news exceeds the capacity of words to express it.

The speaker's pose in this short poem is, however, more deliberate and more calculated than it may first appear. Dickinson's displacement of responsibility for the quality of her expression onto language itself indirectly reflects, I believe, her insecurity about both her abilities as a poet and her provincialism. In "This is my letter to the World," she attempts to cast herself in the romantic role of the "natural" poet who sings naïvely and not by design, and as a denizen of rural Amherst, she would be "expected" to occupy such a position. Dickinson also claims in the poem to carry on a more extensive correspondence with nature than with her fellow man or woman, and the parallelism present at the conclusion of each stanza in her use of "tender"/"tenderly" makes a tacit appeal for the same degree of consideration from us, her readers, that she supposedly has enjoyed from Nature. Her very propinquity to nature earns her the right, Dickinson implies, to have her work judged not as a piece of literature, but as an almost involuntary outpouring of revelation. I need hardly point out, however, that neither her role as a "natural" poet nor her claim to be judged nonliterarily would be entirely compatible with a poetics actually based upon conscious choice, precision of expression, and attention to detail.

An Intrusive Friend

In an almost childlike way, Dickinson's framing of "This is my letter to the World" as an epistle reifies the Transcendentalist notion of "correspondences," and the anthropomorphism that is blatant in Dickinson's designation of nature as "her" and latent in her entire trope of "correspondence" underlies many, if not most, of the poet's poems about nature. Dickinson's "friendship" with nature seems to undergo all the vicissitudes that conventional human relationships do, and although Dickinson and nature exist on cordial terms in "This is my letter to the World," such is not always the case. In some poems, rather than politely asking the poet to "pass along" her news to the world at large, nature monopolizes her attention, and Dickinson's conviction that nature actively sought her out, rather than she it, defines an important distinction between her and Emerson. Compare, for example, a passage from *Nature* with another Dickinson poem (no. 891) about communicating with nature:

> The greatest delight which the fields and woods minister, is the suggestion of an occult relation between man and the vegetable. I am not alone and unacknowledged. They nod to me and I to them.

> To my quick ear the Leaves—conferred—
> The Bushes—they were Bells—
> I could not find a Privacy
> From Nature's sentinels—

> In Cave if I presumed to hide
> The Walls—begun to tell—
> Creation seemed a mighty Crack—
> To make me visible—

The cardinal difference between these two statements is that Dickinson's relationship to nature is hardly "occult," but rather insistently personal to the point of becoming invasive. What is merely a "nod" from the woods to Emerson becomes a ceaseless stream of chatter for Dickinson, who exhibits more than a trace of apprehension as she realizes no hole is deep enough to hide her from her importunate correspondent. Nature pursues her as diligently as she supposed God did in "I never felt at Home—Below," his prying, telescopic vision never failing to find wayward "children" such as herself. The mediatory role that Dicksinson assumes as translator between humankind and nature in "To my quick ear the Leaves—conferred" carries over into her imagery, which hovers halfway between the human and nonhuman. Leaves "confer" with her like confiding friends, the walls of a cave sprout lips, and each natural object appears to her to be a "sentinel" of the news nature has to impart. It is as if a language common to human beings and to nature were intelligible at times to Dickinson, whose "quick" or sensitive ear renders her especially susceptible to nature's efforts to communicate.

Dickinson did not doubt that this sensitivity to sound was an indication that God had chosen her to perform a specific errand, that is, to be the herald of what she had heard. In one of her earlier letters to Higginson she said that "there's a noiseless noise in the orchard—that I *let* persons hear—" (L415, emphasis added). She had already used the image of an orchard in an explanation of how she became inspired to write in a letter sent only a couple of months earlier, in which she said that "a sudden light on Orchards" caused her to feel a "palsy, here" that her "Verses just relieve—" (L408). If she were properly receptive to the voice of nature, and if the message arrived incrementally rather than in a chaotic rush, the overall experience was usually a positive one, as in the following poem (no. 276):

> Many a phrase has the English language—
> I have heard but one—
> Low as the laughter of the Cricket,
> Loud, as the Thunder's Tongue—
>
> Murmuring, like old Caspian Choirs,
> When the Tide's a'lull—
> Saying itself in new inflection—
> Like a Whippowil—
>
> Breaking in bright Orthography
> On my simple sleep—
> Thundering it's Prospective—
> Till I stir, and weep—
>
> Not for the Sorrow, done me—
> But the push of Joy—
> Say it again, Saxon!
> Hush—Only to me!

This poem reproduces the sensation of lying in bed half awake after being roused from sleep by a progression of natural noises. As in "To my quick ear the Leaves—conferred," Dickinson's imagery once again conflates the human and the natural or nonhuman, for crickets are described as laughing, the thunder has a tongue, frogs have arranged themselves (concealed behind a rather florid figure of speech) into choirs, and English itself is apostrophized as a "Saxon." The sublinguistic message nature has to convey arrives first as a series of iterated, inflected calls like the chirping of crickets, the croaking of frogs, or the cry of the whippoorwill. The noise continues to swell until nature addresses Dickinson imperatively through the vehicle of a thunderclap, spelling out its message explicitly through the "bright orthography" of lightning. All of these natural voices constitute the "one phrase" in English that Dickinson has heard, the undifferentiated *ur*-language that can manifest itself, as could nature in "The Veins of other Flowers," through any number of forms.

The immediacy of her inspiration in this poem seems, at least on the face of things, to be fundamentally different from her patient combing of her "Lexicon" to find the words to fit her thoughts, a difference Dickinson herself promoted. Because language formulated through rational deliberation existed at a farther remove from supernatural sources, she treated it with disdain: "'Speech'—is a prank of *Parliament*—," she sneered, a pallid compromise we fashion from among the many voices of our reason. But how different, finally, is the poetic method described in "Many a phrase has the English language—" from Dickinson's more prosaic technique of searching for the right word? The repeated calls with which nature solicits her attention are analogous to the permutations of language appearing in her penciled lists of variants. Yet Dickinson's romantic sensibilities, guided principally by Emerson's endorsement of intuition as the source of "primary wisdom," as he says in "Self-Reliance," prompted her to privilege the spontaneous over the studied, the superrational over the rational, preventing her, at least for a while, from respecting her own poetic resources sufficiently. Consequently, although "Many a phrase" might strike us as an accurate rendition of that transitional moment in which the raw materials for poetry supplied by the unconscious are converted into speech or text, Dickinson prefers to mythologize the experience as a transferral of information from the natural domain to the lexical.

Emerson himself, on the other hand, may have discriminated too finely at times between the realms of nature and of language. In a discussion of the famous "transparent eyeball" passage in *Nature,* Richard Poirier points out a fundamental discontinuity between the ecstasy of the moment being described and the excessive civility of the language Emerson uses to describe it: "In his performances, his structuring of sentences and paragraphs, especially in so early an effort as *Nature,* he often unwittingly evades the struggle with language to which [his] causes would seem necessarily to commit him" (65). Thus Emerson was prohibited from writing a prose as transcendent as his vision had been by his own allegiance to standards of proper conduct, polite address, and even to the conventional forms of literature. Consequently, says Poirier, despite Emerson's self-characterization as a transparent eyeball, "There is no speaking 'I' for the seeing 'eye'" (66).[8]

Dickinson circumvented this incongruity of substance and style by telling herself she belonged to a discourse community that was not exclusively human. She actively courted the primal voice of nature and the compound vision of God by trying to loosen the intellect's grip upon the word-making process, resorting to unconscious sources of language in dreams, daydreams, and moments of spontaneous revelation. In so doing, she took to heart Emerson's injunction in "The Poet" that a poet should unleash the "*dream*-power which every night shows thee is thine own." The wished-for moment of revelation might arrive at any time; divinity might even announce its presence while she was in the midst of trying to select one word from among several variants, thereby obviating the need to continue searching (no. 1126):

Shall I take thee, the Poet said
To the propounded word?
Be stationed with the Candidates
Till I have finer tried—

The Poet searched Philology
And was about to ring
For the suspended Candidate
There came unsummoned in—

That portion of the Vision
The Word applied to fill
Not unto nomination
The Cherubim reveal—

A manuscript variant for the fourth line, "Till I have Vainer tried—," indicates that the poet's search for adequate words had actually been futile from the outset. The vision she seeks is not susceptible to "nomination," a triple pun which succinctly expresses the word-making process, the "electoral" methods employed by the poet in her pursuit of the right word, and the difference between those who have been merely "nominated" for admission to heaven versus those who were already members of the "Elect." That the poet's search for the proper term has ended in failure does not invalidate the quest itself, for the vision she had been pursuing as her ultimate goal announces itself only after the poet has exerted her nominative powers to their utmost. The selection process itself has evidently made the poet's mind elastic enough to comprehend a new "portion" of her vision.

In the midst of such revelatory moments, however, language's capacity to convey meaning was suddenly jeopardized while astonishment, or awe, or fear drove the poet to the brink of inarticulateness, or rather to a condition of romantic sublimity in which words were neither adequate nor necessary.[9] Transcendence being intrinsically at odds with all forms of expression, Dickinson's habit of pushing language to the limits of its expressive power threatened to nullify the entire enterprise. The poet's deemphasizing of her own role in the production of poems finally placed her in a logical dilemma from which it proved difficult to extricate herself. The burden of language prevented her from ascending high enough to achieve the vision of God and eternity she wanted, yet her own criteria for performing adequately as a poet demanded that she exhaust all the significatory possibilities of language. Compiling lists of alternates and variants would be laborious and infrequently rewarding, and the poet could only hope that in the midst of searching through the interplay of words and inflections she might accidentally stumble across the "correct" expression sponsored by God himself. This makes her effort to find the word to fit the thought more than just an attempt to find *le mot juste;* it was a consideration of the multiple possibilities of relation set up by different associations of words, like tumblers in a combination lock. Indeed, numbers themselves provided Dickinson with a second productive paradigm she could use to work out the symbolic connections between her poetry, her self, and heaven.

MATHEMATICAL TROPES

As Gary Stonum observes in *The Dickinson Sublime,* mathematics "occupies a distinctive place in Dickinson's work," with "Roughly two hundred of [her] poems includ[ing] some reference to mathematical terms and ideas, often in a precise and pointed way, and a number of others implicitly depend[ing] on counting, measuring, and quantitatively assessing" (133). Dickinson's fascination with mathematics derived largely, Stonum quite cogently points out, from her interest in the idea of ratios. "Almost every poem in which she counts, measures, reckons, or estimates implies the operation [of computing a ratio], even when the word is absent" (134). The single ratio that most interested Dickinson was, of course, the unknown one obtaining between eternal and temporal values.[10] Thus Dickinson employed the idea of ratios in her poems as part of a larger project to compare earth to heaven, in order to discover which of the two might satisfy her emotional and intellectual requirements more thoroughly.

Then too, figures of speech grounded in mathematics could, like some of her tropes involving nature, be used to imply an incremental, progressive, or evolutionary pattern in which each new ratio permitted the poet to establish a quantity to use in other, further, formulae, resulting in the simultaneous condensation of expression and compounding of meaning she sought. In treating mathematics as a symbolic system analogous to language, Dickinson may have been taking her cue once again from Emerson, who proposed in "The Poet" that many mathematical terms had originally been based upon tropes, in the same way that all language was "fossil poetry": "consider how much this makes the charm of algebra and the mathematics, which also have their tropes, but it is felt in every definition; as when Aristotle defines *space* to be an immovable vessel, in which things are contained;—or, when Plato defines a *line* to be a flowing point; or, figure to be a bound of solid; and many the like." Emerson also praised the universality of mathematical symbols, which contrasted with the narrowness of the hackneyed figures used by poets whose vision had never risen above the parochial. "Let us have a little algebra, instead of this trite rhetoric," Emerson suggested, "—universal signs, instead of these village symbols."

Treating her poetry as a kind of "mathematics" provided Dickinson with yet another appropriate hermeneutic model for her activities as poet. Each poem could be considered a "problem" she had to solve in order to move on to the next, more complex issue.[11] Yet even though her skill in manipulating her "figures" might develop over time, she still faced a major conceptual obstacle in that the "variables" upon which she based her calculations received their value necessarily from God, whose arithmetic might ultimately prove incomprehensible. At her most optimistic, Dickinson could tell herself that God took a personal interest in nurturing the intellectual capacities of his "pupils" (no. 545):

'Tis One by One—the Father counts—
And then a Tract between
Set Cypherless—to teach the Eye
The Value of it's Ten—

Until the peevish Student
Acquire the Quick of Skill—
Then Numerals are dowered back—
Adorning all the Rule—

'Tis mostly Slate and Pencil—
and Darkness on the School
Distracts the Children's fingers—
Still the Eternal Rule

Regards least Cypherer alike
With Leader of the Band—
And every separate Urchin's Sum—
Is fashioned for his hand—

Here Dickinson compares our discovery as children that numerical values exist far in excess of the ten we know experientially from counting upon our fingers to our gradual maturation, in adulthood, as metaphysicians. Moreover, that same hand becomes symbolic, in the poem's final line, of our individual rates of cognitive growth: the conclusions or "sums" each "pupil" reaches are both subjectively and objectively valid, for even though individuals may reach their solutions via different paths, the same salvation in heaven awaits each. The fingers upon which we learn to count are "distracted," however, by obstacles comprising both the clumsy intellectual apparatus, or "Slate and Pencil," with which we must work, and the "Darkness on the School," which could signify either the general state of people's spiritual ignorance or Dickinson's own "schoolroom"/sickroom. Still, darkness, like barriers of gauze, served merely to stimulate the poet's determination to perceive and understand. "I shall vote for Lands with Locks," said Dickinson, "Granted I can pick 'em— " (no. 1195). Dickinson herself may be the "Student" who has acquired the "Quick of Skill" as a poet to unlock greater and greater quantities of revelation, or the "Numerals" "dowered back" to her. Afterwards, these new realizations "Adorn" her "Rule," that is, the frame of reference she had used in the past to measure the grandeur of existence. Simultaneously, however, the "Eternal Rule," or God himself, gauges each individual by a different standard. Thus, even though the procedure by which Dickinson learns about heaven exposes her to successively larger truths, in God's own numerical system the "least Cypherer" is equivalent to the "Leader of the Band," and no standards of comparison are applied.

Dickinson's "peevishness" may be ascribed to the difficulty of her task, the intractability of the "problem" put to her, and to the limitations of her tools. At times, the insusceptibility of themes she wished to address to being expressed in language may have induced a kind of writer's block, as in the following poem (no. 69):

Low at my problem bending,
Another problem comes—
Larger than mine—Serener—
Involving statelier sums.

I check my busy pencil,
My figures file away.
Wherefore, my baffled fingers
Thy perplexity?

I believe this poem is a portrait of the poet at a loss for words, not numbers. As each new philosophical quandary suggests itself, she finds she cannot concentrate adequately on the task at hand, so her fingers become "baffled." "Check" at the beginning of the second stanza probably means "stop" rather than "examine," so that Dickinson would appear to be describing a voluntary cessation of her own writing. When she does stop, however, whatever she has just written seems to dwindle into insignificance, dwarfed by the magnitude of whatever new issue confronts her. Dickinson's "figures" (possibly her "figures" of speech, although a variant line reads "My ciphers steal away") "file away," abandoning the current project because they no longer mean anything, or rather, because they do not mean enough. The steady, intellectually comprehensible progression of dilemmas God poses to his "children" in "'Tis One by One—the Father counts—" has broken down, and Dickinson has been left in the "wilderness of size" we saw in chapter 4.

The "problems" Dickinson endeavored to solve were, of course, philosophical or religious rather than numeric, yet in their degree of difficulty, they may have reminded her of the knotty mathematical equations she had wrestled with as a girl. In the following poem she uses "Algebra" as a catchall term to describe the problem-solving technique she applied to the question of whether heaven would admit her or not (no. 600):

It troubled me as once I was—
For I was once a Child—
Concluding how an Atom—fell—
And yet the Heavens—held—

The Heavens weighed the most—by far—
Yet Blue—and solid—stood—
Without a Bolt—that I could prove—
Would Giants—understand?

Life set me larger—problems—
Some I shall keep—to solve
Till Algebra is easier—
Or simpler proved—above—

Then—too—be comprehended—
What sorer—puzzled me—
Why Heaven did not break away—
And tumble—Blue—on me—

Here Dickinson uses her ingenuous "pupil" persona effectively as a foil for another, older persona, employing childish language primarily in the first two stanzas while she describes the early mystery of the sky's power to maintain its position without visible supports despite its loss of "atoms" (presumably in the form of snow, ice, or rain), but using a sadder and wiser adult tone in the third and fourth stanzas. The problems of adulthood require a good deal more subtlety, she says, and some are still so confounding that she will have to wait either until her power to comprehend has improved or until her death, when God would reveal the solutions like a schoolteacher reviewing an examination with the "class." Nevertheless, even though Dickinson begins by speaking indulgently of her own childish naïveté, saying, in mock seriousness, "For I was once a Child," her quick, ironic twist at the end of the poem, where she wonders why the sky did not fall on *her*, abruptly undercuts the complacency and equanimity of her more "mature" point of view.

Dickinson uses parallelism rather deftly within this poem first to encourage us to distinguish between the "problems" of childhood and adulthood, but then to deny that difference, as her repetition of "Blue" in the final line implies that she has not really made any headway in resolving old questions. Because Dickinson is returned to a state of unknowingness virtually identical to childish ignorance, this poem challenges the rational epistemologies we endeavor to develop all our adult lives, as well as the "progressive" paradigm of cognitive development to which Dickinson subscribes in other poems. Although Dickinson encourages us to smile condescendingly at a child's earnest misapplication of an early lesson in physics, she quickly attacks the grounds of our own knowledge, compelling us to question our adult certainties. As part of Dickinson's program to blur the boundaries between the rational and the supernatural, even the adults who *should* be able to speak with authority about how the world works are trivialized as semimythical creatures or "Giants." The child Dickinson imitates in this poem must always be tilting her head up to find the truth, whether from inquiring of "Giants" or looking up at the sky, a motion that instills in the reader a sense of giddiness the poet can take advantage of in the final stanza, when the narrator suddenly reprises her old childish dilemma about the sky collapsing. This sense of physical disorientation is consonant with the intellectual disorientation the narrator feels after the tools of reason have failed her.

The question of whether poetry was one of those tools that had failed her remains open to question. "Algebra," which Dickinson uses here as a summarizing term for all instruments of rational analysis adults apply to quandaries, would not, of course, be even remotely applicable to the problem in physics the child has raised—why the sky continues to hang, evidently unsupported, above her head. Yet writing poetry is, as poems previously discussed appear to show, a rational means of problem-solving in its own right, which begs the question of whether Dickinson is also doubting the effectiveness of her own avocation here. No matter how many "problems" she solves, other problems will come, each more troubling than its predecessor. Did her poems grant her true insights into the architecture of the universe, or were they merely random assemblages of lexical symbols, uninformed by the presence or the knowledge of divinity? The crux of the problem lay within her poetic methodology itself. Dickinson's valorizing of external sources of inspiration and of the moment of romantic sublimity threatened to make her the permanent victim of forces she could neither see nor comprehend, so that at best, she would continue to serve merely as a passive recipient of "bulletins from Immortality" which, in rare moments of good fortune, she would be able to body forth into language.

Mathematics and language, the two primary symbolical skills for interpreting experience which had been imparted to her by her schooling, may have begun to strike Dickinson as hopelessly inadequate to the task of describing the symbolic function she imagined herself fulfilling as poet. Instead, she may have adopted a paradigm based upon the sacrament, telling herself that the words she used in her poems were literally charged with immortal content. Looking back upon her education, Dickinson realized that rational epistemological tools such as mathematics and language had lacked the crucial ingredient of direct divine participation (no. 728):

> Let Us play Yesterday—
> I—the Girl at school—
> You—and Eternity—the
> Untold Tale—
>
> Easing my famine
> At my Lexicon—
> Logarithm—had I—for Drink—
> 'Twas a dry Wine—. . . .

In adulthood these two inferior forms of the eucharist, "Lexicon" and "Logarithm," had to be replaced somehow by knowledge informed by deity. By using language eucharistically, Dickinson may have hoped to elevate the symbolic content of her poetic language; nevertheless, we shall see her concluding once again that words used in full consciousness of their symbolic content could also threaten the poet's mental equilibrium like the unmoored sky overhead if the moment of romantic sublimity they were intended to release suddenly lapsed into a "wilderness" of unmediated revelation.

THE PREY OF UNKNOWN ZONES

"The cordiality of the Sacrament extremely interested me when a Child," Dickinson wrote to Clara Newman Turner (L835), and the spirit of receptivity and generosity intrinsic to the concept of the sacrament continued to attract her, even after she ceased attending church. Despite her alienation from organized religion, she participated as an adult in what Jane Donahue Eberwein calls "alternative natural liturgies" (187). Dickinson's belief that nature made itself accessible to those who sought consolation in it as Christ did for communicants may have been the chief reason why the poet was prone to describe nature in sacramental or eucharistical terms, as when she characterizes nature as possessing "mystic bread" and "immortal wine" for the spiritually famished in "These are the Signs to Nature's Inns—," "I had been hungry, all the Years—," and "These are the Days when Birds come back—." Yet the sacramental imagery in these poems remains purely metaphorical, for rather than signifying that Christ's body is literally present in nature, Dickinson is simply asserting that there are moments in which more *meaning* is present in nature than at other times. The same would be true of words used in her poems (no. 1452):

> Your thoughts dont have words every day
> They come a single time
> Like signal esoteric sips
> Of the communion Wine
> Which while you taste so native seems
> So easy so to be
> You cannot comprehend its price
> Nor it's infrequency.

At those rare moments when Dickinson's words coincided precisely with what she intended to say, the language she used differed from conventional language in the same way communion wine differs from ordinary wine: its semantic content was infinitely greater.[12]

The infrequency of such inspired moments, implicit in Dickinson's phrase "single time," and her inability to exert much control over them helped confirm the poet's belief that language was at least partially autonomous. When Dickinson first wrote Higginson to ask whether her verse was "alive," her request was consonant with what she says in her poems about language's existence as an independent entity. A word is not "dead" when it is said, as Dickinson put it, but rather begins to "live," so that, in writing a poem, the poet incarnates thought. Making words "live" constituted an important element of Dickinson's metapoetics, and the following poem is an important—albeit obscure—explanation of why Dickinson enjoyed the entire business of writing poetry (no. 1651):

A Word made Flesh is seldom
And tremblingly partook
Nor then perhaps reported
But have I not mistook
Each one of us has tasted
With ecstasies of stealth
The very food debated
To our specific strength—

A Word that breathes distinctly
Has not the power to die
Cohesive as the Spirit
It may expire if He—
"Made Flesh and dwelt among us
Could condescension be
Like this consent of Language
This loved Philology.

The symbolism in this poem is extraordinarily rich and dense. On one level the poem is an exegesis of John 1:1–14, which the poet partially quotes in the first line of the first stanza and in the fifth line of the second stanza. The poem may also turn upon the hoary legend, popular among churchgoing children, that in the mouths of unrepentant or unconfessed sinners, the eucharist becomes poisonous, a danger that would have added even more piquancy to the "crime" of stealing a sip of sacramental wine. Dickinson perhaps employs both allusions to describe the rewards and perils inherent to writing poetry and to invite her fellow poets to acknowledge that they indulge in the same guilty pleasure she does. As it stands, the poem is derived from a transcript made by Susan Dickinson, a woman of intermittently strong religious convictions who shared Emily's enthusiasm for literature.[13] If the poem is indeed addressed specifically to Sue, the first stanza could be an attempt to wring from her an admission that she was a covert participant as well in the "theft of the sacrament" Dickinson imagined the writing of poetry to be. Thus she may be trying to establish complicity among thieves: her "mistake" in the fourth line has been her assumption that the writing of poetry is a practice "seldom" engaged in. On the contrary, she says, "Each one of us" has the capacity and the desire to write poetry at one time or another in our lives. The poem also quite likely draws upon Dickinson's medical history, for the "ecstasies of stealth" with which she approaches food "debated / To our specific strength" are strongly reminiscent of the "delirious" pleasure she experiences while escaping from her sickroom to enjoy the light of day in "The Soul has Bandaged moments—." In "A Word made Flesh is seldom" Dickinson does not rule out the possibility of the poet's coming to grief by writing poems, but she does stress the invulnerability of words themselves, which, once they have become perfectly significant, become practically immortal as the spirit. A word that "breathes distinctly" no longer has the power to die, having been incarnated.[14]

The second stanza of "A Word Made Flesh is seldom" is more cryptic than the first, although I think the very symmetrical form of the poem and its fully executed rhyme scheme show that Dickinson was relatively satisfied with the draft as it stands. One major impediment to intelligibility is the stanza's vague pronoun antecedents. The reiterated "this" in the last two lines is especially confusing, because it is unclear whether Dickinson intends for that pronoun to refer to the writing of poetry or to her biblical quotation. Another difficulty presents itself in Dickinson's inconsistent punctuation. Terminal quotation marks after the citation from John are missing, left out either by Dickinson herself or by Susan Dickinson, whose transcript of the poem constitutes the only extant version.[15] That quotation marks should set off the citation at all represents yet another inconsistency, considering that none are used to enclose the biblical allusion's first appearance in the poem's initial line. But Dickinson's abbreviated punctuation in the second stanza would seem to indicate that she intended to approach the entire quotation homiletically, so that "this consent of language" and "This loved Philology" refer directly back to "Made Flesh and dwelt among us." Christ's incarnation was a "consent of Language" because deity "consented" to be made flesh, an analogy Dickinson employs to describe language's "consent" to manifest itself and be used by the poet. Thus poets do not really "steal" words when they write; rather, words willingly "consent" to making themselves available to poets. "Could condescension be" may be a rhetorical question asking whether any other form of heavenly condescension might be comparable to that first descent of divinity into a human form, to which the implicit answer would be yes—the conversion of ordinary language into the heightened meanings of poetry *was* as wondrous as divinity's transformation of itself into mortal flesh.

In the phrase "loved Philology" Dickinson becomes a philologist in her own right, giving the phrase multivalent meanings. First, the phrase is a tautology, a "loved love of words," or the avocation as poet which she, and perhaps Susan as well, cherished. Secondly, the phrase alludes directly to the passage from John, emphasizing love of Christ as the Word. Thirdly, the entire poem is a philological exegesis, a gloss upon scripture. In this regard, the poem closely resembles no. 1342, which comments upon Enoch's rapture into heaven, described in Genesis 5:24:

"Was not" was all the Statement.
The Unpretension stuns—
Perhaps—the Comprehension—
They wore no Lexicons—

But lest our Speculation
In inanition die
Because "God took him"—mention—
That was Philology—

Overlooking, for the moment, Dickinson's intriguing reference to Webster's lexicon as a garment, we notice a structural similarity between this poem and the previous one: Dickinson begins with a fragment of scripture, puzzles over it, and then goes on to practice "philology" by using the rest of the citation to gloss the fragment. In poem no. 1651, then, Dickinson begins with "The word was made flesh" and ends with the philological explanation "and dwelt among us," so that the true wonder of poetry is not, according to Dickinson, its embodiment of thought as language, but rather its willingness, despite its autonomous nature, to be expressed and used. True poetry would not suffer itself to remain "[un]reported," but rather would discover some avenue of expression, whether from one poet's hand or from another's.

It is not by accident, I propose, that Dickinson speaks to us, in "A Word made Flesh is seldom," as if from the pulpit. If God was the Word and the Word was God, Dickinson had a biblical precedent for believing divinity to be immanent within language, and the poet who manipulated words thus charged could mediate between benighted mankind and God's revelation. Such a poet would preside over the rite of writing like a priest over the ceremony of the sacrament, indispensable to its consecration and yet apart from the mechanism of transubstantiation itself. If sacramental transferrals of meaning were enacted within Dickinson's writing, her poems are indeed churches in miniature, as she would claim (no. 488):

> Myself was formed—a Carpenter—
> An unpretending time
> My Plane—and I, together wrought
> Before a Builder came—
>
> To measure our attainments—
> Had we the Art of Boards
> Sufficiently developed—He'd hire us
> At Halves—
>
> My Tools took Human—Faces—
> The Bench, where we had toiled—
> Against the Man—persuaded—
> We—Temples build—I said—

Here the narrator stipulates that she was born or "formed" a carpenter (that is, a poet) as if such had been her destiny. God created her in the form of a poet, just as she herself creates shapes of wood (or of words). The degree to which Dickinson externalizes her own poetic skills is especially striking: the "Builder," or publisher, even offers to employ the poet and her poetry at "Halves," as if they were independent contractors. Of all the tools of carpentry Dickinson could have selected to represent being a poet, she chooses a plane, perhaps because she envisaged writing poetry as the shaping of the rough lumber of inspiration into the smooth building stock of rhymed trimeter. This facility in the "Art of [planing] Boards" is what a publisher requires of Dickinson and her tools, but after a hurried colloquy they refuse to construct anything so mundane as a house. Writing poems or "building houses" is not a simple, utilitarian venture for her. On the contrary, her poems are "temples," or structures within which the holy spirit may dwell, constructed according to an organic plan resulting from cooperation between the artist and language itself, rather than from a Urizenic process of measurement and assembly.

Dickinson had to receive "cooperation" from the words she used because factors other than her own will and talent were involved, and in order to encourage divine intervention she had to prepare a residence fit for God to dwell in. A poem was thus a simulacrum of heaven, a tangible, physical place in which deity consented to visit, an ark. Yet a poem was not heaven itself, nor ever could be, for to Dickinson, heaven was, by definition, the one thought that could not be expressed in words (no. 581):

I found the words to every thought
I ever had—but One—
And that—defies me—
As a Hand did try to chalk the Sun

To Races—nurtured in the Dark—
How would your own—begin?
Can Blaze be shown in Cochineal—
Or Noon—in Mazarin?

Inaccessible as the noonday sun would be to those whose eyes could not tolerate bright light, heaven resists description. Words could demonstrate heaven's presence only indirectly, like colors superficially imitating the brilliance and depth of "Blaze" or "Noon." Prevented from seeing the sun herself while still confined to her sickroom, Dickinson would have been well aware of the inadequacy and unsatisfactoriness of other people's verbal accounts of what she could not see for herself. "Nurtured in the Dark" like a member of that "Race" she imagines, Dickinson comprehended the division that separated language from experience. Yet because she did know precisely how hazardous exposure to the sun's unadulterated brightness could be, Dickinson also prized the mitigating effect of language, which stood as a sort of flexible bulkhead—or protective blindfold—between her and dangerous divinity. Drawing upon her experience as someone who, like Icarus, had ventured too near the bright light of the sun, Dickinson distinguished between unadulterated meanings sent express from heaven and those screened or tempered by the smoked glass of poetic language. If we were to understand the full import of what we meant, thought Dickinson, our sanity would be put at risk (no. 1409):

Could mortal lip divine
The undeveloped Freight
Of a delivered syllable
'Twould crumble with the weight.

A connection between this small poem and Dickinson's conception of poems as "churches" becomes readily apparent if we add four more lines deleted from a prior draft:

> The Prey of Unknown Zones—
> The Pillage of the Sea
> The Tabernacles of the Minds
> That told the Truth to me—

I would like to treat these two stanzas as a single poem, but to do so we will first have to unravel the rejected stanza's syntax. The dominant image in the poem is that of a statue crumbling under the onslaught of the elements in some "Unknown Zone" or terra incognita upon the map, a desolate and forgotten place near the sea where the waves can "pillage" the ruined idol like barbarians desecrating a church. The poem's first line sets up an implicit contrast between "mortal" and "divine," the two regions which are, in this poem, incompatible. An as-yet unidentified figure has received a "delivered" syllable, that is, one sent straight from God, and the full significance of that single fragment threatens to become the straw whose added weight would cause the entire "statue" to crumble.

In *The Life and Letters of Emily Dickinson*, Martha Dickinson Bianchi made one editorial emendation to this poem that strikes me as being entirely appropriate: the definite article at the beginning of the second stanza's third line is changed to "These," whose pronominal antecedent would be, presumably, "lip(s)." Such an alteration means that "Tabernacles," "Prey," and "Pillage" all modify lips, rather than "syllable(s)."[16] The "Sea" whose one word is "inundation" is that same wilderness of inexpressible meaning we have seen Dickinson shun before, and thus we are justified in concluding, I suggest, that this miniature explorer's saga is intended to be self-referential. Her "pillaged" lips had served as the unstable or infirm "tabernacles" of mysterious "Minds" which told her divine truths, thereby causing, wittingly or unwittingly, her destruction by the forces of unmediated meaning.

Although I do not think that Dickinson harbored any messianic delusions about her position as artist, I do believe she saw herself as a prophetic figure, if only because she could use compound vision to achieve a "prospective" of the eternal world. Her poems are sacramentalized by the presence of divine influence, and often the symbology she uses in her work participates in a larger metaphor of communion. In Dickinson's cosmos, God, nature, and man inhabit spheres which commingle at the edges, so that higher forms can "condescend" to manifest themselves within smaller "circumferences." Divinity condescends to becoming human in the form of Christ, or to becoming a part of language itself as the Word; nature condescends to becoming almost human at times, so that noises in nature can abruptly sound like phrases in English; and one's own thoughts can condescend to becoming expressible in language. Dickinson saw herself as the hub of energies both externally and internally generated, and she strove to find a middle ground, her own charmed circle. As translator of immortal truths she had an almost sacerdotal responsibility, for rather than being a conventional poet developing her art to suit herself or an audience, she might actually be, for all she knew, the "Rivet in the Bands," that is, the linchpin in a rare and eternally significant bond between mankind and deity. As the author of spiritual formulae which might reveal themselves to be as important and true as the equations she had conned in her mathematics textbooks, Dickinson could readily justify her own continued perseverance as a poet. Yet such a rationalization also necessarily prevented her, at least for a while, from seeking to have her poetry published.

If fame belonged to me, I could not escape her—

Dickinson, in a letter to T. W. Higginson, June 7, 1862

"A TUMULTUOUS PRIVACY OF STORM"

Snow, Publication, and the Problem of Romantic Egotism

DURING HER MOST active years as a poet, Dickinson promulgated an image of herself as a messenger or facilitator in the transferral of meaning from eternity to earth. Occupying such a position helped reassure her of her own importance, and, in the aftermath of illness, it may also have represented an effort to persuade herself that she was acting in accordance with the divine will, rather than in conscious or unconscious opposition to it. Moreover, because she did not, for the most part, try to engage the attention of strangers through being published, her articulation to herself of her mission as a writer provided an extraliterary justification for pursuing her avocation. She continued to regard writing as a private and sacramental act, not only because divinity was briefly incarnated in her words but also because her poems represented the corporeal presence of her own body. The fact of this acute self-identification with her work goes far to explain Dickinson's initial hostility to the idea of being published, a hostility she expresses in no uncertain terms. In poems such as "I'm Nobody! Who are you," "Fame is a fickle food," and especially in her famous verse diatribe against the commercial print industry, "Publication—is the Auction," Dickinson condemns the pursuit of literary renown as being inherently selfish. In "Publication—is the Auction" she even says that she would rather die than send "Our Snow" to a publisher. Yet in about 1883,[1] only three years before she actually did die, Dickinson took the (for her) uncharacteristic step of sending a letter accompanied by a few poems to Thomas Niles, an editor at Roberts Brothers in Boston. One of them was entitled, ironically, "Snow." That particular poem was a radical reworking of a piece she had written almost two decades earlier, at about the same time she wrote "Publication—is the Auction—," entitled "It sifts from Leaden Sieves." Was this act of sending a poem entitled "Snow" to a publisher a deliberate gesture, then, of surrender to ambitions she had once stifled? I suggest that, by examining the origins of her use of "snow" to symbolize her poetry, we may encounter evidence of a profound shift in Dickinson's attitude toward the "ownership" of her work during the latter stages of her career that permitted her to accept responsibility for her poems at last, rather than continuing to attribute them to forces largely beyond her control. Only after she could consider her poems to be exclusively hers may Dickinson have been willing to entertain the idea of getting them published.

The image of snow in Dickinson's poems possesses both religious and secular roots which help to explain why she adopted it as a symbol for her poetry. Snow was the stuff of heaven, the garment of angels,[2] a material Dickinson celebrated for its whiteness and purity, as well as for its origin in that quarter of her private cosmography that she assigned to God, the north. Thus Dickinson called her poems "snow" in "Publication—is the Auction" primarily because she believed the power of God to be immanent within them. But the image of snow would also have possessed, for Dickinson, further connotations drawing upon a specifically literary source: Emerson's poem "The Snow-Storm." That particular poem should be viewed, I propose, as a backdrop for Dickinson's "It sifts from Leaden Sieves," even to the extent of searching for images and expressions that the two works possess in common.

Yet evaluating Dickinson's response to any of Emerson's poems is admittedly a highly imprecise affair. Even to discover a wider pattern of literary influence linking the two writers has often proven to be unexpectedly difficult. Harold Bloom, for example, in his Chelsea House volume *Emily Dickinson: Modern Critical Views,* characterizes her and Whitman as twin "Titan[s]" fostered by Emerson, while saying virtually in the same breath that she has "no single, overwhelming precursor whose existence can lessen her wildness for us" (1–2). In this chapter, however, I will consider "The Snow-Storm" as a "precursor-poem" for "It sifts from Leaden Sieves—" to see how Dickinson might have read (or misread), first, what Emerson has to say about snow's aptness as a symbol for poetry and, second, his portrayal of a "surreptitious" artist who enjoys a peculiarly covert relationship to his (or her) audience. A pattern seems to emerge in which Dickinson finally reacts against the romantic egotism implicit within Emerson's portrait of the artist and responds by progressively and deliberately removing her presence from her own poem.

THE ASCENSION

Dickinson's failure to publish has been attributed by some observers to Colonel Higginson's tepid and condescending critical response to the poems she sent him, while others have blamed what they see as the entire century's failure to take its women writers seriously. Some have suggested that Dickinson actively resisted publication, finding it more satisfactory to act as her own publisher by assembling her fascicles and packets in the privacy of her own room.[3] In recent years, attention has turned to a conjectural incompatibility between Dickinson's highly personal and idiosyncratic methods of arranging her thoughts on paper and the conventional print medium's coldly uniform disposition of words and letters upon the page.[4]

But for a while, at least, Dickinson may have been prevented from publishing by her own code of artistic ethics. Because she ascribed her ability to write to heaven, she could regard what she wrote as being not "literature" at all, at least not in the strictest sense of that term, and as being therefore unsuitable for publication. Although she considered her poems objects of worth, or "jewels" that she had polished, they received their valuation not from readers or critics, but rather from an "economy" established in heaven. This distinction between temporal and eternal economies provides the basis for her best-known rejection of the notion that she should ever deliberately seek to have her work published (no. 709, written in about 1863):

Publication—is the Auction
Of the Mind of Man—
Poverty—be justifying
For so foul a thing

Possibly—but We—would rather
From Our Garret go
White—Unto the White Creator—
Than invest—Our Snow—

Thought belong to Him who gave it—
Then—to Him Who bear
Its corporeal illustration—Sell
The Royal Air—

In the Parcel—Be the Merchant
Of the Heavenly Grace—
But reduce no Human Spirit
To Disgrace of Price—

Dickinson's economic tropes maintain an ironical edge throughout. She derides publication as an "Auction" by which the products of human creativity are sold to the editor who makes the highest bid, an infernal industry writers abet by submitting their work in the first place. Sending her work out with the expectation of being paid for it would be not just an act of unforgivable hubris, but an affront to God, since poetic inspiration is given by heaven so freely as to render all economic considerations meaningless. Fame is invalidated as well, for poems and poets resemble snowflakes, the "Royal Air," or heavenly grace in that they constitute an indivisible whole. The concept of ownership is thus reduced to an absurdity, and the most scrupulous posture for a poet becomes resolute anonymity. The sole exception Dickinson is willing to admit to this rigid code of self-abnegation is poverty, and that only grudgingly. She herself would rather starve, Dickinson rather self-righteously declares, than be "rescued" from her stereotypic artist's garret and placed before the public eye—or, to extend her metaphor, regard herself as a form of "property" to be hauled down from the attic and auctioned off.[5]

Dickinson's preferred orientation is upward, toward heaven, and her death, by reversing the direction of the snow's descent, promises to return the "literary property" of her creativity to its rightful owner. Essentially, submitting herself to heaven would help Dickinson avoid committing an act of plagiarism, for just as her own words were the corporeal habiliments of her thoughts, she was the corporeal expression and instrument of God's will, a poem "written" by God, or by his avatar in this poem as lord of the north. Thus, if we take at face value what Dickinson is saying in this poem, she was prohibited from seeking publication chiefly because her poems did not "belong" to her, having more in common with natural phenomena than with the fruits of human labor. In an intensely personal reinterpretation of her role as poet, Dickinson denies her own literariness, removing herself entirely from the commercial arena to shut herself up like the sequestered nun that so many of the mythicizing early accounts of her life made her out to be.[6]

Yet the poem generates a logical difficulty from which Dickinson would have had some difficulty extricating herself. Is she speaking here as a representative poet, or is she identifying herself as an anomaly, a writer who exists outside of conventional definitions of the literary enterprise? Dickinson's concluding admonition in the poem's last six lines implicitly condemns *any* writer who pursues literary fame, and her phrases "the Mind of Man" and "Human Spirit" clearly indicate that she is speaking on behalf of all humanity. Yet Dickinson leaves rather conveniently unresolved the question of how any literature would be produced at all, if every writer were to heed her advice. Whether she likes to admit it or not, Dickinson is indeed making a case in this poem for being treated differently. The kind of "literature" Dickinson describes herself creating would elevate her far above the ranks of her fellow writers—almost literally so, for her melodramatic depiction of her own projected death by starvation in the clichéed artist's garret resembles nothing so much as the Ascension. By serving as a "metaphor" mediating between heaven and earth, Dickinson even replaces Christ in the trinity, a form of self-promotion so extreme as to be justifiably construed not as noble modesty, but as an apotheosis of self-glorification. Thus the poem, rather than conveying a spirit of self-effacement or Christian altruism, can come off sounding like colossal egotism. Although Dickinson represents her own "snow" as being inherently worthless, the poem itself makes a tacit appeal to be considered as a priceless object too good to be trusted to the rough hands of publishers.

This tirade against ambition may also be viewed only too easily as a rationalization for Dickinson's near-neurotic unwillingness to expose herself to the public eye. Dickinson so thoroughly conflated her self with her poems that the prospect of having them appear in public resembled a form of prostitution, and thus the language in this poem connoting virginity and physical purity.[7] Initially, an intense self-identification with her poems may have been what barred Dickinson from participating in the milieu of "serious" nineteenth-century poetry read by a largely male audience, and in this regard she perhaps resembled other women writers who, feeling compelled to define themselves according to men's expectations, eventually had to shatter what Sandra Gilbert and Susan Gubar call "The Queen's Looking Glass," or the "patriarchal voice of judgment that rules the Queen's—and every woman's—self-evaluation" before they could assert their right to a niche in the literary marketplace (38).[8]

Caught, therefore, between an internal conviction of her own possible greatness and a natural diffidence[9] that impelled her to shun the consequences of greatness, Dickinson developed a profound ambivalence about assuming a public role as poet. Even though she admired the heroine of Elizabeth Barrett Browning's *Aurora Leigh* as a woman determined to live an openly literary life, Dickinson herself was prevented from following that same route by an antipathy toward the romantic stereotype of the Byronic poet who, by writing, implicitly puts himself on display. Ironically, Dickinson's poetry derives much of its power from her exquisite consciousness of the self, yet her art's very existence was jeopardized by a painful and debilitating self-consciousness.

A TUMULTUOUS PRIVACY

Although Dickinson's religious convictions and her reticence partially explain why she used "snow" to symbolize both herself and her poetry, we might also look for that image in some literary work we know she admired, and in making such a determination, we could hardly find a more likely candidate than Emerson's popular lyrical portrait of a driving snowstorm.[10] Dickinson's personal history with that piece extended back virtually to her childhood, for "The Snow-Storm" appears in the volume of Emerson's poems that she received from her first literary mentor, Benjamin Newton, in 1850, when she was only eighteen.[11] One line from the poem, "a tumultuous privacy of storm," which Dickinson wrote out on a slip of paper in February 1884, constitutes her only known quotation from an Emerson poem (L928). Although her use of the line was, given the time of year, probably a topical reference, the fact that Dickinson should quote the poem a full thirty-four years after receiving the volume provides at least one measure of its importance to her.

Ostensibly, "The Snow-Storm" takes as its subject a theme Emerson would later revisit prosaically in *Nature* and "The Poet," that is, art's relationship to nature. Without entirely rejecting this conventional interpretation, we may nevertheless also read the poem "as if" we were Dickinson, a deconstructive approach that interrogates what Emerson says in the poem about art and about artists. Even though the poem describes fantastic creations made out of snow, a compelling argument may be made, I believe, that the real subject under discussion is poetry and that the poem itself could be read as Emerson's semiconscious, half-wishful depiction of himself as poet. Dickinson, initially attracted to the poem by its treatment of snow as an artistic medium descending from above, may well have paid close attention to its implicit portrait of the artist, a possibility that seems all the more likely if we recall in what high regard Dickinson held Emerson as both poetic theorist and exemplar. Furthermore, if we read the poem as being about creativity rather than about art's inability to imitate nature, it may be seen as describing a particular kind of snow-artist, one who requires privacy in order to create, yet who also demands an audience that can appreciate him while maintaining a respectful distance. "Tumultuous privacy of storm," the line Dickinson quoted in her letter, may then be read as referring not just to the forced seclusion of the occupants of the snowbound house, but also to the intensely private creative method employed by Emerson's ideal artist.[12]

Here is Emerson's poem (published in 1847):

THE SNOW-STORM

Announced by all the trumpets of the sky,
Arrives the snow, and, driving o'er the fields,
Seems nowhere to alight: the whited air
Hides hills and woods, the river, and the heaven,
And veils the farm-house at the garden's end.

The sled and traveller stopped, the courier's feet
Delayed, all friends shut out, the housemates sit
Around the radiant fireplace, enclosed
In a tumultuous privacy of storm.

Come see the north wind's masonry.
Out of an unseen quarry evermore
Furnished with tile, the fierce artificer
Curves his white bastions with projected roof
Round every windward stake, or tree, or door.
Speeding, the myriad-handed, his wild work
So fanciful, so savage, nought cares he
For number or proportion. Mockingly,
On coop or kennel he hangs Parian wreaths;
A swan-like form invests the hidden thorn;
Fills up the farmer's lane from wall to wall,
Maugre the farmer's sighs; and at the gate
A tapering turret overtops the work.
And when his hours are numbered, and the world
Is all his own, retiring, as he were not,
Leaves, when the sun appears, astonished Art
To mimic in slow structures, stone by stone,
Built in an age, the mad wind's night-work,
The frolic architecture of the snow.

Furnished by an "unseen quarry," snow is an endlessly abundant, highly
plastic material that may be used to transform the landscape into a fac-
simile of the artist's imagination, yet it is also a "valueless" commodity
that will eventually melt away, leaving few traces behind. The north wind
or snow-artist's methods are primarily mimetic, as when he uses snow
as plaster to parody human architectural forms. Emerson deploys his
own mimetic techniques in the poem, although fairly unobtrusively: for
example, the long "i" assonance within the poem's first four lines and
long "e" assonance in the second stanza help to suggest, as many readers have noticed, the shrieking wind. The first stanza's blank verse dramatizes the snow's almost stately entrance, which acquires an air of finality from a series of three parallel absolute phrases, and at the stanza's
very end, unstressed syllables retard the line containing the phrase "tumultuous privacy of storm" to match the stranded housemates' immo-
bility. The poem's tempo picks up again in the second stanza as the blank

verse, now largely unencumbered by periods, piles clause upon clause in imitation of the accumulating snow.

In a poem purporting to say that art can imitate nature only slowly and laboriously, Emerson's nimbly mimetic techniques create a fundamental conflict between form and function that threatens to call undue attention to itself. Emerson cleverly circumvents this problem by subverting his reader's objectivity. For example, the poem's point of view undergoes an abrupt shift at the stanza break, as direct address ("Come see") replaces the first stanza's omniscient perspective, inviting the reader to enter the poem and accept a role as the narrator's "housemate." Further, Emerson's use of conversational, blank-verse rhythm helps to disguise his poem as a spontaneous, natural, "nonpoetic" utterance performed both in real time, while the poem is being read, and in the fictive time the poem describes, as the housemates peer out the window.

If we read the poem as being about poetry itself, rather than about art's inability to match nature's capacity for generating forms, it may be seen to resolve itself into a kind of aporia in which a paradoxical kind of romantic artist or poet is being described, one who works in private while remaining firmly fixed within the public's eye. "Tumultuous privacy of storm," the line Dickinson quoted, may then be read as referring not to the forced seclusion of those occupying the snowbound house, but to the unspoken, highly transient bond established between writer and reader in the moment a poem is read. Furthermore, Emerson displaces onto the domineering figure of his personified snowstorm the constraints he himself imposes upon his reader's field of vision to distract him away from thinking more clearly about the poem's internal contradictions. In the first stanza Emerson characterizes the storm as an invading king "driving" over the fields, claiming new territory by inundating it with snow. This martial emphasis is preserved in the second stanza through the presence of such words as "retiring," "bastion," "turret," in the victorious phrase "the world / Is all his own," and in the poem's final lines, where art's slow imitation of the north wind's "night-work" resembles the rebuilding of a sacked town. Finally, while the storm/sculptor works in a creative frenzy witnessed by the housemates (of which the reader is now one) at their window like visitors to an atelier, he is by turns "fierce," "wild," "savage," and "mad." Thus the thread of similarity connecting king to sculptor in the first and second stanzas is an imperiousness bordering on ferocity.

In his disregard for propriety and his "uncivilized" spontaneity, the personified snowstorm in this reversed reading resembles the quasi-Celtic "kingly bard" of Emerson's "Merlin," who achieves artistic greatness by rejecting rationality and obeying intuition, "leaving rule and pale forethought" to "mount to paradise / By the stairway of surprise." Such an unpremeditated art requires an artist who can wield organic forms rather than measured, proportional strains, or, as Emerson writes of his ideal romantic hero-poet, "He shall not his brain encumber / With the coil of rhythm and number," lines that are highly reminiscent of "The Snow-Storm": "—nought cares he / For number or proportion." Emerson's critics have nevertheless called attention repeatedly to an incongruity between the unfettered imagination Emerson extols in "Merlin" and that poem's highly wrought lines and exact rhymes.[13] A similar kind of disjunction between ostensible meaning and poetic praxis threatens to mar "The Snow-Storm," a poem that implicitly invites readers to admire its technical facility even as it purports to say that all human art is inherently derivative, imitative, and overintellectualized. To be successful and make the world "all its own," Emerson's egocentric yet self-doubting artistry must deny its own existence, or behave "as [it] were not," leaving behind only the irrefutable fact of the poem itself, like the storm's fantastic snow sculptures seen the morning after. Any overt emphasis on technique would break the spell and destroy the hermetic, fictive space in which disbelief has been suspended, a condition acknowledged overtly in the reader's acquiescence to becoming a participant in the poem ("Come see") and covertly through the symbol of the snowbound house itself. Then too, there are advantages to be gained by a poet who figuratively covers his own tracks. By exercising his or her craft surreptitiously, a poet may leave an impression that the poem is an autonomous artifact, as "real" within space and time as the object or event it describes. Furthermore, art that denies it is art evokes more surprise and admiration from readers, who emerge abruptly from the fictive reality created by the poem and realize they have, in effect, been hoodwinked.

"Our Snow"

Through its depiction of snow as an artistic medium, through its emphasis on the way the artist's vision transforms and comments upon the empirical world, and especially through the covert way it approaches its own artistry, "The Snow-Storm" may have exerted a subtle, yet profound, influence upon Emily Dickinson.[14] To a poet who had persistent qualms about being publicly identified *as* a poet, yet who increasingly recognized the scope and rarity of her own talent, Emerson's portrait of the artist may have proven—initially, at least—powerfully attractive. Her response is to be found in "It sifts from Leaden Sieves—," or rather in the two vastly different versions of that poem. The first version represents her own rendering of the scene Emerson painted, even to the point of recycling some of his language and images, while her second, written two years after the first and, evidently, *after* "Publication—is the Auction," represents an abrupt shift in attitude that prepared her to send the poem, twenty years later, to Roberts Brothers, with the title "Snow" appended to it.

"It sifts from Leaden Sieves—" appears to have possessed considerable personal significance for Dickinson: not only did she include it among the few pieces she deemed worthy enough to send to Thomas Niles, but she also awarded it pride of place among her own manuscripts, the first version of the poem (written about 1862) leading off fascicle 24. Within that first version, however, any mention of the word "snow" remains conspicuously absent, perhaps because "snow" is the elided answer to Dickinson's verse conundrum:

It sifts from Leaden Sieves—
It powders all the Field—
It fills with Alabaster Wool
The Wrinkles of the Road—

It makes an even face
Of Mountain—and of Plain—
Unbroken Forehead from the East
Unto the East—again—

It reaches to the Fence—
It wraps it, Rail by Rail,
Till it is lost in Fleeces—
It flings a Crystal Vail

On Stump—and Stack—and Stem—
The Summers empty Room—
Acres of Joints—where Harvests were—
Recordless—but for them—

It Ruffles Wrists of Posts—
As Ancles of a Queen—
Then stills it's Artisans—like Swans—
Denying they have been—

Like Emerson, Dickinson personifies the snow, emphasizing its ability to transform the landscape and concluding with a meditation upon the snow's transitoriness. Her poem and his also share particular images, such as the swan, the road filling up with snow, and the veil thrown over the landscape. Nevertheless, the urgency of Emerson's poem is missing from Dickinson's calm, deliberate, repetitive lyric. This difference in mood is matched by a difference in rhythm: Emerson's headlong pentameter line contrasts with Dickinson's more laconic rhymed trimeter, broken up by the tetrameter in each stanza's third line. Finally, whereas Emerson's emphatically masculine snowstorm is, by turns, magisterial, fierce, mocking, and frolicsome, Dickinson's feminine snow is tender, solicitous, maternal, and inclusive. Virtually all of Dickinson's imagery is derived either from the domestic arts or the toilette, for the snow "sifts" like flour from "Sieves," fills wrinkles like a facial powder or vanishing cream, and wraps the fence in "fleeces" sewn into "ruffles." Whereas "veil" in Emerson's poem is a verb, Dickinson's "vail" [*sic*] is a specific garment embellishing such mundane objects as stumps, woodpiles, and corn shocks. From her window the poet's or observer's gaze travels downwards and inwards from the mountains and the horizon to objects more near at hand, such as farmers' fields and fences. Simultaneously, however, a composite portrait is being drawn of a woman—first her face, emphasized by tropes involving makeup; then her forehead, made even by the snow/facial powder; then her limbs, reaching out to wrap the fence in "Fleeces," reemphasized by "Wrists"; finally, her "an[k]les."[15]

The woman represented in this poem must be, I think, Dickinson herself. If Emerson's poem may be considered a window through which he conspiratorially invites the reader to look with him at an artist modeled perhaps upon himself, Dickinson's poem resembles a mirror the author holds up to her own face, making her sole witness to her creative act. As opposed to Emerson's sculptor/architect who assembles the landscape in his poem, Dickinson's artist "dresses" the landscape like a lady's maid, evoking human characteristics latent within the landscape itself such as the "joints" in fields and the "wrists" of fenceposts. Dickinson was already accustomed to picturing the act of writing as "dressing" her thoughts, as she explained in an early letter to Higginson in which she claims not to have had a sufficiently objective perspective of her own work: "While my thought is undressed—I can make the distinction, but when I put them in the Gown—they look alike, and numb" (L404). Dickinson's relatively consistent employment of hymn form in her poems helps to explain why they looked alike to her after she had committed her thoughts to the page. That consistent, even static, format also provides a stylistic equivalent for her predilection for wearing white frocks, an intentional routinization of both the appearance of her thought and her appearance in public (or at least, to the very private "public" to whom Dickinson consented to show her person).

Because snow has its origins in the north, that quadrant of Dickinson's highly localized cosmos the poet habitually associated with a supervisory God, this "habit" (in a double sense) of white or "Uniform of Snow" (no. 126) codified Dickinson's dedication to her task as mediator while simultaneously symbolizing her allegiance to heavenly, rather than mundane, concerns. Thus the poet's religiously derived literary idiom, her physical presence, and her imagined reason for writing all converge in the single image of a snowy garment, and publication, by threatening to contaminate Dickinson's understood rationale for continuing to write, would have its figural equivalent in being "stripped." Significantly, Dickinson is said to have compared the idea of being published to appearing undressed in public (Leyda, 2: 482).

In "It sifts from Leaden Sieves—," the snow-artist's apparent objective is to establish an identity between all the objects in the landscape, so that the snow does not merely *transform* the landscape, it *incorporates* it by making it part of itself. Thus a cardinal difference between Emerson's and Dickinson's poetic methodologies in these poems is that she projects her body and herself into the landscape, accomplishing a transferral of "sacramental" meaning through the vehicle of the poem. Reciprocity between artist and subject reaches a peak in the poem's third stanza, in which a reader may have difficulty sorting out all the various "its." What, finally, gets "lost in Fleeces"—the fence or the snow itself? Confusion between observer and observed is a natural outgrowth of Dickinson's poetic method, which is to bring order to disparate phenomena by making them extensions of the self. Dickinson uses the supremely plastic medium of snow/poetry to make the landscape part of herself, so that what she sees becomes, in the queenly phrase she uses in "Publication— is the Auction," "*Our* Snow," succinctly expressing both her pride of ownership of her poetry and the sense of aggrandizement the act of writing gave her. An urge to incorporate her subject, which may have had its genesis in her experience as a convalescent, when she tried to avoid "consuming" the landscape, also suffuses the tropes Dickinson uses in "It sifts from Leaden Sieves—" and in what she says about the transformative power of metaphor. In Emerson's poem, the snow functions metaphorically by reconciling opposites, so that snow makes the thorn resemble a downy swan, the lowly kennel acquires a classical edifice, and the barnyard gate becomes a castle's turret. In contrast, Dickinson's tropes work to establish the same kind of uniformity and consistency that must have been imposed upon the poet's field of vision whenever the white "vail" of her bandages descended over her eyes again: her snow fills wrinkles and roadways, smooths bumps, and robs fence rails of their individuality.

Although the controlling poetic consciousness in Emerson's poem embellishes the barnyard with fantastic inventions of the imagination while Dickinson radically simplifies the rural countryside by merging with it, both poets express a sense that they achieve a kind of supremacy in their art, characterizing their appropriated landscapes in terms denoting royalty or aristocracy. Both also exercise a kind of romantic tyranny of the "I" over the reader, either immobilizing him in a posture of passive appreciation, in Emerson's poem, or dispensing with him altogether, in Dickinson's. To prevent their poems from becoming purely solipsistic, however, both poets employ strategies of transferral, displacing their own techniques onto nature. By "denying they have been," they successfully sidestep uncomfortable issues posed by a more obvious authorial presence, although Dickinson, by failing to mention the word "snow" in her poem, leaves the door open for a second possible answer to her riddle: not snow, but her own poetic vision.

A "Chill Gift"

So long as she remained unpublished, Dickinson could continue writing poems with omitted centers, or riddles she didn't need to answer because she recited them only to herself. Yet such poems lacked true identities of their own as literary commodities, and Dickinson did ultimately become ambitious enough to want her poems to stand on their own without her help. Although she took the intermediate step of sewing her poems into fascicles, a form of self-publication that permitted her to retain strict control over the "body" of her work, not until she could divorce her poems from heaven, and herself from her poems, would Dickinson finally become comfortable submitting them to an actual publisher. This shift in attitude toward her role as a poet may have evolved over the course of several years, or it may have developed quite suddenly, shortly after her initial outburst of creativity in 1861 and 1862. In any case, the version of "It sifts from Leaden Sieves—" she sent to Thomas Niles at Roberts Brothers in 1879 was a very different poem from the poem we have been examining. Written, probably, in 1864,

only one year after "Publication—is the Auction," her second version of
the poem continues in the vein of self-effacement begun in the first version. Rather than disappearing into the landscape by "clothing" herself
with it, however, Dickinson removes virtually all traces of her own presence:

> It sifts from Leaden sieves
> It powders all the Wood
> It fills with Alabaster Wool
> The Wrinkles of the Road.
> It scatters like the Birds
> Condenses like a Flock
> Like juggler's Flowers situates
> Upon a Baseless Arc—
> It traverses—yet halts—
> Disperses, while it stays
> Then curls itself in Capricorn
> Denying that it was—

This dramatically shorter draft preserves only the first four lines from
the original, with the minimal alteration of "Field" in line 2 back to
"Wood," a variant she had considered using while in the early stages of
writing the poem. No longer does the poem suggest a self-portrait; in
fact, almost all of the previous version's "feminized" details have been
expunged, to be replaced by a compact series of largely unrelated, rapidly shifting similes. Save for the genderless figure of the "juggler," all
references to people have been dropped, and a new emphasis upon animal traits predominates. Finally, the storm described in this poem is
patently more turbulent than its predecessor, a truly "tumultuous" event.
Why might Dickinson have made such far-reaching changes during the
two-year interim between versions, and what is this new poem about?

Dickinson appears to have returned to her protopoem's definition/
riddle structure, interpolating a new series of parallel declarative statements beginning with "It." Yet her attempt to weld new lines to old is
only partially successful. Although the new words "scatter," "juggler,"
and "flower" do rhyme seamlessly with the preexisting "Alabaster" and
"powder," and her modification of "been" in the first version's last line
to "was" in the second version gets a rhyme with "stays," the poem's
underlying topic has changed. Rather than describing how the landscape
has been transformed by snow, this poem describes the kinetic movements of the snow itself; correspondingly, verbs, and not nouns, are

emphasized, and geometric abstractions, rather than specific objects within the landscape. Specific words like "rails" and "Ruffles" in the first version disappear in favor of more abstract terms such as "situates," "Arc," and "traverses," as if the poem were no longer serving to record a remembered scene, but rather to analyze an intellectual problem. The wheeling, circular motion introduced through the image of the juggler's "Arc" is recapitulated at the poem's end as the departing storm curls itself into the constellation Capricorn, on the southern horizon, a movement that is symbolically equivalent to the poem's own passage from its heavenly point of origin in the "north" to a new, independent status in the carnal south.

The overall trend toward abstraction in Dickinson's editing of the poem is consistent with a new conceptual emphasis upon snow itself rather than its effects, or, I propose, upon the mechanism of poetic language rather than the poet's controlling vision. When Dickinson sent this poem to Thomas Niles, one of her very few last-minute changes besides dividing the twelve-line poem into three four-line stanzas and appending a title of "Snow" to it was to replace "Flowers" in line 7 with "Figures," another generality. "Figures" may also be read in the sense of "figures of speech," or tropes, as if Dickinson were commenting on the manipulation of metaphor by a "juggler" or poet who seems to make concrete objects rest upon a "baseless arc" of nothingness. Poetry, and not the poet, performs and then disappears. Like the surreptitious poet invisible in the poem's wings, poetry itself succeeds most completely, Dickinson appears to be saying, while it remains elusive, magical, and intangible. In effect, then, Dickinson "secularized" her first version of "It Sifts," removing the "sacralizing" presence of her own body from it so that it could assume a life of its own. No longer does her "snow" belong to heaven, or even to her; significantly, poetry *itself* now denies that "it was," whereas in the previous version, it had denied that its "Artisans," the shapers of poetry, "have been."

Yet the second draft of Dickinson's poem may also be interpreted as a deliberate evasion of romantic egotism. The earlier draft of "It sifts from Leaden Sieves—" is, like Emerson's poem, a "covert" portrait of the artist in which the power of the artist's vision to transform the empirical world receives major emphasis. The feminine artist whose presence is implied in the poem imposes her own personality upon her subject matter, so that what she describes becomes "hers" by having been made part of her. Only a year or so after writing "It Sifts," however, Dickinson uncovered, in "Publication—is the Auction," an inherent flaw in this approach. In making what she saw part of her, she merely produced more versions of herself, multiple reflections whose tautological confusion of observer and observed, figure and ground results in a romantic solipsism and self-regarding subjectivity similar to that lying beneath the shiny technical veneer of Emerson's poem. Therefore, her second version of "It sifts" represents Dickinson's departure from regarding her poetry as being either sacramental or self-referential: her second snowstorm is not only not feminine, it is scarcely human, her new tropes focusing upon animal movement rather than cosmetics or dress. In her second version the snowstorm is no longer the poet, but poetry itself, a physical force fully integrated with the forces of nature. The umbilical connection between herself and her poem having been severed, Dickinson could finally baptize her poem "Snow" and send it off, ultimately, to Thomas Niles, saying, "I bring you a Chill Gift—My Cricket ["Further in Summer than the Birds"] and the Snow."[16]

Rather than concern herself overmuch with the poet's role, Dickinson learned to concentrate instead upon her poetry, and in this regard she surpassed her "precursor-poet" Emerson,[17] who was too often somewhat intimidated by what he saw as the grave significance of the poet's office. Dazzled by the bardic ideal of the "natural" Sayer, Emerson persuaded himself that the poetic tools he possessed had to be invalid simply because they *were* tools, and he finally transferred his formidable skills in deploying rhythm, symbolism, and ironic paradox to prose, instead. Dickinson, on the other hand, who never doubted she was a real poet, needed to remove herself completely from her poems and escape the prison of her own "tumultuous privacy" to seek the objective readership she once had shunned. Willing, finally, to let her poetry be itself rather than an extension of her body, she released what had been exclusively "*Our* Snow" to the world. It is finally intriguing to wonder whether, when Dickinson made that queenly reference to "her" snow, she may have been distinguishing between her poetry and someone else's—perhaps Emerson's. His poem was already well known among New England households; could she have been explicitly contrasting his "snow poem" with "It sifts from Leaden Sieves—," which she was initially determined to keep locked up in its "garret" of obscurity? If so, her "Chill Gift" of the poem to Thomas Niles many years later may represent a deliberate effort to turn her face away from heaven and join, albeit belatedly, the ranks of recognized American poets from whom she had previously held herself aloof.

Even though only two years separate the very different versions of "It sifts from Leaden Sieves—," Dickinson's separation of her own body from the body of her work probably took place over a number of years. Perhaps the impulse to identify so closely with her work had its origins in her illness, when Dickinson's freedom of movement became so circumscribed that she had to use her poems as prosthetic extensions of herself and of her senses. Then too, all the visible world having been denied her, Dickinson may also have used her imagination to annex physical space, reincarnating it for herself upon the blank white surfaces of her writing paper. As the memory of having been ill receded, however, Dickinson depended less and less upon the perceptual compensations of compound vision or the sacramental aspects of her role as translator of divine meanings. As her poetics matured, she turned her attention progressively outwards, not only toward the possibility of publication but also toward the desirability of using her poems to gain ends much more worldly than those of the poet who had envisioned herself handling, as she worked, the substance of heaven. Now that Dickinson had taken ownership of her work, she no longer needed to dread God's interference or worry about securing his approbation. Similarly, she no longer needed to use her poems to serve primarily as statements of identity, drawing all things to her to make them accessories of the self. Instead, her poems acquired identities of their own, and, as such, they could be assigned specific duties in the real world. They became emissaries not of God's word, or even of the "simple News that Nature told," but rather of the poet's will.

Quite empty, quite at rest,
The Robin locks her Nest, and tries her Wings.
She does not know a Route
But puts her Craft about
For *rumored* Springs—
She does not ask for Noon—
She does not ask for Boon,
Crumbless and homeless, of but one request—
The Birds she lost—

No. 1606, written in March, 1884,
after Lord's death

A CHARTER FOR
HEAVEN ON EARTH

Law, Property, and Provincialism
in Dickinson's Poems and Letters
to Judge Otis Phillips Lord

TO OTIS PHILLIPS LORD, Dickinson wrote, "in Heaven they neither woo nor are given in wooing—what an imperfect place!" (L728). After her affair with Judge Lord commenced, heaven became, in her letters and poems to him, more obviously a heaven of physical love. Having been made acutely aware in middle age both of the transitoriness of earthly experience and of the rarity of physical, passionate love, Dickinson could no longer countenance a heaven without physical substance, either of the earth or of the flesh. The long conflict waged within her poetry between heaven on earth and a deferred, purely conceptual heaven had been decided long before, with an earthly paradise clearly to be preferred. Only in the hope of having the beloved dead, such as her nephew Gilbert Dickinson or her parents, returned to her did Dickinson persist in clinging to her old notion of a consolatory, materialistic heaven. In writings addressed to Lord, however, heaven, which had once been represented by the reconciliation of the two fleshless lovers in "There came a day at summer's full," is differently transmuted into a specific "property" represented by the poet's own body, or by the body of her beloved, or by the "place" created by the union of the lovers' two bodies. Therefore heaven, rather than being a representation of "the imagination of God," as Charles Wadsworth would have had it, became the *body* of the Lord—Lord's body.

Although references to her optical illness faded away from letters and poems written after about 1866, some of the tropes Dickinson had adopted perhaps as a result of having been ill persisted, yet in contexts that are distinctly more positive. For example, the carcerative images we saw her associate in her poems with sickroom confinement reappear in her communications with Judge Lord in a completely different guise, as a form of erotic play.[1] Similarly, imputations of guilt for having committed some sort of trespass that characterized some of her earlier poems referring to the loss of her eyesight are reconfigured into jubilant imagined "plunderings" of the judge's person and property. During her final decade, the impulse toward a desacralizing of her poetry also continued, and the uses to which she put it could hardly be more secular: she employs her poems as instruments of persuasion and seduction, or as mock legal documents. All in all, these letters and poems reveal a matured "version" of Emily Dickinson, who possesses an earthy sense of humor, a disputatious turn of mind, and a keen sense of pride in her identity as poet.

THE "JUDGE LORD BRAND"

Family duties in Amherst and a busy docket in Boston compelled Emily Dickinson and Judge Otis Phillips Lord to pursue their autumnal love affair largely on paper rather than in person.[2] They maintained a weekly correspondence of which only scraps survive, all written by her to him, yet these few remnants show that Dickinson and Lord negotiated at length with each other over such issues as how much sexual license she would grant him during his visits, if and when their relationship might be formalized, and whether she might ultimately move into Lord's house at Salem.[3] Serious as all these topics were, the negotiations themselves are often couched in facetious metaphors based upon the law, an area in which Dickinson possessed considerable lay expertise. Drawing upon her knowledge of the law in her communications with Judge Lord was a rhetorical strategy that may have originated in a series of humorous poems Dickinson began writing during the early 1860s, almost two decades before the affair began. In them, Dickinson's use of legal terms and concepts prepared the ground for her later use of them in her letters to Judge Lord.

Although we cannot be certain that he was indeed her lone, intended audience for these poems, circumstantial evidence and the frequency with which certain themes recur argue that she at least had Judge Lord in mind. The poems usually describe comic legal disputes over titles to rural properties or bold incursions made into rural spaces by characters who had once been tenants, and they conclude, typically, with an entreaty to some unnamed authority to determine who is the property's rightful owner and who the trespasser is. Dickinson apparently deployed these legal and rural tropes as part of a campaign to combat Lord's real or imagined disdain for all things provincial, including herself. Attracted to the poems initially by Dickinson's use of what she called "the Judge Lord brand" of humor and by the intrinsic interest of the legal issues she raised, Lord may also have been persuaded to listen more attentively to what Dickinson had to say about the advantages and drawbacks of small-town life, as well as what she had to tell him about the importance, to her, of being a poet. Many years later, after she and Judge Lord had begun exchanging love letters, the subjects of rural property ownership, the legal concept of trespass, and Dickinson's demands for Lord's respect reappear in a new, much more overtly erotic context.

Dickinson's affection for Otis Phillips Lord dated from a period during which he became, according to Millicent Todd Bingham, her father's "best friend" (3). Edward Dickinson probably met the slightly younger

Lord shortly after the latter's appointment to the Superior Court of Massachusetts in 1859. Mutual interests drew the men together: they shared an old-fashioned Calvinistic morality, conservative (even "hunkerish") Whig political convictions, and a deep concern for what today would be called "law and order" issues, including all manner of criminal behavior ranging from public drunkenness to incitement to riot. Lord soon acquired a reputation for the severity of his sentences as well as for being, in Richard B. Sewall's words, "notoriously hard on divorce seekers" (648).[4]

Work or pleasure brought the judge to the Amherst area frequently, either to preside over trials in Northampton or to attend alumni functions at Amherst College, from which he had graduated in 1832, when Dickinson was only a year old. On some of these occasions Lord and his wife Elizabeth called at the Homestead, where they were received by Mrs. Dickinson and her adult daughters, whom Lord called his "Playthings" (L727). With Emily he engaged initially in what Martha Dickinson Bianchi called "adventures in conversation," or witty banter that arose, quite possibly, out of an almost comic inability to comprehend each other (*Face to Face*, 36). His sense of humor may have been what first endeared the judge to Dickinson, who told him, "you have a good deal of glee . . . in your nature's corners" (L695), and, according to Bianchi, Dickinson labeled the judge's unique strain of humor "the Judge Lord brand" (*Life and Letters*, 69–70). Inferring from what we know about Judge Lord, we could summarize "the Judge Lord brand" of humor by saying that it involved a fondness for the slightly risqué, deflations of overbearing authority (especially men's over women's), and stories told at the expense of stereotypically rural New Englanders. All of these themes merit further examination for any light they might shed on the basis of Dickinson's relationship with Lord.

Perhaps as a result of having witnessed the entire gamut of human behavior in his courtroom, the judge apparently enjoyed the occasional bawdy joke. According to at least one colleague, he could be "piquant and racy in conversation" (Bingham, 36–37). A predilection for indelicate subject matter also helps to explain the Judge's special fondness for the passage in *Hamlet* describing Ophelia's garland-weaving before her death:[5]

> Therewith fantastic garlands did she make
> Of crow-flowers, nettles, daisies, and long purples
> That liberal shepherds give a grosser name,
> But our cull-cold maids do dead men's fingers call them.[6]

While Dickinson thoroughly enjoyed this roguish side of the judge's character, she remained more than a little intimidated by his stern public demeanor and rigorous standards of professional conduct. As she said in eulogizing him, "Calvary and May wrestled in his Nature" (L861), a paradoxical combination which, as Richard Sewall points out, could just as well have been applied to her own father.[7]

Emily Dickinson and Judge Lord both enjoyed poking fun at pomposity, perhaps because he had a reputation for being a stuffed shirt himself on occasion,[8] yet was good-natured enough to laugh about it. They scorned those who wielded power without exercising common sense,[9] and such is the tenor of two comic anecdotes they exchanged early in their correspondence. According to Bianchi, they "relished" the first of these fictitious stories, a dialogue between a doctor and a nurse, for "its portentous inference lacking fact" (*Life and Letters,* 70):

> "Nurse," says [the doctor], kind of high and haughty-like, "what is your opinion?"
> "Doctor," says [the Nurse], kind of low and deferential-like, "I am of your opinion."
> And what was his opinion? asked the listener.
> "Lord bless you, my dear [says the Nurse], he hadn't any!"

Dickinson wrote upon the second anecdote, a newspaper clipping she kept pinned to her workbox, "Returned by Judge Lord with approval!"

> NOTICE! My wife Sophia Pickles having left my bed and board without just cause or provocation, I shall not be responsible for bills of her contracting.
>
> *SOLOMON PICKLES*

> NOTICE! I take this means of saying that Solomon Pickles has had no bed or board for me to leave for the last two months.
>
> *SOPHIA PICKLES*

The women in these anecdotes sarcastically challenge men's fitness to rule in either the professional or the domestic spheres: the nurse abruptly reveals that the doctor is an uninformed quack, while Sophia Pickles's *quid pro quo* with her husband reinterprets his public announcement of her desertion of him as an admission of his own shiftlessness. Implicit within both stories is the idea that women should not subordinate themselves to men, a point that will reappear in a slightly different semblance in poems Dickinson may have written expressly for Judge Lord's benefit.

The third component of the "Judge Lord brand" of humor, a satirical treatment of rural New England manners, is exemplified by the second anecdote, which invites us to laugh at Solomon and Sophia Pickles, nineteenth-century equivalents of Ma and Pa Kettle, not only for their unsophisticated airing of their dirty laundry in public, but also for their bickering over an insignificant amount of personal property. Nevertheless, the anecdote does not gainsay the legitimacy of making property ownership a precondition for continuing normal marital relations. In fact, Sophia Pickles's common-sense interpretation of "bed and board" reifies a domestic arrangement which had become lost amid the abstractions of her husband's legal boilerplate. For Dickinson herself, preserving domestic happiness was always contingent upon possessing actual, tangible property, and her communications with Judge Lord refer repeatedly to the susceptibility of rural domestic spaces to violation by intruders, loss through bankruptcy, or occupation by uninvited guests.

The Rustic Life

The "Judge Lord brand" of humor is much in evidence in a poem Dickinson wrote as early as 1863, "The Judge is like the Owl—." At the time, her friendship with the judge was almost certainly still platonic,[10] yet the poem is already overtly flirtatious, and the pose Dickinson strikes seems calculated to pique the judge's interest in her (no. 699):

> The Judge is like the Owl—
> I've heard my Father tell—
> And Owls do build in Oaks—
> So here's an Amber Sill—
>
> That slanted in my Path—
> When going to the Barn—
> And if it serve You for a House—
> Itself is not in vain—
>
> About the price—'tis small—
> I only ask a Tune
> At Midnight—Let the Owl select
> His favorite Refrain.

Dickinson deliberately misconstrues her father's clichéd reference to the judge's "owlish" sagacity and offers him appropriate "nesting" material consisting of an "amber sill," or a spray of oak leaves gathered on her way to the barn. Yet posing as a country ingenue who takes her father's figure of speech only too literally permits Dickinson to mock both men for having underestimated her. Further, by rejecting her father's simplistic summary of the judge's character and then extending her own invitation to him to meet her at midnight, Dickinson makes an implicit claim to the intellectual respect and the romantic prerogatives due a grown woman. Daring the judge to treat her either as a "Plaything" or an adult, Dickinson teasingly asks him in the final stanza to compensate her for the "Sill" of oak leaves, or rather for the poem itself.[11]

Because Judge Lord evidently enjoyed having his judicial gravity twitted, quite likely he congratulated Dickinson for her little sally. Yet the poem is more than just a *bon mot*, and Dickinson is asking for more than just the judge's applause. "The Judge is like the Owl— " is actually a complex work of self-representation that establishes, through an urbane manipulation of persona and tone, the intelligence and sophistication of someone who transcends her environment even as it affirms, through accurate naturalistic observations, the narrator's rural origins. Accordingly, even though Dickinson invites the judge to laugh at her for her rusticity, she asserts the validity of country life; indeed, the bough she offers the judge is symbolic of the domestic happiness to be found in a rural setting. Attached to the bough, the poem becomes a kind of legal document, specifically, an offer to sell. If the judge agrees to her terms, he can buy a "country retreat" for a song, yet the "price" being negotiated actually involves his entire reevaluation of her, both as someone who, although of the country, possessed talents and abilities consistent with a far more cosmopolitan outlook, and as a mature woman capable of bargaining with him independently on her own terms.

Dickinson's provincialism nevertheless remained, at least in her eyes, a potentially formidable barrier between her and the judge. Unsure herself at times whether she truly "belonged" in the country, Dickinson used her poems as vehicles to dramatize her ambivalence about living in the comparative isolation of western Massachusetts. In them, she converted doubts about her own provincialism into legal debates, often employing the "Judge Lord brand" of humor and mobilizing a cast of nonhuman rustic characters to ensure that an ironic distance would be maintained between herself and the poems' narrators. "Alone and in a circumstance," composed in about 1870, is written in this vein (no. 1167):

Alone and in a circumstance
Reluctant to be told
A spider on my reticence
Assiduously crawled

And so much more at Home than I
Immediately grew
I felt myself a visitor
And hurriedly withdrew

Revisiting my late abode
With articles of claim
I found it quietly assumed
As a Gymnasium
Where Tax asleep and Title off
The inmates of the Air
Perpetual presumption took
As each were special Heir—
If any strike me on the street
I can return the Blow—
If any take my property
According to the Law
The Statute is my Learned friend
But what redress can be
For an offense nor here nor there
So not in Equity—
That Larceny of time and mind
The marrow of the Day
By spider, or forbid it Lord
That I should specify.

The poem's subject matter is certainly earthy enough to amuse the judge: it is someone's description of being interrupted by a spider while using the privy.[12] The narrator, who had beaten a hasty retreat, returns armed with broom and dustpan, only to discover that the privy has been occupied during the interval by even more spiders and insects. The rest of the poem then becomes a mock problem in civil procedure, an appeal to an offstage judge to hear the case. Even though the spider's intrusion has not technically robbed the narrator of any property, she protests she has lost "time and mind," intangible goods for which she might ask compensation from a court of chancery.[13]

In addition to its inherently comic setting, the poem depends for its humor on a county court stereotype of the timid countrywoman compelled to appear, knees shaking, upon the witness stand. In the poem's narrative, which is constructed as a deposition, the witness-narrator testifies she was in circumstances "reluctant to be told," as if modesty prevented her from specifying for the court where she was when the alleged larceny took place. At the end of the poem she also asks the court's indulgence for having refused, out of squeamishness, to name the particular bugs that had molested her.[14] Nevertheless, a contrast in tone similar to what we saw in "The Judge is like the Owl—" lets the reader know that the narrator's diffidence is not meant to be taken at face value. The poem's diction and style are insistently urbane, wittily combining puns such as "reticence" (for "residence") with ironical euphemisms such as "articles of claim" for broom and dustpan. Such felicities of speech signal the presence of a keen intelligence that is so sharply at odds with the narrator's putative backwoods origin that we are clearly meant to distinguish the poem's author from its narrator.

The poem's underlying conceit also weaves a sophisticated legal argument about property ownership. The narrator compares the privy to an abandoned residence now occupied by squatters whom the rightful owner is attempting to evict, even though her own "claim" to the property is tenuous, since she has failed to keep up the taxes on it. Her uninvited tenants have, she complains, vandalized the property by treating it more like a "Gymnasium" than a residence and by behaving in general as if they owned the place. Unable to make a statutory claim at law or an equitable claim in chancery, the speaker comically vents her frustration at the futility of her situation.

Although it cannot be proven indisputably that Dickinson intended this poem for Judge Lord, the narrator's appeal for redress from someone she calls "Lord" is provocative, for two reasons. First, the poem's rural situation and broad humor are decidedly of the "Judge Lord brand." Second, because the poem is framed as an appeal to a judge, "Lord" suggests to mind the British legal honorific "milord," a possible punning reference to Judge Lord's name. In her later love letters to the judge, Dickinson showed she was perfectly capable of contriving puns based upon the judge's surname. For example, in the following letter scrap, written almost a decade after "Alone and in a circumstance," Dickinson compares Judge Lord to Christ on the cross, while characterizing herself as one of the two crucified thieves:

> I know you [are] acutely weary, yet cannot refrain from taxing you with an added smile—and a pang in it. Was it to him the Thief cried "Lord remember me when thou comest into thy Kingdom," and is it to us that he replies, "This Day thou shalt be with me in Paradise"?
> The Propounder of Paradise must indeed possess it—(L754)

If the Judge is "Lord," heaven has now become Salem, Massachusetts, where Lord resided, and Dickinson is the "thief" suing for admission there. Paradise was to be "possessed," in both a sexual and a proprietary sense, and Dickinson appears to be daring the judge both to "own" her and be "owned."

An assumption that "Alone and in a circumstance" was indeed written for Judge Lord's benefit renders the poem's meaning somewhat clearer: Dickinson is expressing her ambivalence about her rustic heritage by alluding to the legal concept of adverse possession, or "squatter's rights." Definitively humorous symbol of everything rural, the privy represents the backwoods culture in which Dickinson does not feel entirely at home, yet which she cannot bring herself to renounce. Significantly, the narrator feels herself to be both victim and intruder, property owner and uninvited "visitor" suddenly alienated from a setting she had once occupied comfortably. Dickinson's alienation from her environment finds an analog in the disposition of her legal complaint, which fails to qualify for a hearing in any existing courtroom. Or, to view her situation from the court's standpoint, her alienation has its counterpart in the "judge's" inability to provide a remedy, for the case is in nature, outside of his "jurisdiction."

WITHOUT LEGAL REMEDY

Other poems possibly written for Lord's benefit are similarly framed as legal questions for which, even though they have been brought to a judge's attention, no legal answer exists. Despite Lord's and Dickinson's mutual admiration for order and common sense, she was capable of challenging the epistemological limits of the law in order to affirm the inherent value and mystery of nature, or that portion of rural life Dickinson treasured most and for which she claimed to be able to speak with some authority. For example, in this next poem, Dickinson uses a semiserious discussion of the dangers attendant upon rural isolation to impugn the law's analytical methods (no. 1202, ca. 1871):

The Frost was never seen —
If met, too rapid passed,
Or in too unsubstantial Team —
The Flowers notice first

A Stranger hovering round
A Symptom of alarm
In Villages remotely set
But search effaces him

Til some retrieveless Night
Our Vigilance at waste
The Garden gets the only shot
That never could be traced.

Unproved is much we know—
Unknown the worst we fear—
Of Strangers is the Earth the Inn
Of Secrets is the Air—

To analyze perhaps
A Philip would prefer
But Labor vaster than myself
I find it to infer.

This miniature murder mystery portrays the autumn frost as a "stranger" who progressively infiltrates outlying "villages" of vegetation before ultimately invading the "town" and murdering its flower-inhabitants in their "beds." Although the flowers realize that something is amiss and give the alarm not by barking, like watchdogs, but by wilting, each time the homeowner searches for evidence, his or her own steps efface all traces of the frost's "footprints." Finally, one October night after the family has retired, a hard frost destroys the garden with a single, untraceable "shot," and the culprit escapes.

Traveling throughout Massachusetts on official business would have familiarized Judge Lord with crimes committed in remote villages as well as with the difficulties involved in finding witnesses and amassing evidence. Frightened towns would buzz with rumors about suspicious strangers passed upon the road or put up at the local inn, or about deep, secret plots which, especially in the wake of Lincoln's assassination, seemed to be hatching everywhere. But because the mystery Dickinson points to in her poem is natural and not criminal, her use of terms drawn from law enforcement to describe a normal, annual event ultimately serves to interrogate, or even parody, the aims of man-made law. For example, although the frost's arrival in town is imperceptible supposedly because his "Team" is too slow or too fast or too "insubstantial," all these *prima facie* conclusions are raised simply to show how laughable they are. The entire Earth is an "Inn" housing mysteries we will never understand, Dickinson says, capitalizing upon her small-town experience to show that all human beings are as isolated within the universe as the townsfolk of any lonely hamlet.

At the poem's end the speaker refuses to speculate any further, citing her own purported inadequacies as a detective and deferring to an external authority, a "Philip," to unravel the mystery. One indication that Dickinson customarily addressed Judge Lord by his first name may be present in her possession of a ring, mentioned by Jay Leyda in *The Years and Hours of Emily Dickinson*, that had the name "Philip" engraved within it (1: lix). Yet Thomas Johnson and other commentators have identified "Philip" in this poem not as Judge Lord, but as the disciple Philip, who asked Jesus for proof of God's presence in him. I think that Dickinson is probably referring in this line to both the judge *and* the disciple, knowing that Lord would catch her biblical allusion. It is worth noting that John 14: 8 reads, "*Philip* saith unto him, *Lord*, shew us the Father, and it sufficeth us" (emphasis added).

If Dickinson did indeed intend this poem for "Phil Lord," however, her deference is ironic, for no civil authority could ever "solve" this "crime," nor, for that matter, would anyone wish to have it solved. Natural and transcendental events often exceed man's powers of analysis, Dickinson says, but, by doing so, they remind us of the importance of wonder, or even dread. Because such subjects fall more properly within the poet's domain rather than the jurist's, or even the scientist's, Dickinson's message to Lord would appear to be that, despite her disclaimer in the poem about her own limitations as a thinker, the heuristic method implicit in her poetics was equal or superior to the empirical, evidentiary procedures of law.

Dickinson's almost proprietary interest in nature prompted her to sympathize with her nonhuman protagonists, despite their occasional repulsiveness. The spiders in the privy, for example, are to be admired for their industry and initiative, and their status as tenants rivals the poet's own. Similarly, in the following poem, Dickinson pays homage to the rat (no. 1356, ca. 1876):

The Rat is the concisest Tenant.
He pays no Rent.
Repudiates the Obligation—
On Schemes intent

Balking our Wit
To sound or circumvent—
Hate cannot harm
A Foe so reticent—
Neither Decree prohibit him—
Lawful as Equilibrium.

As someone whose own habits of reticence and conciseness were a by-word among her friends and family, Dickinson had ample reason to feel an oblique kinship with the rat, who lives according to an idiosyncratic set of rules as internally consistent as the laws of physics. While he abides by them, the rat remains as immune to criticism as "Jack Frost" is to criminal law in "The Frost was never seen—," secure within his sphere of subrational activity as Dickinson was within her own creative element. Even though the rat "trespasses" within our households, he, like the spiders, enjoys a legitimate claim to the premises that laws and decrees cannot erode.

The rats, spiders, and owls in these poems are Dickinson's surrogates for herself, indigenous yet exotic creatures whose behavior or appearance may inspire disgust in observers who fail to comprehend them in the context of their natural habitats. Such is the theme of yet another poem written during the 1870s about a household pest, no. 1388:

> Those Cattle smaller than a Bee
> That herd upon the eye—
> Whose tillage is the passing Crumb—
> Those Cattle are the Fly—
> Of Barns for Winter—blameless—
> Extemporaneous stalls
> They found to our objection—
> On eligible walls—
> Reserving the presumption
> To suddenly descend
> And gallop on the Furniture—
> Or odiouser offend—
> Of their peculiar calling
> Unqualified to judge
> To Nature we remand them
> To justify or scourge—

That this poem was written for Judge Lord's benefit is suggested by its ironic use of legal terminology ("objection," "judge," "remand") and by its implicit reference to a cause of action with which the judge would have been only too familiar, the widespread country complaint of livestock vaulting fences to graze upon someone else's property. Then too, the barnyard humor is very much of the "Judge Lord brand," broad and scatological, if by "odiouser offend" Dickinson means *flyspecks*. As in previous poems, attention is trained here upon creatures ordinarily thought of as vermin who "trespass" on our domestic spaces. Like the rat, however, houseflies live in innocence of human laws, so that they are "blameless" of stalls and have a "peculiar calling" all their own. Yet the plea for mercy, or at least for understanding, Dickinson makes for her "clients" in "Those Cattle smaller than a Bee" could be intended as much for her own sake as for theirs. Her own "peculiar calling" of writing poetry makes her a natural advocate for all marginalized rural creatures such as flies, errant cattle, rats, or spiders, and their "rude" behavior in her poems indirectly reflects her own fears that Judge Lord might perceive her as rural, fumbling, and peculiar. Her apparent ungainliness, Dickinson managed to imply, lay at least as much within the eye of the beholder as it did within the figure she cut either in public or in private.

"INCARCERATE ME IN YOURSELF"

By appealing to Lord directly as a judge in her poems, Dickinson could not only defend herself, but gently prod him toward reexamining his own prejudices about poets, poetry, and provincial culture. She may have continued using her poems to entertain and educate the judge right up until the death of his wife in late 1877. After that time, however, Dickinson suddenly no longer needed to use her poems as a subtle form of propaganda, or as she herself said in a letter written probably in 1878, shortly after the affair began, "My lovely Salem smiles at me. I seek his Face so often—but *I have done with guises*" (L614, emphasis added). Yet the same legalistic paradigms she had used in her poems to Lord continue to appear. For example, one letter uses the trope of "trespassing" to tell Lord that concerns about how he regarded her rusticity had begun weighing heavily upon her mind long before they became lovers:

> Our Life together was long forgiveness on your part toward me.
> The trespass of my rustic Love upon your Realms of Ermine, only
> a Sovereign could forgive—(L727)

Here the Judge's ermine-trimmed robe is more than just a badge of office: it is the regalia for the "realm" he rules over, that is, his entire identity as a judge on the Massachusetts Supreme Court,[15] an identity which, Dickinson may have feared, Lord might consider compromised by a public admission of their affair. Yet her reference to his robe possesses a sexual dimension as well, for it is also a garment upon which Dickinson has "trespassed" in seeking to embrace him, and virtually all of the legal tropes in Dickinson's surviving letters to Lord are similarly freighted with new, more manifestly erotic meanings.

As she had in her poems, Dickinson continued to address Lord in her letters directly as a judge, but rather than "consulting" him for a legal opinion, she began casting herself as a "felon" appearing before his bench as part of a game of sexual role-playing in which crime and punishment become delightful pastimes. Her passion for him threatens to "bankrupt" her, Dickinson tells Lord, asking, "Will you punish me? 'Involuntary Bankruptcy,' how could that be Crime?" or "Incarcerate me in yourself—rosy penalty" (L615). Sometimes the roles are reversed, and she sits in judgment upon him: "my Naughty one, too seraphic Naughty, who can sentence you?" (L616). Considering the judge's age, it is not surprising, perhaps, that a vestige of filial love may even be discerned within this game of mild domination and submissiveness, for in one letter she addresses Lord as "Papa," saying, "Papa has still many Closets that Love has never ransacked" (L728).

Thus incarceration, rather than suggesting the claustrophobia-inducing "prison" in which Dickinson had been compelled to spend her time while recovering from her optical illness, is transformed instead in these letters into a means of forcefully occupying a highly coveted piece of "property." A house to be broken into as well as a jail to which she might happily be confined, the judge's person becomes a physical edifice to which Dickinson lays siege. "I have been in your Bosom," she was to write, proud to accomplish at last the invasion she had desired to make for so long (L727). Furthermore, the concept of interdicted property is pressed into service in these poems and letters as a shared metaphor Dickinson and Lord could use while negotiating the sexual terms of their relationship. For example, in a rough draft of a letter she wrote after Lord's wife had died, Dickinson describes her body and Lord's as "territories" that might be conjoined to form a new "country": "—we went to sleep as if it were a country—let us make it one—we could make it one, my native Land—my Darling come oh *be* a patriot now . . . Oh nation of the soul thou hast thy freedom now" (L615). The independent "continent" Dickinson had once sought to establish through the medium of her poetry has now evolved into a republic, specifically the American republic, liberated from the "imperialistic" power of Lord's late wife.

But this new "country" required its own charter, a set of legally defined property rights to each others' bodies upon which both could agree. While tantalizing Lord repeatedly with the possibility of intimacy, Dickinson professed her reluctance to grant him full access to the "property" of her body before their marriage negotiations had been finalized. Until then she barred him from "trespassing" upon the country meadow she used to symbolize her own body: "The 'Stile' is God's—My Sweet One—for your great sake—not mine—I will not let you cross—but it is all your's, and when it is right I will lift the Bars, and lay you in the Moss—" (L617). Significantly, Dickinson's rusticity has now become an embellishment rather than an impediment, a prize to be won and enjoyed rather than a fault for which she had to make excuses.

Yet nothing ever came of Dickinson's and Lord's utopian scheme of living together upon ground held in common. Even though both parties appear to have been amenable to the idea of marriage, events frustrated their plans repeatedly. Emily and Lavinia became much involved in nursing their mother, who suffered a stroke in 1875 and required virtually constant attention until she died in November 1882. Soon afterwards, perhaps within a week,[16] Dickinson wrote her famous reply to Judge Lord's humorous suggestion that she call herself "Emily 'Jumbo,'" proposing instead that they amend it to "Emily Jumbo Lord" (L747). Judge Lord's response to this pointed hint was probably encapsulated in a letter sent the following month, to which she in turn made this reply, in early December 1882:

> You said with loved timidity in asking me to your dear Home, you would "try not to make it unpleasant." So delicate a diffidence, how beautiful to see! I do not think a Girl extant has so divine a modesty.
>
> You even call me to your Breast with apology! Of what must my poor Heart be made? . . . the tender Priest of Hope need not allure his Offering—'tis on his altar ere he asks. (L753)

Nearly two decades after she had first offered Judge Lord a "house" of oak leaves, after she had used her poems to justify and defend her own provincialism, Dickinson may have finally been preparing to leave the Homestead and create a "paradise" in Salem with Judge Lord. The "stile of 'Pearl'" over which Dickinson had hoped to be lifted in "'Arcturus' is his other name—" had matured into the "Bars" Dickinson herself would lift to allow the judge "lawful" access to her own person.

But Dickinson and the judge had already delayed too long. In poor health already, Lord was felled by a fatal stroke in March 1884, only a little more than a year after inviting the poet to live with him. Dickinson, already seriously ill herself with kidney disease, would die soon afterwards, in 1886. At her funeral, Lavinia Dickinson placed two heliotropes in her sister's hands to take "to Judge Lord," apparently in appreciation of Dickinson's prolonged efforts to join the judge in some mutually satisfactory location. Thus the twin impulses toward a heaven on earth and toward secularization that had begun characterizing Dickinson's poems in the years after her illness went into remission reached their logical terminus: physical, temporal love had completely supplanted poetry as the "eucharist" to be consumed, and rather than journey toward a cold, forbidding Lord of Hosts who always managed to remain somehow out of sight, Dickinson could imagine herself, at her death, setting out in the direction already taken by the highly tangible, emphatically physical Judge Lord.

CONCLUSION

EVEN AFTER Emily Dickinson's eyes apparently no longer troubled her, attitudes formed by the experience of being ill persisted as ingrained modes of thought and avenues of expression. She remained fascinated for the rest of her life not only by differences between the seen and the unseen, but also by the problem that, as Dickinson phrased it in poem no. 1071, "Perception of an object costs / Precise the Object's loss— "; that is, the act of looking always entails a forfeiture. Dickinson goes on in that poem to explain that perceptions are inherently worth more than the objects perceived because their value is directly proportional to the degree of difficulty involved in achieving them, while the "Object Absolute," she says, "is nought—." The instant removal of the objects of perception from view is powerfully evocative of Dickinson's experience as a patient, when gazing briefly at the sun could result in being forbidden to look outside again for days on end. The perceptual paradox of looking for sustained periods of time upon an unwitnessable object, as if one were to measure the sun, became the central problem Dickinson tried to address in much of her poetry.

While she was ill, her poems became adjuncts of the self that Dickinson could wield to accomplish ends she was prevented from achieving physically. Her poems compensated her not just for the loss of her perceptual freedom but also for the diminution of her physical space. A consideration of Dickinson's poems as tools also reminds us that, while the poet remained ill, writing presented her with a form of useful work. Prohibited for a time from making her customary contribution to the Dickinson household beyond performing such rudimentary chores as "bang[ing] the spice for cake" (L302), Dickinson could still call writing her special area of expertise. By characterizing herself as a laborer, as when, for example, she says "Myself was formed—a Carpenter—," Dickinson even distances herself somewhat, at times, from the province of art. Although she admits in "I cannot dance upon my Toes—" to having an aptitude for dance and in "I would not paint—a picture—" a susceptibility to the splendors of pictorial art and music, she is actually more likely to invite comparisons in her poems between herself and scientists or attorneys, professionals who seek the truth in either the physical world or in society. These forms of self-identification reach to the very core of a poetics based upon perception, in which to see truly is to see well. Although "compound vision" resembles neither the scientific method nor the Socratic, it nevertheless attempts in its own way to get at the truth behind appearances. Dickinson's emphasis upon professionalism also indirectly reflects a growing sense that, as poet, she played a role in society as well as in eternity. Through her poems she spoke not just for herself but for others, too, as when, in "Had we our senses," she universalizes her state of sensory deprivation during illness to warn her readers that, unless they were careful, they might impose upon themselves a state of willful insensitivity to the beauties of the world.

Dickinson's various responses to illness, as recorded through the medium of her poems, reflect an overall shift from feeling victimized to taking an active role in her own recovery and salvation. When her eyes first began failing her, Dickinson interpreted illness Calvinistically as a divine punishment meted out to her for having loved the visible, earthly paradise too well. As she fought to regain unlimited eyesight, Dickinson somewhat desperately concluded that she could retain the visual world only by affecting to renounce it, generating a cognitive dissonance in her poetry that manifests itself through manifold layers of irony, through the voices of her various personae, and through her doomed attempt to develop an imagination independent of visual imagery. As her cyclical convalescences repeated themselves, however, Dickinson manufactured a more optimistic mythologic explanation for having fallen ill that portrayed God not as her Punisher, but rather as a doctorlike Preceptor who instructed her in the ways of seeing "infinitely." Concurrently, Dickinson became increasingly sensible of intrinsic conceptual and artistic strengths that could help to counterbalance her physical weakness. Although her eyes were "finite," she had an extraordinary "gift" for writing poetry, an indication to her that God had chosen her for a special mission. Her poetry, and not her eyes, became the new locus for interactions between the mundane and the divine, and words themselves could be substituted for empirical phenomena Dickinson had once "consumed" during the perceptual binge which had, she came to believe, precipitated her optical problems. Then too, the idea of "consumption" metamorphoses smoothly into communion, or the assimilation of charged fragments of divinity. Thus the ceremony of the sacrament became Dickinson's preferred analog for her conversion or transubstantiation of potentially destructive meaning into the less hazardous medium of language.

Yet by adopting this paradigm of communion for her activities as poet, Dickinson also necessarily surrendered some degree of control over her literary productions. As an exponent of compound vision, Dickinson had to represent herself to herself as being continually receptive to intervention by supernatural agencies whose presence she could only intuit, at best. Thus Dickinson may have envisioned herself as collaborating, over the course of several years, with the same supernatural forces that had once inflicted intense pain upon her eyes. Still, Dickinson never completely submerged her awareness of her own merit as a poet to a religiously determined code of self-abnegation and obedience. Instead, she used elements of a myth contrived to explain her own existence as an artist to justify, retroactively, methods for writing poetry that she had already realized worked well for her, as when, for example, she rationalized her policy of choosing between several variants as the nomination of the "elect" from among several candidates hoping to enter heaven.

Indeed, a poem itself was a little heaven, a paradise of order established within a "wilderness" of white, dimensionless space. The promised land that Dickinson feared she would be prohibited from entering, even after having achieved, like Moses, one tantalizing glimpse of Canaan, she could nevertheless shape for herself out of the infinitely plastic "snow" of poetry. As Dickinson matured as a poet, however, the sacramental model for understanding both what she did as a poet and her mediatory position between heaven and earth began to portend an ultimate artistic stagnation. First, the centrality of her position as translator threatened to produce a numbing sameness of outlook born of subjectivity, which, in its most extreme form, could manifest itself as a romantic "tyranny of the I" similar to that which lay just beneath the surface of Emerson's "The Snow-Storm." Secondly, as Dickinson grew older and became more interested in "Disseminating [her own] Circumference—" by lighting the "lamp" of her poetry, she perhaps realized that poems, in order to survive, had to be divorced not only from heaven, but from their authors, as well. Put another way, poems had to be trusted to succeed on their own, like adult children removed from their parents' monitoring presence. This attribution of increased independence to her poems as self-sufficient artifacts liberated Dickinson to use them in achieving a new spectrum of artistic ends. Nevertheless, these uses often remain contiguous with her previous employment of her poetics to make her art the locus of her interactions with God. Thus, for example, in her poems and letters written for Judge Lord, the poet reclaims and transforms the physicality of material desire that had characterized her quest for God and Paradise from the beginning.

The evolutionary pattern of Dickinson's poetics demonstrates a progressive entering of the world, even as she physically withdrew into her family's house. For this reason, I think it is a mistake to interpret Dickinson's self-seclusion as a renunciation. Instead, her withdrawal was consistent with modes of behavior already established during young adulthood, when illness inured Dickinson to staying at home and taught her to exploit all the possibilities for perception and self-expression that were available there. Her poetics are finally those of simple survival, for she continued to write in spite of obstacles which continually arose to block her progress. In the bucolic Amherst of her youth, for example, Dickinson had comparatively little incentive to develop into a poet of merit. Save for a few friends such as Benjamin Newton or Susan Dickinson, she lacked local literary mentors or exemplars of sufficient caliber either to recognize her talent for what it was or to stimulate it by commending innovative contemporary authors to her attention. Later, during her optical illness, the simple physical act of writing may have presented problems for Dickinson, and her imprisonment in the state of sensory deprivation that was her sickroom threatened as well to cut off her access to the visual stimuli her imagination required to retain its vividness. Language itself was menaced with extinction when its symbolic value was fully realized and Dickinson suffered the vision for which her words had been, she believed, only the forerunners. Still another motivation to continue writing was eliminated by the patriarchy's refusal to believe that women could ever become noteworthy poets, as well as by Dickinson's own resistance to being published.

Although Dickinson could have found any number of reasons for lapsing into silence, she did not, of course. Having become accustomed to surmounting obstacles, Dickinson lifted up her poetics again and again to respond to new challenges. Her poems often seem to have emerged suddenly from the midst of crisis or to have been dashed off during stolen hours or minutes, and this furtive quality gives Dickinson's poetry a sense not so much of spontaneity, but of great urgency. Hers are the poetics of the imperiled interval, the moment of sunrise before dawn bursts upon the landscape, or the long waning of sunlight before the curtain of a real or an artificial night falls across the poet's eyes. The most characteristic time in Dickinson's poems is the instant right before the end, the wobble which precedes a plunge, the final throes of hypothermia. Although Dickinson's poetics do not, as a whole, concern themselves with the Day of Reckoning, they do, by constantly anticipating their own nonbeing, speak repeatedly and reverentially of last things.

NOTES

INTRODUCTION

1. Wilbur's essay "Sumptuous Destitution," which first appeared in *Emily Dickinson: Three Views,* edited by Wilbur, Louise Bogan, and Archibald MacLeish (Amherst: Amherst College Press, 1960), and which was reprinted in *Emily Dickinson: A Collection of Critical Essays,* ed. Richard Sewall (Englewood Cliffs, N.J.: Prentice Hall, 1963), remains the definitive explanation of Dickinson's distinctive response to privation of all kinds.

2. For the sake of convenience, throughout this book I will use the numbering system established by Thomas Johnson in his three-volume variorum edition of Dickinson's poems. In almost every case, versions of poems appearing in these pages also draw upon that edition.

3. Wendy Barker's book *Lunacy of Light: Emily Dickinson and the Experience of Metaphor* is an incisive investigation of a pervasive ambivalence toward

the sun in Dickinson's poems and letters. Barker begins her discussion as follows:

> When in 1859 Emily Dickinson casually asked a friend "Are you afraid of the sun?" she poses a question that metaphorically reverberates throughout the canon of her seventeen hundred–odd poems. Sounding rather like an encoded test for entrance to a private club, Dickinson's question in fact reveals a major theme of her poetry. Repeatedly in Dickinson's writing, images of sun dazzle only to abandon, beckon only to burn, while images of darkness—although at times suggesting the awful finality of death—frequently provide quiet refuge from the often-frightening and obliterating rays of the sun. (1–2)

4. I have in mind here Josephine Pollitt's *Emily Dickinson: The Human Background of Her Poetry;* Genevieve Taggard's *The Life and Mind of Emily Dickinson;* and George Frisbie Whicher's *This Was a Poet: A Critical Biography of Emily Dickinson.*

5. *Social Values and Poetic Arts,* 43. Of Dickinson herself, McGann says:

> The retreat of Emily Dickinson is eloquent with social meaning, and her poetic methods—the refusal to publish, the choice of album verse forms, the production of those famous manuscript fascicles—are all part of a complex poetic statement which is explicated in the context of her world, and which carries significance into our day when we are able, not to enter, but to face and come to terms with that world. ("Visible Language," 48–49)

CHAPTER 1

1. Among the various references to illness appearing in the writings of nineteenth-century women, those describing optical illnesses were, as Gilbert and Gubar point out, especially prevalent:

> Eye "troubles" . . . seem to abound in the lives and works of literary women, with Dickinson matter-of-factly noting that her eye got "put out," George Eliot describing patriarchal Rome as "a disease of the retina," Jane Eyre and Aurora Leigh marrying blind men, Charlotte Brontë deliberately writing with her eyes closed, and Mary Elizabeth Coleridge writing about "Blindness" that came because "Absolute and bright, / The Sun's rays smote me till they masked the Sun." (58)

2. For much of the information in these pages concerning Dickinson's optical illness I am indebted to Sewall's biography.

3. A suggestion that Dickinson's eyes may have begun bothering her as early as 1851 is raised by a visit the poet made to Boston that year to consult Dr. William Wesselhöft, a homeopathic doctor (Sewall, *Life,* 435). Fifteen years later, in 1866, she wrote to Higginson that she had promised to visit her "Physi-

cian" in Boston for a "few days in May," but had ultimately decided not to go because her father was "in the habit" of having her nearby (L450). 4. St. Armand says, "Whether or not we believe her condition to have been psychosomatic, Dickinson knew who was responsible for her traumatic loss of vision. Master had put out her eye with his blinding image of romantic love" (104).

5. Other diagnoses have been offered. In "'Banished from Native Eyes': The Reason for Emily Dickinson's Seclusion Reconsidered" (41–48) Jerry Ferris Reynolds attributes her symptoms to systemic lupus erythematosus. Gerald W. Jackson proposes that Dickinson's illness was a form of iritis, or inflammation of the iris (master's thesis, 7–20), a diagnosis with which biographer Polly Longsworth and Dr. Norbert Hirschhorn concur in their jointly written article, "'Medicine Posthumous': A New Look at Emily Dickinson's Medical Conditions." The causes of iritis (also called uveitis) are, as Longsworth and Hirschhorn point out, often bacterial, rooted in infections elsewhere in the body, such as tuberculosis or syphilis (304). Nevertheless, because the women in Dickinson's mother's family, the Norcrosses, apparently had a history of suffering from exotropia (see p. 11 in this volume), I believe iritis probably was not the primary culprit in the poet's optical difficulties.

6. Ackmann presented her paper "'I'm Glad I Finally Surfaced': A Norcross Descendant Remembers Emily Dickinson" on August 6, 1995, during the second meeting of the International Conference of the Emily Dickinson International Society, hosted by the University of Innsbruck, Austria.

7. As Ackmann was kind enough to point out in a letter to me, Viano's guesses about her ancestors' apparent optical maladies were unusually well informed, since she had received professional training in physiology during the 1930s and had worked for a while as a physical therapist.

Viano died on August 30, 1995.

8. Wand and Sewall also speculate that poor vision may have been largely to blame for the deterioration of Dickinson's handwriting into a barely decipherable scrawl (404). At about the time during which the symptoms of Dickinson's illness first became acute, that is, in about 1861, her handwriting underwent what Thomas Johnson calls a "Noticeable change in appearance: letters elongated and uneven, as if written with excess of nervous energy" (*Poems,* 1: liv). In subsequent years, Dickinson's handwriting continued to be markedly more irregular than it had been during her youth and early adulthood. If illness did indeed affect her handwriting, the validity of recent calls for reproductions of Dickinson's poems to be made more faithful to the autograph originals must be questioned. For example, McGann has written in *Black Riders: The Visible Language of Modernism* that he believes Dickinson's written texts are examples of what Charles Olson called "composition by field," or "a poetic deployment of writing within the given space of the page" (27), so that any attempt made to "regularize" her poems by printing them mechanically upon the page could po-

tentially do violence not only to the poems' forms, but to the meanings she intended for those forms to help convey. In looking too closely for evidence of conscious design in the figures Dickinson's poems make upon the page, I think we stand in some danger, however, of falling victim not to the "intentional fallacy," but rather to the "fallacy of intentionality." The way Dickinson's words are arranged on the page may not always have resulted from a series of deliberate artistic choices. If, for example, Dickinson's deteriorating eyesight compelled her over the years to write in a larger hand so that fewer words fit upon a line, we should not automatically assume that certain words carry over into the next line of a manuscript because she explicitly intended for a line break to be inserted there.

9. In an attempt to prevent my biographical readings from becoming too narrow, however, I will heed the advice offered by such critics as Elizabeth Phillips, who, in her study *Emily Dickinson: Personae and Performance,* finds evidence for a connection between Dickinson's optical illness and her poetry's subject matter, but also warns that biographical readings can threaten to become reductive and simplistic if they are not combined with a recognition that some of the material is strictly imaginative in origin (61–75). Similarly, in *Lunacy of Light,* Barker says, "Although, to be sure, physiological difficulties may have provided the impetus for her frequent association of light with pain, nevertheless, to rely solely upon a medical rationale for the profusion of these images throughout the poems would be to ignore the pervasiveness and complexity of Dickinson's metaphorical associations and their correspondences to similar metaphors occurring in the works of other writers" (4).

10. See also poem no. 930:

There is a June when Corn is cut
And Roses in the Seed—
A Summer briefer than the first
But tenderer indeed

As should a Face supposed the Grave's
Emerge a single Noon
In the Vermillion that it wore
Affect us, and return—

Two Seasons, it is said, exist—
The Summer of the Just,
And this of Our's, diversified
With Prospect, and with Frost—

May not our Second with it's First
So infinite compare
That We but recollect the one
The other to prefer?

11. In his book *The Dickinson Sublime* Gary Stonum remarks on Dickinson's preference for "power" rather than "glory" or "the kingdom" (53–54). He points to a note Dickinson sent to Susan Gilbert in about 1878 in which she says, "Cherish Power—dear . . . Remember that stands in the Bible between the Kingdom and the Glory, because it is wilder than either of them" (L631). Stonum suggests that Dickinson relished power as a sign of having achieved mastery over a force greater than hers, a victory that provided her with a route to romantic sublimity in her poetry. Although I agree that Dickinson was acutely aware of her own powers of the imagination, I question whether she ever felt she had achieved mastery over them.

12. In her book *Rowing in Eden* Martha Nell Smith sees this poem as alluding to Milton's *Samson Agonistes*. Smith points out that Dickinson refers to Milton "throughout her correspondence" (247n.10). The question of whether Dickinson's interest in the great blind poet stemmed in part from her concerns over her own eyes remains unanswered, however.

13. I disagree with John Cody's psychobiographical interpretation of this poem in his book *After Great Pain: The Inner Life of Emily Dickinson*. According to Cody, Dickinson avoided the sun because, as I mentioned, she unconsciously associated it with an unacknowledged male component in her personality that she feared would be castrated (437). But attributing Dickinson's eye difficulties to a form of penis envy strikes me as being needlessly elaborate, considering the relatively high frequency of optical problems among the population at large both in her own era and in ours. Also, the persistence Dr. Williams showed in scheduling sessions with Dickinson in Boston indicates some confidence on his part that the illness was treatable using conventional medical techniques.

14. The sense of exhaustion the narrator's presence induces in her "friend" brings to mind Higginson's description of Dickinson after having visited her in Amherst: "I never was with any one who drained my nerve power so much. Without touching her, she drew from me. I am glad not to live near her" (L476).

15. Barker and Barton St. Armand integrate Dickinson's fondness for making sunrise and sunset the topics of her poems within their larger arguments about what the image of the sun represented for the poet. Of sunsets, Barker says that "through sunset imagery Dickinson covertly asserts that feminine imaginative energy can emerge when masculine solar power has retreated" (109). St. Armand writes at greater length about sunset in his book's eighth chapter, "The Art of Peace: Dickinson, Sunsets, and the Sublime." He describes the sunset as being, for Dickinson, a "sacred experience" during which the "masculine and Christ-like" sun encountered its own mother, day, who, like Mary, "stood as a sometimes agonized, sometimes ecstatic witness of her child's birth, death, entombment, and resurrection" (276). While I do not entirely disagree with Barker's, St. Armand's, and John Cody's observations about Dickinson's gendering of the sun as a male in her poems, I think that all too often such arguments are

apt to be skewed by virtually unverifiable assumptions about just how comfortable or uncomfortable Dickinson felt in the presence of men.

16. The theme of Dickinson's perceptual "avarice" being the result of a heightened awareness of the world's mutability appears as well in the following poem (no. 1682), which is so similar to "My first well Day" that they might be considered companion pieces:

> Summer begins to have the look
> Peruser of enchanting Book
> Reluctantly but sure perceives
> A gain upon the backward leaves
>
> Autumn begins to be inferred
> By millinery of the cloud
> Or deeper color in the shawl
> That wraps the everlasting hill
>
> The eye begins it's avarice
> A meditation chastens speech
> Some Dyer of a distant tree
> Resumes his gaudy industry
>
> Conclusion is the course of All
> At *most* to be perennial
> And then elude stability
> Recalls to immortality—

Here Dickinson personifies summer as the reader of a particularly exciting novel who notices with regret that only a scant number of pages remain. In the second stanza, the "leaves" of the book metamorphose smoothly into the leaves that are changing color on a nearby hill, which is represented, as in "My first well day," as a brightly colored shawl. The eye, alerted to summer's disappearance, begins its "avarice," taking in as much as it can before winter arrives. This phenomenon of accelerated perception reminds Dickinson that conclusion is the rule for all things, although some few are "perennial" or cyclical, that is, capable of returning briefly, but they will ultimately "elude stability" and cease to exist.

CHAPTER 2

1. In a study of Dickinson's diction, William Howard found that out of the 770 words the poet borrowed from special sources for her poems, the largest group came from contemporary technology or science (230).

2. No evidence has emerged thus far to indicate that Dickinson ever wore glasses. In any case, as Wand and Sewall point out, exotropia is generally not alleviated by the wearing of corrective lenses (405–6).

3. In her essay "'Compound Manner': Emily Dickinson and the Metaphysical Poets," Judith Banzer says, while suggesting that a continuity exists between

Dickinson's poetry and that of metaphysical poets such as Donne and Herbert, "The discipline that wrought many of her poems was the metaphysical one of a 'Compound Vision' by which the eternal is argued from the transient, the foreign explained by the familiar, and fact illumined by mystery" (417). M. M. Khan makes a similar point about Dickinson's love poems in his essay "Romantic Tradition and the Compound Vision of Love in Emily Dickinson's Poems," in which he finds both similarities and differences between Dickinson's poems and those of such seventeenth-century writers as Donne and Shakespeare.

4. Richard Sewall devotes considerable space in his biography to emphasizing just how important Hitchcock was as an influence upon all the young minds of Amherst. Sewall's opinion is seconded by Cynthia Griffin Wolff, who says in her own biography of the poet that "More or less directly as a result of his [Hitchcock's] presence in Amherst, Emily Dickinson became conversant with the most sophisticated science then available in North America" (79).

5. On May 16, 1848, Dickinson wrote a letter to her friend Abiah Root saying that she was studying astronomy at Mt. Holyoke (L67).

6. In his variorum edition Thomas Johnson proposed a date of composition for this poem of about 1859 (*Poems*, 1: 56).

7. Christine Avery raises an important point about the conflict underlying this poem: who is more destructive, the scientist or the poet?

> There is one odd and interesting feature of the poem. It is almost startlingly obvious that she is not repeating Wordsworth's accusation that 'we murder to dissect.' On the contrary, it is the poet who destroys, by 'pulling' a flower from the woods; presumably as the gardener militant she 'slays' a worm, and then captures a butterfly in her hat, which seems quite as unfortunate for it as being pinned in a display case. It is the scientist who murmurs 'Resurgam,' implying the continuation of life, and the scientist who says 'Centipede,' thus re-enacting the first and most pleasant of the tasks of Adam in Paradise, the giving of names to animals. (48)

8. Avery thought Dickinson's habits of orderliness were conducive to making scientific inquiries:

> [Dickinson] had an essentially exact mind, naturally delighting to entertain both logical and scientific concepts. An aspect of science deeply sympathetic to her was its free, constantly conjecturing spirit. She recurrently uses the word 'experiment' to suggest action which is a kind of adventure of wholly uncertain result: applied to creation it makes this a living issue, and not a drearily automatic winding up to a foregone conclusion. (51)

9. In chapters 2 and 3 of *Lunacy of Light: Emily Dickinson and the Experience of Metaphor,* Barker comments extensively and persuasively on Dickinson's associations of the sun with, variously, God's watchful eye, male seduction, and divine retribution. In chapters 3 and 4 of *Emily Dickinson and Her Culture,* Barton St. Armand interprets the aggregate image of the sun in Dick-

inson's poems and letters as "Phoebus," a male figure whom Dickinson both loved and feared.

10. David Peck Todd, professor of astronomy at Amherst College and husband to Dickinson's future editor, Mabel Loomis Todd, hoped to lead one of the U.S. Naval Observatory's expeditions to photograph the 1882 Transit. Although circumstances conspired against his participation on that particular occasion, he did succeed in using a photoheliograph to take pictures of the Transit from Mt. Lick observatory in California (Longsworth, 64–65).

11. Preparations for sending expeditions to witness the Transit would almost certainly have been reported in Samuel Bowles's *The Springfield Republican,* which Dickinson read faithfully.

12. Either at Amherst Academy or at Mt. Holyoke, Dickinson may very well have seen a classroom demonstration of the principle of parallax involving the use of a candle flame to represent the sun and requiring two students to stand at different locations in the room. By sighting along a common intermediate object, such as a ruler, they could observe the flame's apparent displacement.

13. See, for example, the final stanza of poem no. 959, "A loss of something ever felt I—":

And a Suspicion, like a Finger
Touches my Forehead now and then
That I am looking oppositely
For the site of the Kingdom of Heaven—

14. "Bankruptcy" was an inherited, well-remembered fear for the entire Dickinson family. The poet's grandfather, Samuel Fowler Dickinson, came so perilously close to bankruptcy that he had to leave Massachusetts to take a new position in Ohio (Sewall, *Life,* 37).

15. Jack Capps, in his study of Dickinson's reading, said that although "she makes fewer substantial references to Revelation than to Matthew or John . . . the vision and prophecy of Revelation were for her a return to the images of Eden . . ." (56–57).

16. William Shurr says that "One reads the fascicles of Emily Dickinson with the growing sense that there came to be one day in her life which she considered to be unique. Many poems in the fascicles celebrate that day and analyze its importance." Shurr calls this momentous day the "Marriage day" (10). About this particular poem, Shurr says that "two of Dickinson's most striking themes . . . are started here: that the lovers will meet beyond the grave, and that the intervening years of separation will be suffered as their Calvary" (14).

17. Rowena Revis Jones reads this poem as a reenactment of a baptismal rite, rather than of the blessed sacrament or the sacrament of marriage: "The lovers belong within the 'Sealed Church,' or invisible body of those who have experienced regeneration, and their admission is sealed by a private 'baptismal' pledge confirming their mutual devotion" (42).

CHAPTER 3

1. St. Armand also sees, in this poem, a refusal by Dickinson to overanalyze what may be a holy moment:

> To Dickinson, the great amateur of sunsets, what is seen hovering upon the western hills is imaged (and preserved) as an immense floral specimen, a blossom related to that most persistent and characteristic of New England exotics, the lilac. The crucifixion that is implicit in the romantic typology of sunset is here subsumed by Dickinson's study of the overwhelming, passional color of the scene. To analyze this phenomenon, in fact, would itself be a kind of crucifixion of her subject by the devoted artist, who can only admire and try her skill in her chosen medium of poetic reproduction. (289)

2. Greg Johnson, who also discusses the centrality of compound vision to Dickinson's poetic practice in the ninth chapter of his book *Emily Dickinson: Perception and the Poet's Quest,* interprets compound vision as being essentially a fresh appreciation of experience brought about by a heightened awareness of death's imminence (156–76). I, on the other hand, remain persuaded that both the term itself and its underlying significance to her emerged directly from her experience as a patient.

3. In proposing immortality for the pine tree by her window, Dickinson may have been imitating Thoreau, whose writings she admired (Capps, 119). In *The Maine Woods* Thoreau famously (or infamously) proposed that a pine tree might have a spirit of its own that would "go to as high a heaven [as he would], there to tower over me still" (685).

4. Shurr somewhat bizarrely suggests that the puzzling phrase "Screw of Flesh" refers not to Dickinson's own body, but rather to that of a child the poet imagines herself bearing (176–77).

5. Shurr says that "Seven years from 'around 1861' would bring us near to the time when she is assumed to have first met the Reverend Charles Wadsworth, 1855, although the dating also coincides with the departure of Henry Vaughan Emmons from Amherst (an early candidate for the beloved) and the arrival in Amherst of one of her favorite clergymen, Reverend E. S. Dwight" (16).

6. According to various accounts, Dickinson reserved her nights for writing. She may have done so simply as a matter of preference, or else out of necessity, either because household chores demanded her attention during the day or because, while she was ill, the bandages over her eyes were removed only at nightfall. A thorough analysis of Dickinson's predilection for nighttime and darkness may be found in the third chapter of Barker's book, *Lunacy of Light: Emily Dickinson and the Experience of Metaphor.*

7. In attributing Dickinson's own use of carcerative images in her poetry to a case of agoraphobia (606–50 passim), Gilbert and Gubar also anticipate and pave the way for Maryanne Garbowsky's book *The House without the Door.*

8. A variant for "Circuit," "Measure" could suggest to mind the feet of a poem as strongly as the feet of a prisoner, raising the question of whether Dickinson might be describing here her own tightly circumscribed, comparatively uniform poetic idiom. Perhaps the regularity of her style offered her a solace similar to that which the sonnet's "scanty plot of ground" offered to Wordsworth, when he "felt the weight of too much liberty."

9. Maryanne Garbowsky interprets the narrator's anguished acceptance of an imprisoned life as being typical of the feelings harbored toward their residences by agoraphobes (85–87).

10. In his variorum, Thomas Johnson notes that a different first stanza of this poem appears in a letter Dickinson wrote in late January 1875 to Mrs. J. G. Holland (922). There, that moiety of the poem becomes a direct reference to her father's death during the previous year:

Mother is asleep in the Library—Vinnie—in the Dining Room—Father—in the Masked Bed—in the Marl House.

How soft his Prison is—
How sweet those sullen Bars—
No Despot—but the King of Down
Invented that Repose!

The fact that Dickinson chose to insert only the first stanza of the poem in her letter to Mrs. Holland suggests to me that she somewhat opportunistically selected a stanza from a previously existing poem written on another topic (her confinement) and modified it slightly for the occasion. This practice was not unusual for Dickinson.

11. See, for example, Cheryl Walker's explication of the poem in her book *The Nightingale's Burden* (112–15) or Shurr's in *The Marriage of Emily Dickinson* (87–88).

12. In *Emily Dickinson's Gothic: Goblin with a Gauge,* Daneen Wardrop interprets the "other" appearing in Dickinson's prison melodramas as a "Doppelgänger" of the self, whose creation is consistent with the Gothic literary convention of "character doubling," which "bifurcates the world into inner and outer states—most frequently the acceptable, social self as opposed to the unsocialized, libidinous self" (97).

13. In her chapter "The Humor of Excess" in *Comic Power in Emily Dickinson* (written in collaboration with Suzanne Juhasz and Martha Nell Smith), Cristanne Miller connects Dickinson's use of irony to her particular brand of humor by tracing in both the presence of an underlying skepticism born of experiences with suffering and with pain (117–18).

CHAPTER 4

1. See, for example, the following comment by Inder Nath Kher in *The Landscape of Absence: Emily Dickinson's Poetry:*

In discussing absence as *distance* or *beyond,* I have implied throughout that Emily Dickinson does not evince any posture of escape from the world. On the contrary, like a true existentialist-romanticist, she gazes upon the world so intensely, and encounters its mystery and paradoxes so passionately, that the whole external world becomes a concrete metaphor of her life and art. Like Hopkins, she dramatizes the notions of *inscape* and *instress.* (62)

2. See, for example, Stonum's comment in *The Dickinson Sublime:*

Unlike Wordsworth . . . who moves on to a visionary affirmation, Dickinson lingers with the sublime and with a poetry that hovers between determinate states. Indeed, the theoretically necessary in-between quality of the sublime can be said to be literalized in the usual spatial and temporal siting of Dickinson's poems. Temporally . . . the poems prolong the otherwise vague interval between a traumatic phase and an anticipated reactive phase. Spatially, the notorious scenelessness of many of her poems exemplifies the indeterminate relation between those two moments. (180)

3. In her article "'The One Thing Needful': Dickinson's Dilemma of Home and Heaven," Robin Riley Fast shows how Dickinson invested the "consolation" writers' heaven of "glorified domesticity" with a sense of mystery derived from heaven's impermanence and inaccessibility (160).

4. St. Armand provides a thorough description of Dickinson's hypothetical "landscapes" for heaven in *Emily Dickinson and Her Culture.* There, he also approaches the problem of understanding how Dickinson linked the temporal world with eternity by positing a "mystic day" for her, in which time and eternity are collapsed (278). He assembles a tabular schema comprising many of Dickinson's most prominent symbols and themes, including "noon," which he associates with "Summer," "Maturation," "Faith," and "Conversion" (317).

5. Dickinson may also be giving voice in this poem to a realization that she would have been entirely willing to exchange her "present" condition of bandaged, obfuscated sight for the "imperfect," impaired vision she enjoyed before being treated.

6. Dickinson's fondness for the west may also have been attributable to the fact that she looked out a west-facing window while seated at the writing desk in her room (Mudge, 50).

7. Betsy Erkkila's lucid and highly useful essay "Emily Dickinson and Class" analyzes the poet's perception of herself as a member of Amherst's, and America's, "aristocracy." Erkkila observes that "In her letters and poems, Dickinson assumes an aristocratic order of rank and difference as the natural order of things" (300). Erkkila interprets Dickinson's aristocratic pretensions as an expression of Whiggish antidemocratic sentiment:

Whereas . . . many of the women writers of her age, including Stowe, Fuller, Child, and Jacobs, embraced the democratic language of republican ideology even as they turned that language to a critique of the actual practice of the American government, Dickinson returned to a pre-Revolutionary and aristocratic language of rank, titles, and divine right to assert the sovereignty of her self as absolute monarch. Not only does she set herself against what F. O. Matthiessen calls [in *American Renaissance*] "the possibilities of democracy" invoked by other writers of her age (ix), but at a time when a woman, Victoria, was the queen of England, Dickinson's royalist language also bears witness to the political irony that it is under an aristocratic order of hereditary and divine right rather than under a democratic order of contract and inalienable rights that a woman was entitled to political power and to rule. (305–6)

8. See, for example, Stonum in *The Dickinson Sublime* (174–75).

9. Images of drowning also appear in Dickinson's letters written during the mid-1860s. Thomas Johnson says that "tropes involving water are especially predominant in messages written during the period that ED was under treatment for her eyes" (L441).

10. R. W. Franklin speculates that the following stanza is a continuation of "A Pit—but Heaven over it—" (*Editing*, 44–46):

'Twould start them—
We—could tremble—
But since we got a Bomb—
And held it in our Bosom—
Nay—Hold it—it is calm—

I am persuaded, as Franklin was, by the textual similarities between this stanza and the aforesaid poem. In terms of my own exegesis, I believe she is declaring herself unafraid of the "Pit's" hazards because she has nothing more to lose by falling. Since she has suffered an emotional calamity ("a Bomb"), the prospect of venturing her life in the "Pit" no longer appalls her, although she can understand the terror others might feel ("'Twould start them") in the same situation.

11. Barker makes just such an argument in *Lunacy of Light* (76).

12. In her essay "Spiders in the Attic: A Suggestion of Synthesis in the Poetry of Emily Dickinson," Joanne DeLaven Williams provides an insightful exposition of Dickinson's spider/artist poems in which she notes that this particular poem describes the conflict between "the spiritual ideality of the imagination and the concrete reality of human existence." The artist's efforts are futile from the start:

The positive, constructive action of the artist-spider is countered by the negating influence of the external world of "Nought." The outcome of the creator's "Trade" is therefore "unsubstantial"; it is hardly of the substance of the real world, though subject to its hazards. No longer does his creative imagination enjoy the sanctuary of the separated, passive, ideal state. Having been necessarily exposed to the real world through creative action, it becomes vulnerable to the disintegrating forces there. (23–24)

13. Of such efforts to supplant physical reality with art's "artificial" boundaries, Richard Poirier writes the following in *A World Elsewhere: The Place of Style in American Literature:*

> The idea that through language it is possible to create environments radically different from those supported by economic, political, and social systems is one of the sustaining myths of any literature. It is a myth in one sense because it is historically invalid: the enormous contrivances of style called forth by this effort are themselves an admission that the environment thus created has an existence only in style. Not God, not religion, not reality, history, or nature, but style is its only authority. (16–17)

CHAPTER 5

1. In *Emily Dickinson: A Poet's Grammar,* Miller provides a thorough contemporary analysis of Dickinson's compressive style (24–44).

2. Dickinson sent the first stanza of the poem from which this phrase is drawn, "The Only News I know" (no. 827), to Higginson during her convalescence in the summer of 1864. The poem in its entirety succinctly summarizes both the sensory limitations imposed upon Dickinson by her confinement as well as her loneliness, while she remained isolated in her rented room:

> The Only news I know
> Is Bulletins all Day
> From Immortality.
>
> The Only Shows I see—
> Tomorrow and Today—
> Perchance Eternity—
>
> The Only One I meet
> Is God—The Only Street—
> Existence—This traversed
>
> If Other News there be—
> Or Admirabler Show—
> I'll tell it You—

3. It is helpful to think about Dickinson's use of symbolism in light of Charles Feidelson's original and still-useful distinction in *Symbolism and American Literature* between "symbolistic program" and "symbolistic principle" (66). The former term could be used to describe Hawthorne's use of the letter "A" in *The Scarlet Letter* or Maule's Well in *The House of the Seven Gables,* that is, the deployment of symbols whose meanings remain relatively constant throughout

a text. "Symbolistic principle," on the other hand, describes an approach taken toward language itself, a property generic to the way words are used. Language informed by the symbolistic principle gains complexity of meaning often at the expense of clarity, for when words no longer exist monolithically or in antinomies, they tend to overlap and mutually reflect, rendering definitions more and more untenable.

4. See Capps (116).

5. Vivian C. Hopkins, in her book *Spires of Form: A Study of Emerson's Aesthetic Theory*, sees the spiral as being the central pattern governing Emerson's theories about both art and nature. The spiral, she says, "admirably hits the combination of circular movement with upward progress which is the heart of his aesthetic" (3).

6. Robert D. Richardson Jr. traces Emerson's emphasis upon organic unity and metamorphosis in nature to the influence of Goethe, particularly his *Metamorphosis of Plants*. Richardson quotes Emerson's restatement of Goethe's insight:

> Goethe suggested the leading idea of modern botany, that a leaf or the eye of a leaf, is the unit of botany, and that every part of the plant is only a transformed leaf to meet a new condition, and by varying the conditions, a leaf may be converted into any other organ and any other organ into a leaf.

This view seems to me remarkably similar to the vision of botanical nature expressed in Dickinson's "The Veins of other Flowers." Furthermore, what Richardson says of Emerson's emphasis upon the "process of growing" instead of "the grown product" and his interest in "metamorphosis rather than taxonomy" (172) could be applied with equal validity to many of Dickinson's statements about nature.

7. Miller points out in *Emily Dickinson: A Poet's Grammar* that the poet's "artlessness" in this poem is a transparent pose:

> This poem modestly represents the poet as a neighborly correspondent. She passes on Nature's "Message" or "simple News" in a friendly letter, and we are to judge her "tenderly" for the sake of the original speaker, Nature, not for her gifted translation of nature's truths. The writer disappears behind the supposed transparency of her message. In the fiction of the poem she does not create, she gossips. (8)

8. The "transparent eyeball" image, certainly the most famous in all of his writings, is Emerson's representation of himself during a moment of purely egoless perception. The importance of perception may have been driven home for Emerson, as it probably was for Dickinson, by an optical illness. Richardson says in *Emerson: The Mind on Fire* that "The eye disease that struck Emerson in early 1825 [when Emerson was twenty-two years old] was almost certainly uveitis, a rheumatic inflammation of the eye that gave the sufferer headaches and was often linked with rheumatism" (63).

9. Stonum's book *The Dickinson Sublime* is a detailed and thoughtful study of the romantic sublime in Dickinson's poetry.

10. One example that could be adduced from among many other potential candidates is the following (no. 88):

As by the dead we love to sit,
Become so wondrous dear—
As for the lost we grapple
Tho' all the rest are here—
In broken mathematics
We estimate our prize—
Vast—in it's fading ratio
To our penurious eyes!

11. Greg Johnson provides a trenchant discussion of variable ratios within Dickinson's poetry in "Broken Mathematics: Ratio, Transience, Essence," the second part of his book *Emily Dickinson: Perception and the Poet's Quest*. He ties together the concepts of *distance* in Dickinson's poetry with her interest in ratios:

Dickinson's mature quester . . . focuses her abundant energies upon an exhaustive analysis of human perceptual values. From her acknowledgment of the distance between perceiver and perceived, and her awareness that this distance gives any perception its value, she evolves one of her central poetic ideas: she insists that the value of the perceived object is directly proportionate to its distance from the perceiver. For the purposes of Dickinson's religious quest, to know that perception of an object costs precisely its loss is not enough, for the element of time places this relationship in constant flux: thus the concept of a flexible ratio, implying movement and change through the temporal dimension, can measure the value of perception within any human context. And, since natural existence and its conditions are important only within the "larger function" of her quest for spiritual knowledge, Dickinson offers the empirical truth of these "measurements" (having proved their validity in her poems) as a metaphor for spiritual reality. (81)

12. Although I would contend that Dickinson merely resituates the concept of the sacrament from the body of Christ to the material world and to words themselves, E. Miller Budick argues, in *Emily Dickinson and the Life of Language*, that the poet's use of sacramental imagery instead constitutes an attack upon the misapplication of Christian symbolism to worldly matters such as nature and language ("The Dangers of Sacramental Symbolism," 45–77).

13. See Sewall, *Life* (200–201).

14. A contrastive and insightful reading of this poem may be found in the fifth chapter of Miller, *Emily Dickinson: A Poet's Grammar*, "The Consent of Language and the Woman Poet" (171–72).

15. See Thomas Johnson's comments in *Poems,* 3: 1129.

16. Webster's *Third New International Dictionary* defines "tabernacle" as "a receptacle for the consecrated elements of the Eucharist." Thus the connection Dickinson made between creating poetry and consuming the eucharist becomes apparent again in this poem.

CHAPTER 6

1. The date of this letter is uncertain. Thomas Johnson's justification of the proposed date assumes that Dickinson's letter represents a form of thanks for a George Eliot biography Niles had sent her (L768).

2. See, for example, the final stanza of no. 126:

We trust, in plumed procession
For such, the Angels go—
Rank after Rank, with even feet—
And Uniforms of Snow.

3. In *Dickinson and the Strategies of Reticence,* Joanne Dobson suggests that the poet's refusal to publish "is consistent with the contemporary cultural ideology of feminine reticence" (130).

4. See, for example, Marta Werner's book *Emily Dickinson's Open Folios,* McGann's essay "Emily Dickinson's Visible Language," or Erkkila's essay "Homoeroticism and Audience: Emily Dickinson's Female 'Master'." McGann says, "I think [Dickinson] rejected a market-model of publishing, with its medium of print, because she came to see how restrictive and conventional that medium had become" (*Journal,* 43). Erkkila proposes that Dickinson "appears to have been engaged in a kind of cottage industry, a precapitalist mode of manuscript production and circulation that avoided the commodity and use values of the commercial marketplace" (174).

5. The "Auction" trope itself indicates that Dickinson did indeed set a premium upon her reputation within the Dickinson household for being a poet. Typically, items to be sold at auction are stored in attics or upstairs rooms, such as the room in which she did most of her writing. Therefore her activity as a writer makes her a tangible "asset" to the Dickinson family.

6. Robert Smith, in *The Seductions of Emily Dickinson,* resists, however, the idea that Dickinson is speaking in this poem about herself:

. . . aside from the fact that Dickinson, at various times in her poetic "career," expressed a more acutely ambiguous response to the idea of publication, it is extremely dangerous for the critic to assume that in this poem he or she hears the voice of *the* poet as opposed to the voice of *a* poet. The fact that the narrator of this particular poem at one point identifies with the instantly recognizable starving artist in the obligatory "Garret" would make her only problematically Dickinson herself. In fact, reading the poem as an ingenuous complaint, or rather marvelous rationalization, of an unpublished poet may give the poem a neatly ironic, cutting edge. (114)

7. A similar point is made by Smith on p. 115 of *The Seductions of Emily Dickinson.*

8. In her poem "A Mien to Move a Queen," Dickinson candidly discusses men's inability to reconcile her appearance with the intellectual rigor of her conversation. She characterizes herself in that poem as having two levels of address, an inconspicuous and introverted voice that "on the Ear can go / Like Let of Snow," and a confident, extroverted voice that can "shift supreme / As tone of Realm."

9. Susan Howe has resisted the idea that Dickinson's modesty prevented her from seeking publication, interpreting her refusal instead as being consistent with an American Puritan tradition of finding salvation through self-revelation. Howe says: "The decision not to publish her poems in her lifetime, to close up an extraordinary amount of work, is astonishing. Far from being the misguided modesty of an oppressed female ego, it is a consummate Calvinist gesture of self-assertion by a poet with faith to fling election loose across the incandescent shadows of futurity" (49).

10. It should be pointed out, however, that Gilbert and Gubar see in the name of Lucy Snowe, heroine of Charlotte Brontë's *Villette,* another possible literary source for Dickinson's self-identification with snow (620).

11. See Sewall, *Life* (543).

12. At least one critic, Mario D'Avanzo, correspondingly interprets the eponymous snowstorm as "a metaphor for the tumultuous life of the creative spirit, which is 'unseen' but form-making in a 'tumultuous privacy'—a privacy of spirit that is kindred to Emily Dickinson's intensely creative seclusion" (279).

13. See, for example, Matthiessen's comments in *American Renaissance* (45–46).

14. In *Emily Dickinson: A Poet's Grammar,* Miller says that Dickinson "borrowed from" Emerson's poem, but Miller does not specify where or how (24).

15. Gilbert and Gubar emphasize the essential femininity, for nineteenth-century writers, of the color white: "despite its importance for Melville, white was in the nineteenth century a distinctively female color, frequently chosen as emblematic by or of women for reasons that Dickinson seems to have understood quite well" (615). Gilbert and Gubar also address the provocative question of whether Dickinson's symbolizing of her poetry and herself as "snow" had anything to do with her decision to wear white dresses almost exclusively during the last decade of her life (634–38).

16. That Dickinson's second version of the poem appears only rarely in anthologies of her work seems to me contradictory to what the poet herself would have wished. Although a persuasive case could be mounted that the first version of the poem is artistically superior to the second, Dickinson's evident satisfac-

tion with the later draft is reflected by her willingness not to alter it further during a twenty-year period and by her selection of the poem as one of her better efforts to be sent to Niles.

17. Joanne Feit Diehl writes, in *Dickinson and the Romantic Imagination,*

> What most strongly determines Dickinson's sense of isolation, the need to subvert the Romantic vocabulary and refuse its consolations, depends upon her sense of self as "other." How could a woman without the faith that she too was a member of that great male company of poets, a woman living such an externally provincial existence, hope to vie with the powerful forces that awakened her imagination? Repeatedly her poems acknowledge the need for another presence to inform her own, yet she must banish *his* authority in order to assert *her* individual freedom. (185–86)

CHAPTER 7

1. Despite my several disagreements with the "version" of Dickinson constructed by Camille Paglia in her by-now notorious essay "Amherst's Madame de Sade: Emily Dickinson" (in *Sexual Personae*), I do think Paglia's deliberately *outré* discussion of the poet's sexuality is occasionally "on point": in particular, I think she is accurate in reading some of the poems as "sexual scripts" (648). Nevertheless, I cannot concur with her dismissive, derisive treatment of Dickinson's relationship with Judge Lord. Paglia rejects, despite the evidence presented by Dickinson's surviving letters in manuscript as well as the testimony of some of the poet's contemporaries, even the idea of a romance between the two as "improbable." Instead, Paglia suggests that Dickinson somehow exploited the Judge's interest in her because she wanted him to be "a cinematic rematerialization of her father's forbidding presence" (670). This theory strikes me as being a form of wishful thinking in its own right; moreover, I think experience teaches us that even the most unlikely of couples can become lovers.

2. Werner, in her book *Emily Dickinson's Open Folios,* issues a valid warning against putting too much trust in published versions of the poet's drafts of letters to Lord. The letter fragments themselves are, as Werner reminds us, heavily scissored and, therefore, censored. Moreover, Millicent Todd Bingham's arrangement of some of these same fragments in her book *Emily Dickinson: A Revelation* (1954) and Thomas Johnson's splicing together of them in his 1958 edition of Dickinson's letters are themselves based upon those two authors' unspoken determination to construct a sort of coherent narrative out of intrinsically inchoate materials (43–45). Nevertheless, I believe that, incomplete though they may be, these particular remnants of Dickinson's late correspondence exhibit enough internal consistencies for us to conclude, albeit somewhat advisedly, that Dickinson intended them for Judge Lord. Furthermore, these consistencies are often composed of iterated images and themes that suggest the presence of an already established, shared vocabulary of coded references for the two correspondents' behaviors toward each other.

3. Dickinson's letters to Lord first appeared in Bingham's *Emily Dickinson: A Revelation,* published in 1954.

4. Most of the information about Lord contained in this paragraph is drawn from Sewall's biography (643–49).

5. In a letter to Lord's niece Abbie Farley, Dickinson wrote, "'An envious Sliver broke' was a passage your Uncle peculiarly loved in the drowning Ophelia" (L1006).

6. Although the Judge was not an especially literary man, he was typical of his profession and his era in being a bardolator. Dickinson was an equally ardent admirer, and for Christmas 1880, Judge Lord gave her Mrs. Cowden Clarke's *The Complete Concordance to Shakespeare* (Sewall, *Life,* xxvi). While *Hamlet* remained the Judge's favorite play, Dickinson especially liked *Othello*. Whether she saw in the differences in age and in race between Othello and Desdemona any analogies for the disparity between Judge Lord and herself remains an intriguing, though imponderable, question.

7. Sewall writes, "As she had with her father, Emily Dickinson saw much more than the public side of Otis Lord, and, in both men, a paradox. 'River God' as Edward Dickinson might have been to the people of Western Massachusetts, to his daughter he was lonely, misunderstood, often bewildered, sometimes comical, and a little pathetic" (*Life,* 649).

8. Martha Dickinson Bianchi remembered him as "pompous Judge Lord" (*Face to Face,* 33).

9. Sewall writes, "Emily Dickinson shared [Lord's] exalted view of [common sense]. . . . 'Common Sense,' she wrote, 'is almost as omniscient as God'" (*Life,* 651).

10. See, however, Wolff's comment that "there is the persistent intimation that the passion that became open in 1878 had its origins much earlier" (401) and John Evangelist Walsh's suggestion that "a passionate attachment was already in progress some years before the death of Lord's wife" (186). Walsh even hypothesizes that Dickinson and Lord could have met clandestinely during her extended visits to Boston in 1864 and 1865 to receive treatment from Dr. Williams (190).

11. Dickinson liked to strike a teasing pose in her poems, particularly in those evidently directed toward a male audience. As Suzanne Juhasz points out in her analysis of Dickinson's comic power, teasing is Dickinson's response to patriarchal power, a "defense as well as [an] invitation" in which Dickinson renegotiates her relationship to the reader outside of more traditional hierarchies (*Comic Power,* 27).

12. Other readers have also identified the "dwelling" described in the poem as a privy. See, for example, David Porter, "The Crucial Experience in Dickinson's Poetry" (285).

13. The "time and mind" of which the narrator has been deprived may refer to lost reading time. The manuscript version of this poem is unique among Dickinson's papers for having embedded within it a postage stamp and two small

strips of paper saying "George Sand" and "Mauprat." Although we may conjecture that Dickinson herself had been reading Sand's novel *Mauprat* in the privy when she was so rudely interrupted, the novel may also have suggested itself to her because it tells the story of Bernard Mauprat, "special Heir" to the Mauprat estate. Further, Sand's novel disparages class differences in France during the *ancien régime*, contrasting the cruelty of Bernard's aristocratic uncle, John de Mauprat, with the humanity of Gaffer Patience, the rustic philosopher. Variants within the poem, such as "Peasants" for "inmates" and "impertinently" for "Assiduously," show that Dickinson did indeed plan for the poem to be read as a miniature, comic account of civic revolt narrated by a member of the imperiled "aristocracy," although this particular aristocrat's villa is, ironically, a privy.

14. Wardrop provides an exegesis of this poem in which the narrator is the victim of a sexual assault (79–80).

15. Sewall notes that Otis Lord was appointed to the Massachusetts Supreme Court in 1875 (*Life*, 647).

16. Thomas Johnson attributes this date to the letter draft based upon its handwriting, upon Dickinson's topical reference within the letter to a snowstorm, and upon some corroborating chronological evidence contained in a penciled draft of a letter (L800) to another, unknown correspondent on the letter's opposite side (*Letters*, 747).

WORKS CITED

Avery, Christine. "Science, Technology, and Emily Dickinson." *Bulletin of the British Association for American Studies* (December 1964): 47–55.

Banzer, Judith. "'Compound Manner': Emily Dickinson and the Metaphysical Poets." *American Literature* 32 (January 1961): 417–33.

Barker, Wendy. *Lunacy of Light: Emily Dickinson and the Experience of Metaphor.* Carbondale: Southern Illinois University Press, 1987.

Bianchi, Martha Dickinson. *Emily Dickinson Face to Face: Unpublished Letters with Notes and Reminiscences.* Boston and New York: Houghton Mifflin, 1932.

———. *The Life and Letters of Emily Dickinson.* Boston and New York: Houghton Mifflin, 1924.

Bingham, Millicent Todd. *Emily Dickinson: A Revelation.* New York: Harper and Brothers Publishers, 1954.

Bloom, Harold, ed. *Emily Dickinson: Modern Critical Views.* New York: Chelsea House, 1985.

Browning, Elizabeth Barrett. *Aurora Leigh.* 1856. Reprint, ed. Margaret Reynolds. Athens: Ohio University Press, 1992.

Budick, E. Miller. *Emily Dickinson and the Life of Language.* Baton Rouge: Louisiana State University Press, 1985.

Capps, Jack. *Emily Dickinson's Reading.* Cambridge: Harvard University Press, 1966.

Cody, John. *After Great Pain: The Inner Life of Emily Dickinson.* Cambridge: Belknap Press of Harvard University Press, 1971.

D'Avanzo, Mario. "'Unto the White Creator': The Snow of Dickinson and Emerson." *New England Quarterly* 45 (1972): 278–80.

Dickinson, Emily. *The Letters of Emily Dickinson.* Ed. Thomas H. Johnson and Theodora Ward. 3 vols. Cambridge: Belknap Press of Harvard University Press, 1958.

———. *The Poems of Emily Dickinson.* Ed. Thomas H. Johnson. 3 vols. Cambridge: Belknap Press of Harvard University Press, 1955.

Diehl, Joanne Feit. *Dickinson and the Romantic Imagination.* Princeton: Princeton University Press, 1981.

Dobson, Joanne. *Dickinson and the Strategies of Reticence.* Bloomington: Indiana University Press, 1989.

Eberwein, Jane Donahue. *Dickinson: Strategies of Limitation.* Amherst: University of Massachusetts Press, 1985.

Emerson, R. W. "Historic Notes of Life and Letters in New England." *Atlantic Monthly*, 1883. Reprinted in *The Portable Emerson*, ed. Carl Bode. New York: Penguin Books, 1981.

———. *Nature.* 1836. Reprinted in *The Portable Emerson*, ed. Carl Bode. New York: Penguin Books, 1981.

———. "The Poet." In *Essays*, Second Series. 1844. Reprinted in *The Portable Emerson*, ed. Carl Bode. New York: Penguin Books, 1981.

Erkkila, Betsy. "Emily Dickinson and Class." *American Literary History* 4, no. 1 (1992): 1–27. Reprinted in *The American Literary History Reader*, ed. Gordon Hutner, 291–317. New York and Oxford: Oxford University Press, 1995.

———. "Homoeroticism and Audience: Emily Dickinson's Female 'Master.'" In *Dickinson and Audience*, ed. Martin Orzeck and Robert Weisbuch, 161–80. Ann Arbor: University of Michigan Press, 1996.

Fast, Robin Riley. "'The One Thing Needful': Dickinson's Dilemma of Home and Heaven." *ESQ* 27, no. 3 (1981): 157–69.

Feidelson, John, Jr. *Symbolism and American Literature.* 1953. Reprint, Chicago: University of Chicago Press, 1962.

Franklin, R. W. *The Manuscript Books of Emily Dickinson.* 2 vols. Cambridge: Belknap Press of Harvard University Press, 1981.

———. *The Editing of Emily Dickinson*. Madison: University of Wisconsin Press, 1967.

Frye, Northrop. *Anatomy of Criticism*. 1957. Reprint, Princeton: Princeton University Press, 1973.

Garbowsky, Maryanne M. *The House without the Door*. Mississauga: Associated University Presses, 1989.

Gelpi, Albert. *Emily Dickinson: The Mind of the Poet*. 1965. Reprint, New York: W. W. Norton, 1971.

Gilbert, Sandra M., and Susan Gubar. *The Madwoman in the Attic: The Woman Writer and the Nineteenth-Century Imagination*. New York: W. W. Norton, 1985.

Higginson, Thomas Wentworth. "Emily Dickinson." In *Carlyle's Laugh*. 1909. Reprint, Freeport: Books for Libraries Press, 1968.

Hopkins, Vivian C. *Spires of Form: A Study of Emerson's Aesthetic Theory*. Cambridge: Harvard University Press, 1951.

Howe, Susan. *My Emily Dickinson*. Berkeley: North Atlantic, 1985.

Howard, William. "Emily Dickinson's Poetic Vocabulary." *Publications of the Modern Language Association* 72 (1957): 225–49.

Jackson, Gerald W. Master's thesis, Wake Forest University, 1974.

Johnson, Greg. *Emily Dickinson: Perception and the Poet's Quest*. Tuscaloosa: University of Alabama Press, 1985.

Jones, Rowena Revis. "'A Royal Seal': Emily Dickinson's Rite of Baptism." *Religion and Literature* 18, no. 3 (1986): 29–51.

Juhasz, Suzanne, Cristanne Miller, and Martha Nell Smith. *Emily Dickinson's Comic Power*. Austin: University of Texas Press, 1993.

Khan, M. M. "Romantic Tradition and the Compound Vision of Love in Emily Dickinson's Poems." *Panjab University Research Bulletin (Arts)* 9:1–2 (1978): 53–69.

Kher, Inder Nath. *The Landscape of Absence: Emily Dickinson's Poetry*. New Haven: Yale University Press, 1974.

Leyda, Jay. *The Years and Hours of Emily Dickinson*. 2 vols. New Haven: Yale University Press, 1960.

Longsworth, Polly. *Austin and Mabel: The Amherst Affair and Love Letters of Austin Dickinson and Mabel Loomis Todd*. New York: Farrar, Straus and Giroux, 1984.

Longsworth, Polly, and Norbert Hirschhorn. "'Medicine Posthumous': A New Look at Emily Dickinson's Medical Conditions." *New England Quarterly* 69, no. 2 (1996): 299–316.

Matthiessen, F. O. *American Renaissance: Art and Espression in the Age of Emerson and Whitman*. 1941. Reprint, Oxford: Oxford University Press, 1972.

McGann, Jerome. "Emily Dickinson's Visible Language," *Emily Dickinson Journal* 2:2 (1993): 40–57. Reprinted in *Black Riders: The Visible Language of Modernism*, 26–41. Princeton: Princeton University Press, 1993.

———. *Social Values and Poetic Acts: The Historical Judgment of Literary Work.* Cambridge: Harvard University Press, 1988.

Miller, Cristanne. *Emily Dickinson: A Poet's Grammar.* Cambridge: Harvard University Press, 1987.

Mudge, Jean McClure. *Emily Dickinson and the Image of Home.* Amherst: University of Massachusetts Press, 1975.

Nicolson, Nigel. *Vita and Harold: The Letters of Vita Sackville-West and Harold Nicolson.* New York: G. P. Putnam's Sons, 1992.

Orsini, Daniel J. "Emily Dickinson and the Romantic Use of Science." *Massachusetts Studies in English,* 7.4–8.1 (1981): 57–69.

Paglia, Camille. *Sexual Personae: Art and Decadence from Nefertiti to Emily Dickinson.* New Haven: Yale University Press, 1990.

Phillips, Elizabeth. *Emily Dickinson: Personae and Performance.* University Park: Pennsylvania State University Press, 1988.

Poirier, Richard. *A World Elsewhere: The Place of Style in American Literature.* London: Chatto and Windus, 1967.

Pollitt, Josephine. *Emily Dickinson: The Human Background of Her Poetry.* New York: Harper and Brothers Publishers, 1930.

Porter, David. "The Crucial Experience in Dickinson's Poetry," *ESQ* 20, no. 4 (1974): 280–90.

Price Herndl, Diane. *Invalid Women: Figuring Feminine Illness in American Fiction and Culture.* Chapel Hill: University of North Carolina Press, 1993.

Reynolds, Jerry Ferris. "'Banished from Native Eyes': The Reason for Emily Dickinson's Seclusion Reconsidered." *Markham Review* 8 (1979): 41–48.

Richardson, Robert D. *Emerson: The Mind on Fire.* Berkeley: University of California Press, 1995.

Rosenbaum, S. P. *A Concordance to the Poems of Emily Dickinson.* Ithaca: Cornell University Press, 1964.

St. Armand, Barton Levi. *Emily Dickinson and Her Culture.* Cambridge: Cambridge University Press, 1984.

Sewall, Richard B. *The Life of Emily Dickinson.* 2 vols. 1974. Reprint, New York: Farrar, Straus and Giroux, 1980.

———, ed. *The Lyman Letters: New Light on Emily Dickinson and Her Family.* Amherst: University of Massachusetts Press, 1965.

Shurr, William. *The Marriage of Emily Dickinson: A Study of the Fascicles.* Lexington: University Press of Kentucky, 1983.

Smith, Martha Nell. *Rowing in Eden: Rereading Emily Dickinson.* Austin: University of Texas Press, 1992.

Smith, Robert McClure. *The Seductions of Emily Dickinson.* Tuscaloosa: University of Alabama Press, 1996.

Stonum, Gary. *The Dickinson Sublime.* Madison: University of Wisconsin Press, 1990.

Taggard, Genevieve. *The Life and Mind of Emily Dickinson*. New York: Alfred A. Knopf, 1930.

Thoreau, Henry David. *Journal*. 4 vols. Princeton: Princeton University Press, 1981.

———. *The Maine Woods*. 1848. Reprint, New York: Library of America, 1985.

Wadsworth, Charles. *Sermons*. Presbyterian Publishing Co., 1882.

Walker, Cheryl. *The Nightingale's Burden: Women Poets and American Culture before 1900*. Bloomington: Indiana University Press, 1982.

Walsh, John Evangelist. *The Hidden Life of Emily Dickinson*. New York: Simon and Schuster, 1971.

Wand, Martin, and Richard B. Sewall. "'Eyes Be Blind, Heart Be Still': A New Perspective On Emily Dickinson's Eye Problem." *The New England Quarterly* 52 (September 1979): 400–406.

Wardrop, Daneen. *Emily Dickinson's Gothic: Goblin with a Gauge*. Iowa City: University of Iowa Press, 1996.

Werner, Marta L. *Emily Dickinson's Open Folios: Scenes of Reading, Surfaces of Writing*. Ann Arbor: University of Michigan Press, 1995.

Whicher, George Frisbie. *This Was a Poet: A Critical Biography of Emily Dickinson*. New York: Scribner's, 1938.

Wilbur, Richard. "Sumptuous Destitution." In *Emily Dickinson: Three Views*, ed. Richard Wilbur, Louise Bogan, and Archibald MacLeish. 1960. Reprinted in *Emily Dickinson: A Collection of Critical Essays*, ed. Richard B. Sewall, 127–36. Englewood Cliffs, New Jersey: Prentice-Hall, 1963.

Williams, Joanne DeLaven. "Spiders in the Attic: A Suggestion of Synthesis in the Poetry of Emily Dickinson." *The Emily Dickinson Bulletin* 29 (1976): 21–29.

Wolff, Cynthia Griffin. *Emily Dickinson*. New York: Alfred A. Knopf, 1986.

POEMS CITED

INDEX

Ackmann, Martha, 11, 179n.5
Astronomy: nineteenth century's fascination with, 36–38, 51; as stimulus for ED's interest in lenses and telescopes, 33–36, 53–56; ED's education in, 34, 38; in ED's poems, 36, 41–48, 54, 101. *See also* Science
Avery, Christine, 183nn.7,8

Bandages: worn by ED as part of treatment, 9, 29, 46, 101, 133; allied terms for, 61; as barriers to perception and to heaven, 61–69, 124; as obstacle between ED and her "twin," 71–73, 107; mentioned, 78, 85, 87, 90, 98
Banzer, Judith, 182n.3
Barker, Wendy, 11, 177n.3, 180n.9, 181n.15, 183n.9, 185n.6, 188n.11
Bianchi, Martha Dickinson, 134, 157, 158, 195n.8
Bingham, Millicent Todd, 156, 195n.3
Blindfolds. *See* Bandages
Bloom, Harold, 138

Browning, Elizabeth Barrett: and influence of *Aurora Leigh* upon ED, 50, 141; mentioned, 8
Budick, E. Miller, 191n.12
Byron, George Gordon, Lord. *See* "Prisoner of Chillon, The"

Capps, Jack, 184n.15, 190n.4
Civil War, 67, 68, 82
Cody, Dr. John, 3, 10, 181*nn.13,15*
Clouds. *See* Bandages
"Compound vision": defined, 28, 35–36; as basis for ED's poetic methodology, 33, 53, 60, 76, 112, 172–73; as used by ED to redefine concepts of time and space, 35–36, 42; as replicating scientific scrutiny, 54, 103; mentioned, 31, 58, 61, 75, 90, 94, 153
"Covered vision": defined, 17; inferiority of, to normal vision, 22; as antithesis of "compound vision," 94; mentioned, 35, 62, 98